To
   Jim
From
      Anne and Bill
With Best Wishes
      Christmas 1994.

The
Northumberland
Village Book

THE VILLAGES OF BRITAIN SERIES

Other counties in this series include:

*Published in conjunction with County Federations
of Women's Institutes

The Northumberland Village Book

Compiled by the Northumberland
Federation of Women's Institutes from notes
and illustrations sent by Institutes in the County

Published jointly by
Countryside Books, Newbury
and the NFWI, Newcastle

First Published 1994

© Northumberland Federation of Women's Institutes 1994

Countryside Books
3 Catherine Road
Newbury, Berkshire

ISBN 1 85306 302 9

Cover photograph of the river Till near Wooler

Produced through MRM Associates, Reading
Typeset by The Midlands Book Typesetting Company, Loughborough
Printed in England by J. W. Arrowsmith Ltd., Bristol

Foreword

Welcome to Northumberland – England's most northerly county which covers almost 2,000 square miles of beautiful and varied landscapes. The triangular shape of the county contains rolling hills, forests, fertile agricultural land, a beautiful coastline and in contrast, before pit closures, one of the largest coal mining areas in England.

The coastline and long boundary with Scotland have influenced its history; a most fought over area of land, with castles, keeps and pele towers built to protect against the Border reivers to the north and the Danes from the sea. The Romans built Hadrian's Wall along the southern boundary to protect themselves from the Scots and Picts as early as AD 122. Christianity came to Holy Island with St Aidan in the 7th century, and after the establishment of the monastery there, the monks spread the word west along the Tweed valley and south to Durham and York.

I would like to congratulate and thank the members of the Northumberland Federation of Women's Institutes who have researched and compiled the story of their much loved county. They are sharing with you, the reader, the interesting and often forgotten details of their villages and countryside.

I hope that you will enjoy reading this book and be encouraged to visit and explore spacious Northumberland – an area of England not to be missed.

Margaret Cadzow
County Chairman

Acknowledgements

There have been many contributors to this book – too many to name individually – from all the Women's Institutes in Northumberland, and thanks are due to every one of them for the research and background information they have provided on their own localities. The black and white illustrations are also original sketches done by WI members, as is the frontispiece map. Collating the material was done by Mrs Kathleen Beale, who found it a fascinating and rewarding task.

Northumberland

Berwick

Holy Island

Farne Islands

Bamburgh

R. Tweed

R. Till

North Sea

R. Aln

Alnwick

R. Coquet

Rothbury

R. Rede

Kielder Water

R. North Tyne

Morpeth

R. Wansbeck

R. Blyth

Hadrian's Wall

Newcastle

R. South Tyne

Hexham

R. Tyne

R. West Allen

R. East Allen

Acklington

Acklington 🐚

The parish of Acklington can be found off the A1, north of Felton, close to the river Coquet. It takes its name from Aeccel, whose sons farmed the land in early times. Open field agriculture was practised and it is recorded that in 1248 the bondsmen of Acklington each held 30 acres but had to work three days a week on the demesne land belonging to Roger Fitzjohn, harvesting corn which was ground at a windmill nearby. During the same period the land south of the river was set aside as a deer park by the Lords of Warkworth, whose barony included Acklington. Gradually this became pastureland and farms developed. Three hundred years later it was let leasehold as one large pasture farm. The period of agricultural improvement and increased demand during the Napoleonic Wars led to much of the land becoming arable.

Little industry has affected the landscape. In the early 1700s a colliery was sited at Acklington, but later, in Victorian times, mines at Broomhill and Radcliffe, east of the village, were developed, so leaving Acklington unmarked. An iron and tin foundry was erected in 1775 by a group of speculators, who also built a dam and weir to provide power. Sadly the business did not flourish but these works can still be seen today. The waterfall which was constructed is a wonderful sight.

In the 1840s a railway was built to run through the village and a small agricultural market was created close to the station. This has expanded and still brings local farmers twice weekly to its sales. Although the station buildings have been converted to a house a few trains still stop there daily. This line is the main eastern route from London to Edinburgh.

The village today remains unspoilt. Two cottages, Rookery Nook and Pump Cottage, are over 400 years old. At the eastern end of the village stands the smithy. In the 17th century it was one of two village inns, the blacksmith being the farrier and cartwright as well as the innkeeper. Two pumps still catch the eye of the visitor. The one at the centre of the village has a little roof over it. Strangers will be told that this is to keep the water dry when it rains! The water is sweet and cool, coming from seven little springs below.

In 1938 the Ministry of Defence built an airbase just outside the village. Three Hurricanes from the base were shot down in 1940 by the first German plane over British soil. They were led by Flt Lt Peter Townsend, whose name was later linked with Princess Margaret. After

9

the war the airfield was an armament practice station and then a training school. A helicopter rescue service also operated from here. Following its closure in 1969, the site was taken over by the Home Office who later established two prisons, one Category C and the other for young offenders.

The landscape around Acklington has remained virtually unchanged since it was part of a royal estate 1,200 years ago and it still provides a rural, peaceful haven for residents and visitors alike.

Acomb 🌰

Acomb means 'the place where the oaks are'. The village was in the Archbishop of York's regality of Hexhamshire, until this was abolished by Henry VIII in the 16th century. Inhabited by copyholders who held by border tenure, which required them to turn out with horse and armour to defend their homes against the Scottish raiders, it was destroyed by the Scots several times – the last being in 1584. However, the village prospered in Elizabethan times from the mining of lead and coal. After the 17th and 18th century enclosures the old medieval farmsteads, which lined the main street running up the hillside, were partly superseded by farmhouses out in the fields. The gaps between were filled up with cottages to house miners. The oldest houses in the village are of this period. The earliest surviving is at Charehead, 1691.

The arrival of the Newcastle and Carlisle Railway in 1846 enabled an increased production of coal for transport to Scotland and Cumberland by rail. Acomb reached its peak of population in the 1850s with lead and coal mining, coke ovens, brickworks, and a chemical plant with a 40-foot chimney. Despite the collapse in the price of lead the mine continued to produce witherite (barium carbonate), attracting miners from the Alston Moor mines.

About the turn of the century the population was somewhat higher than now, but packed in a third of the houses. Several rows of workers' houses were built along the main road to Hexham, at the foot of the hill which is the old corn road, built as a toll road to carry corn from Hexham to the Alnmouth port. The first council houses were built in the 1930s and later both council and private estates were added. With the closure of the witherite mine and later the coal mines the population turned to transport and rural services and an increasing proportion became commuters to Hexham and Newcastle.

Today, the population is almost back to the 18th century level and houses vary from the original two-room cottages to the modern executive-type detached houses. There are three pubs and a hotel, a youth hostel and a popular caravan site, which accommodates many visitors to the Roman wall and the historic abbey at Hexham. About half the villagers work in the surrounding countryside, or in Hexham two miles away.

Hexham is the social centre for the area providing theatre, cinema, art, music, a library, sport, a leisure centre and varied shopping. The village maintains a primary school but older children go daily to Hexham.

The parish church of St John Lee stands high on a hilltop about a mile from the village, on a beautiful site which was formerly a clearing in the oak wood which gave Acomb its name. It was used as a retreat by St John of Beverley when he was Bishop of Hexham. The present church was rebuilt in 1843. The Methodist chapel is over 120 years old and was built at the cost of £300.

The village hall was originally built and maintained by a levy on the miners' wages and it was given to the village on nationalisation. In 1992 the parish council accepted responsibility for its upkeep.

Allendale 🐑

This attractive North Pennine village is the centre of East Allen parish. The river East Allen starts some 600 metres above Allenheads and flows northwards through beautiful moorland scenery, home for blackcock, pheasant and grouse, and now a designated area of outstanding natural beauty very popular with walkers. The parish covers an area five miles east to west and twelve miles north to south and must be one of the largest in England.

There are few visible signs to indicate this was a very important lead mining area in the 18th and 19th centuries. The spoil heaps are overgrown and the flues from the smelt mill have fallen in, while the chimneys are disintegrating with the wind and lightning which strikes across the fell. Once there was a population of 6,000, now there are just under 2,000 people in the dale.

Today this rural community depends not only on agriculture, but on light industry and tourism-related occupations. A high proportion of people are retired, and others commute to larger towns like Hexham. There are two schools, one for five to nine year olds and one for ten to 13 year olds. The first school was an 1879 Board school but had extensive alterations in 1974, while the middle school was built in 1959. Senior schoolchildren travel to Haydon Bridge or Hexham.

There must have been a church in Allendale since early times as a chapel and graveyard were recorded as part of Hexham Priory. Parish records only exist from 1662. The present St Cuthbert's church was built in 1873 to replace one built in 1807. It stands in a prominent position overlooking the river Allen and is in the centre of Britain, as indicated by a sundial on the wall of the tower. This well cared for building has a mosaic reredos depicting The Last Supper and a commemorative sculpture by the 19th century sculptor John Lough.

Two visits by John Wesley in 1748 and 1749 encouraged the growth of Methodism in the dale but a declining population has seen many chapels close. Trinity church was the third (1875) on this site and underwent an interior renewal in 1989. The memorial windows were designed by Victor Noble Rainbird in 1920. There is also a meeting house belonging to the Society of Friends. They were established in

Mill Bridge

the area before 1660 and were frequently punished for non-payment of tithes to the church.

The railway never reached the town; it ended at Catton a mile away, but was closed in 1950. The buses were frequent at that time, but now even they are becoming fewer. There are still eight shops and most essential items are available, and there is one bank left. The post office has recently had its sorting office facility taken to Hexham.

The village hall, once a temperance hall built in 1905, is still the focus of community activities and has recently been extended and modernised, hopefully for the next century. The village is growing and has two large modern estates.

There are five hotels and two inns round the market place, with always a welcome for the traveller. Many people come for the New Year's Eve Tar Barrel Festival. This is carried out by 40 men dressed in fancy costumes who carry flaming tar barrels on their heads. The procession, accompanied by the band, marches round the village and then the barrels are thrown onto a huge bonfire at midnight, to the strains of *Auld Lang Syne!*

Allenheads 🌿

Tucked away in the deepest corner of Northumberland hides Allenheads, thriving between the high Pennine hills where the river East Allen starts its journey to the Tyne.

The road leaving Allenheads to nearby Coalcleugh must have one of the finest views in the country on a clear day. The Cheviots can be seen from here, 70 miles away. Rolling hills, stone walls, patches of woodland and the heather provide every colour on a sunny day. Allenheads is reputed to be the highest village in England, and documented history only reveals a settlement from around 1670. Beneath the stunning moorland lies the secret of why people came – the veins of argentiferous galena, or silver-bearing lead ore.

Estates around the Allenheads area were sold to the Blackett family towards the end of the 17th century. Family fortunes were increased by the mine in the village, which yielded lead and silver, and at one time was responsible for one seventh of total British lead production. Lead mining expanded and made the dale a busy place during the 18th and 19th centuries, as miners ran farmsteads to supplement their incomes. The Blackett and Beaumont families were joined through marriage and the mining continued into the last years of the 19th century. Wentworth Blackett-Beaumont became Lord Allendale in 1906 and his family still own Allenheads Hall and estates. As the lead mining petered out, farming has carried on and many of the smaller farms have been combined to help farmers make a living from the land.

But what was described as a dying village, in more recent years has fought back. The Allenheads Trust, formed within the last decade, has helped transform the village centre. A former bus garage and barn has become a heritage centre used by local groups, while the nearby blacksmith's shop has been restored and opened to the public. The project also added a children's play area, café and craft shop in restored buildings, along with a trout farm and nature trail. During the restoration, an engine house was built to house the Armstrong engine, used to drive a sawmill, and which is once again in running order. The mine yard is still in the centre of the village, and some of the buildings have been used to create workshops for local businesses. Old people's bungalows, the first new homes in the village for 150 years, were built in keeping with the traditional stone farms and cottages of Allenheads.

The 18th century Allenheads Inn is steeped in history – more recently the landlord has discovered a hidden room. Ramblers find the hills around Allenheads a constant lure, as do nature lovers. The variety of flora and fauna in this unspoilt corner of England is stunning, and it is a designated area of outstanding natural beauty.

Farming in Allenheads is challenging and rewarding. Often after a rough winter the pleasure of seeing the lambs and young calves running around in the fields is a reward in itself for the hard work that winter entails. And summer brings the work of providing hay and silage for the inevitable bad weather. Sheep are a vital essence of the surrounding fells as they help regulate the growth of the heather which in turn feeds the grouse. The fells cater for grouse shooting which brings vital income to the area and helps manage the moorland.

The neighbouring hamlet of Sparty Lea takes its unusual name from the spart grasses found on the fells, where walkers can enjoy some spectacular views. St Peter's church is disused but villagers have maintained the churchyard, where burials are still carried out. The 30 or so houses dotted around the valley have their own post office and Methodist chapel, and share them now with the tranquil Swinhope valley, bearing the scars of its industrial heritage. Sparty Lea can also boast its own caves – known as the Elf Holes – at a disused quarry.

Everyone who has lived in the Allenheads area has a story to tell about the harsh winters, of months being cut off, food being brought by sleigh, but coping as best they can. Now winters seem milder and the snow blowers and ploughs soon cut a path through to civilisation, keeping this part of England's Last Wilderness in touch. Some would say, let the snow stay awhile.

Alnham 🐑

Alnham, Aln Hame, Yeldom – all mean 'home of the river Aln or Yelwater'. The strength of the village is Alnham Farm together with Pennylaws, Castlehill, Ewartly Shank, and more recently (1980s) Hazelton Rigg.

It is a sprawling, peaceful village, with a single house at the top of the hill, then further along the semi-detached Havannah Cottages, a recent name. Not far from them is Denecroft, formerly Tully's, the local shop and carrier. All the smallholdings have disappeared. They were once occupied by tradesmen – a cobbler, builder, and blacksmith, but the land has been added to Alnham Farm and the houses sold off to owner-occupiers.

The parish church of St Michael and All Angels (1664) was refurbished and reroofed in the 1950s and 1960s, and is still used. Services are taken by the vicar of Alwinton, once a month. The church bell – November 1759 – is still rung today. The lovely lychgate is still at the churchyard gateway.

Nearby is the fortified pele tower (listed), later the vicarage. It was used as a youth hostel, and then in the early 1960s sold for a private residence and called Tower House.

Children of the district were educated in the Church of England school, built in 1870 and situated halfway up the bank, with house adjoining and the playground over the road – not very safe for the 1990s! There were enough pupils to employ a headteacher and an infants teacher but sadly numbers decreased in the 1950s and early 1960s and the school was closed in July 1967. The children were transferred to the new timber-structured county primary school over at Netherton, opened at Easter 1965 – and taken down in August 1993.

Alnham Memorial Institute is known locally as 'the hall', and was erected by a local voluntary workforce. In the entrance porch is the stone memorial tablet for the 1914–18 war. The stone-built hall was opened in 1922. One popular event is the Old Folks Ball. A variety of other social gatherings are held, such as school or family parties, whist drives, dances and concerts – some by the amateur dramatic group 'We Are Seven'. The hall is also used as a polling station for local and general elections. After the annual harvest thanksgiving service, a harvest supper was sometimes held in the hall.

Just across the field opposite is a former smallholding, now a shepherd's cottage, named after the family who lived there for many years – Oliver's. Further down are two more houses, one of which was the blacksmith's; the blacksmith's shop was pulled down. Back out on the roadside, again at the foot of the bank, is Pennywell Cottage, and this was the site of the inn or public house. There is also the bothy (listed), a place used as accommodation by hired men whilst working locally.

Blackchesters, on Caisley Moor, was the shepherd's cottage for Alnham until about 1960, when it became a weekend cottage. Two new farmworkers' cottages were built at Alnham in 1955. The local population today is about 30.

In fields around Alnham and out behind Castlehill can be seen the outline of former settlements; there must have been a castle or fort around this area in the distant past.

It is sad to record the double tragedy of 1962. After the hill-sale at Rothbury Mart on Saturday, 17th November 1962, two experienced hill shepherds returned to Castlehill, but tragically both died later than night in a severe snow blizzard, whilst going out to their home at Ewartly Shank.

About a mile away is Prendwick, where once a regiment could be mustered, and in the 1930s more than eleven footballers could be fielded. The hill shepherds now live at Prendwick and their former cottages, North Field Head and Prendwick Chesters, are now used by the Scouts. In olden days the gamekeeper's house was a school. On summer evenings a favourite pastime for the men of these country areas was to play quoits. The population of Prendwick is about 15.

Alnmouth

The village of Alnmouth was formerly an ancient borough. It first appears in historical records in Saxon times when it was probably called Twyford, which means 'the place of the two fords'. It was here that St Cuthbert was chosen to be Bishop of Lindisfarne in AD 684 in the presence of King Ecgfrid and Archbishop Theodore.

In the 8th century the Vikings raided the Northumbrian coast and the remains of one of their winter camps can still be seen in the Nightfold Field. They were pagans but the Anglo-Saxons soon converted them to Christianity. In 1789 fragments of a carved stone cross were found at the foot of Church Hill, dated to the time of the Vikings.

The Normans laid out a new town in the early 12th century and called it St Waleric after the saint to whom the church was dedicated. The borough soon became known as Alnmouth because of its position at the mouth of the river Aln and prospered so well that in 1207 it was granted a charter to have a port and a market. In 1316 the bailiff of Alnmouth was ordered to provide vessels for the defence of the kingdom.

In 1348 the Black Death struck and Alnmouth was devastated. Around that time, during the wars with Scotland, Alnmouth, along with many other settlements in Northumberland, suffered considerable damage. In 1336 Alnmouth was set ablaze and is reported to have been almost completely destroyed.

By the end of the 15th century, Alnmouth was once again exporting coal, wool and other produce, but the Scots and English Borderers still raided one another's territory and in 1567 the burgesses were ordered to keep a watch on Wallop Hill by day and by night, and to have ready sufficient wood to light a fire for a warning to the countryside.

The late 17th and 18th centuries were the heyday of Alnmouth's prosperity. At one time there were 16 granaries in the town. It is surprising to learn that during this period Alnmouth was exporting more corn than Newcastle. Fishing also remained a vital part of the town's prosperity. In 1753 a turnpike road was constructed that ran all the way from Hexham to Alnmouth. This greatly improved the carriage of produce into the town and for a time the main street of Alnmouth was called Hexham Road. There was a tollbooth at Lesbury and from there the road into Alnmouth was round the eastern bend of the river past Foxton.

John Wesley visited Alnmouth in 1748 and described it as 'famous for all kinds of wickedness'. As a result a chapel was built and it still stands in Chapel Lane. Besides holding services on Sundays, it opened a school which was used for the children of the village until the new school was built in 1876.

On Christmas Day 1806 a great storm arose and the river broke through to form the channel that exists today; thus cutting off Church Hill from the rest of the village. During the same storm the church was blown down so that the village was left without an Anglican church. Much later, the Duke of Northumberland eventually took pity on the villagers and having bought the former granary which is now the Hindmarsh Hall, he converted it into a temporary church. At the time the Duke was having Alnwick Castle altered by the architect Anthony Salvin and he was commissioned to take charge of the alterations to the granary. This explains why the building that is now the village hall, and which started life as a granary, looks so like a church.

Meanwhile the breakthrough of the river was to prove a disaster for the port. The new channel was not so deep as the old one and ships found it increasingly difficult to enter the harbour so the port was used less frequently and went into decline. Coupled with this, the age of steam had arrived and the railway up the east coast, built in the mid 19th century, proved a much swifter and simpler method of transporting goods.

The railway, however, also brought salvation. Easy transport from Newcastle made an unspoilt seaside town or village such as Alnmouth an attractive holiday resort. In 1864 a new road was built from the station into the village with a bridge across the river, called Duchess Bridge as the Duchess of Northumberland contributed to the cost of its erection. This dispensed with the necessity of having to travel all the way to Lesbury and Foxton to reach the village. A new church was built in 1876 and the temporary one became the village hall. Many of the old granaries, which were well constructed stone buildings, were converted into houses. In 1918 the Alnmouth Women's Institute was founded, one of the earliest in the county.

Times change and it is no longer the railway that brings the visitors to Alnmouth but the motorcar. Alnmouth, however, is very much the same unspoilt seaside village that captured the hearts of the Victorians.

Looking at the quiet village today, it is difficult to imagine that in the 18th and early 19th centuries Alnmouth was a busy port. There would have been the hurly-burly of carts and horses rattling up and down the cobbled streets and the busy quayside activity as men unloaded barrels of beer, timber etc and then loaded such items as corn, pork, eggs, wool and coal. Traffic became so congested that Alnmouth court had to introduce a law that carts were not allowed to stand in the street for more than one and a half hours, the forerunner of today's yellow lines.

Alnwick

Although Alnwick is a town it still has a village atmosphere, with a population of only 7,000. The name is made up of 'Aln' after the river on which it stands (aln is probably from the word 'alain' meaning white, bright or clear) and 'wic', which is Old English for a workplace or trading place – thus it is the trading place on the bright, clear river.

The medieval castle, originally a motte and bailey enclosing about seven acres, is believed to have been built on the site of a Saxon fort and has since 1309 been the home of the Percys and Earls of Northumberland, the most famous of them being Harry Hotspur. The castle is now part of a beautiful estate, part of which was designed by 'Capability' Brown. It has many art treasures and is a popular site for tourists as well as being host to a department of an American university.

Alnwick Abbey was built in 1304 for the Premonstratension white canons. Situated in the beautiful Hulne Park, the gateway is still standing and in use. Hulne Priory, also in the Hulne Park, was one of the earliest Carmelite orders, founded about 1240. It is mostly a ruin except for the modern part built about 1777, which is still inhabited. The monks and priors tended the sick at nearby St Leonard's Hospital, also a ruin. There is now a modern local hospital with a new maternity unit provided by public demand and subscription.

St Michael's parish church dates from 1140 and was largely rebuilt in the 15th century. It was restored by Anthony Salvin in 1863. St Paul's, designed by Salvin, was originally Anglican but is now owned by the Roman Catholic Church. The Methodist chapel, built in 1786 and restored 1886, has a pulpit from which John Wesley preached. The Presbyterian church had a meeting house in Canongate in 1639. After a few moves a new church was built (St James's) in 1895 and it is now St James's United Reformed church after merging with the Congregational church in 1972.

There was a school in Alnwick as far back as 1448. It was called the chantry school and was the first grammar school, where a chaplain from the parish church taught poor boys of the burgesses of Alnwick. In later years there was the Duchess's grammar school for girls – now the comprehensive high school, and the Duke's grammar school for boys, now a middle school. In recent times there was also a secondary modern school which is today also a middle school, and various infants and junior schools, now first schools.

Alnwick used to have a thriving cattle market, but now has only Saturday market stalls and an annual 'medieval' fair, revived 25 years ago. On the west side of the market place is the town hall, built by the freemen of Alnwick in 1731. It is surmounted by a clock and bell tower and was used for quarter sessions, county courts, council meetings and gatherings. In later years prisoners were held below the hall and a curfew bell is rung there every evening at 8 pm. There is a modern police station and courts.

On the south side there is the Northumberland Hall which was started in 1764 as a market house or shambles for the market. This was demolished in 1826 to become the Northumberland Hall with butchers' shambles below and a fish market on the eastern end. Now it houses the Tourist Information Centre, small shops and public toilets.

In 1850 a two and three quarter mile double-track line linked Alnwick with Alnmouth station, as a branch line of the Newcastle and Berwick Railway. Freight and passengers were carried, and the terminus at Alnwick boasted a splendid station building in 1887. Steam working was retained until 1965, but the line was closed by BR in 1968. Today the station is used as warehouses and outlets for agricultural products, books and carpets.

There are three bridges over the river Aln. Lion Bridge carries the Great North Road across the river, near the castle. The present bridge was built by John Adam, but a bridge had existed at this point since 1347. The bridge has three circular arches with embattled parapets and look-outs. In the middle of the east parapet stands a cast-lead lion with a stiff extended tail – the Percy Lion. Westwards out of Alnwick lies Canongate, so called because it was the way used by the white canons of the abbey. The bridge carrying the road westwards to Eglingham was rebuilt in 1821 and has three rounded arches and a plain parapet. The road leading to Dunstanburgh and Bamburgh crosses the river by Denwick Bridge. Dated 1766, a fine view of Alnwick Castle is afforded from this bridge.

A column was erected on Cooper's Hill in 1678. The present South Road was cut through the hill. In 1816 the Duke reduced the tenants' rent by a quarter after the hardships of the Napoleonic Wars. In gratitude the tenants had the present column, designed by David Stephenson, built on what is now called the column field – not really a field but a well laid out garden with seats for the public. It is believed that the Duke decided that if the tenants could afford to pay for the column they could pay higher rents and promptly put them up again, thus the column is also known as Farmer's Folly.

These are only a few of Alnwick's finer qualities. It is a lovely little market town with one foot still in the past and many new buildings hopefully toning in with the old. It is rapidly becoming a popular place to retire to, being not far from the sea, the hills, the country, towns and city.

Amble 🐚

Amble lies at the mouth of the river Coquet, which flows down from the Cheviot Hills through moorland, woodlands and pastures and through pretty villages until it reaches the North Sea. Follow the newly signposted 'Coastal Route' and you will find yourself in Amble.

The focal point is the harbour. The large seine-netters used for deep sea fishing are tied up here while the smaller inshore fishing boats, known locally as cobles, are tied up in the recently renovated dock. A little further upriver is the very attractive yachting marina, another recent acquisition and proving to be very popular for weekend sailors. Two local yachting clubs have premises nearby. On the south side of Amble is the large council-owned caravan site. To both the north and the south lie some very fine beaches of golden sand, wonderful for taking brisk walks but not ideal for sunbathing or swimming. It can be rather cool!

The name is derived from 'Anna's promontory'. Relics of prehistoric times have been found on the sand dunes, known as the 'links'. A recent discovery was a stone coffin complete with skeleton. This appeared after heavy seas had swept sand from the dunes. To the west is Gloster Hill where a Roman altar was found, suggesting that there may have been an encampment here.

Amble has probably been a harbour for centuries but it was in 1839 that the harbour as we have known it was built at a cost of some £200,000. This was done to accommodate the shipping required for exporting coal from the privately owned collieries which had opened in the district. Railway lines were built to transport the coal from the mines to the port, officially known as Warkworth Harbour, where the coal waggons eventually arrived on raised lines, known as staithes, at the quayside and the coal was loaded into the holds of specially built ships, the colliers. Prior to the Second World War, colliers with names belonging to the local companies such as *Togston, Amble, Chevington* and *Hauxley* transported coal to the Continent and to industrial areas around the British Isles. In its heyday over 300,000 tons of coal annually was being shipped out of Amble, which, meanwhile, was growing, and for many years the population remained at approximately 5,000. With the decline of the mining industry the harbour ceased to be used for coal shipments and 1969 saw the last shipment leave Amble.

Mention the name Amble to anyone who grew up there in the days prior to the Second World War and it is almost certain that an outstanding memory will be 'The Feast'. This was the local annual holiday when 'the shows' came to town. These were the fairground amusements, owned at that time by Walter Murphy. Young and old alike took great pleasure in riding on the brightly painted hobby horses and the diving dolphins while the Wurlitzer organ banged out such music as the *Stein Song*. Pay your money at one of the prize stalls and if the tin clock Messerschmidt landed on your number you could win a set of pans or a plastercast 'Cherry Boy' or Alsatian dog ornament. The lucky recipients of the latter prizes would often find that by the time they reached home the boy had lost his cherries or the dog his nose!

Also during this week, sports were held in the local Welfare Park and in the harbour. These were very popular, attracting hopeful young sportsmen from outside the area as well as the locals. The highlight of these events was more fun than competitive. This was the greasy pole. A wooden telegraph pole was erected and held by ropes on a bit of land adjacent to the harbour. At the top was pinned some prize money but the pole was thickly coated with engine grease making it difficult for anyone to climb! It was great fun watching the young men make numerous attempts to climb only to slip down again. It was quite some time before the top was reached and that was only after they had covered themselves with dirt and coal dust from the waggons to combat the grease and had stood on each other's shoulders to help someone else to get higher! When the goal was finally reached it was to great cheers from the onlookers. But more fun was yet to come because all these dusty, dirty, greasy but happy young men would run to the harbour and jump in. All part of 'The Feast', Amble's local holiday.

Another memorable social occasion was the 'Late Night'. This was an evening of dancing in the Legion hall. The dancing, however, was preceded by a display called 'The Grand March'. Young men and young ladies from Amble and surrounding villages, dressed in correct evening wear, would parade, with their partners, to music in a series of set sequences around the dance floor, separating from and rejoining their partners, creating various formations and providing a wonderful spectacle for the onlookers who had willingly paid to witness such a colourful event.

Amble could boast of its own cinema at one time, the Coquet Hall. It was later to become a bingo hall but today stands derelict and boarded up. In its day it provided for many people a few hours of escape from the harsh realities of everyday life in the working class community of this little town.

Although residential areas are growing outwards to the south and west of Amble, the main street, Queen Street, still remains the shopping centre and the heart of the town. On Sunday mornings a market is held on the quayside.

Coquet Island, lying out from the harbour, with its now automated lighthouse, is a sanctuary for sea birds and boat trips can be made there although landing is not permitted. The coastline and organised fishing trips make Amble a very popular venue for sea anglers.

Amble's most recent claim to fame was the arrival in the late 1980s of a bottle-nosed dolphin. This created enormous interest and soon visitors and television crews were flocking to the harbour to see Freddy, as he was christened, playfully following the boats at the harbour entrance. He happily joined the divers who came from great distances to swim with him. A local resident received a letter saying Freddy had appeared on television in Sydney, Australia. Sadly, after giving everyone so much pleasure for these few years, he disappeared as mysteriously as he had arrived.

Ashington 🐾

Ashington was once known as the 'biggest mining village in the world'. It dates from the mid 19th century, when a coal shaft was sunk on land belonging to the Duke of Portland. The first long rows of terraced houses were built at the west end of the town. These rows were simply numbered from First to Eleventh Row. Some were demolished in the 1960s to make way for new housing, but the rest of these first colliery houses remain.

The population of Ashington continued to grow, and in the early years of the 20th century more long rows of terraced houses were built at the east end of the town. Unlike the earlier rows around the colliery, these were named rather than numbered, after trees and Shakespearian characters.

It would be thought that with a base of mining, Ashington would have been a dull unattractive town, with a limited social life, but this was and is not so. There were, and are, parks and recreation grounds, with football, cricket and rugby clubs. There were dance halls, including the Harmonic Hall and the Princess Ballroom. At one time, Ashington boasted five cinemas and the Miners Theatre. Mining is thirsty work, and at one point there were nearly 30 working men's clubs in the town, though some have closed in recent years. Women are still not allowed to be full members, and in earlier years had to be content with the many church socials and the Operatic Society, which is still flourishing.

Ashington colliery closed in 1988, and the miners employed there either took redundancy or were transferred to neighbouring Ellington colliery. There is little evidence now that a colliery existed in Ashington. The site has been transformed into a business park which hopes to bring new industries to the town. The former colliery spoil heaps, which looked like miniature Alps when it snowed, have been levelled and turned into parkland. The main street of Ashington, Station Road, has been made into a pedestrian precinct, the subject of much debate for and against.

Ashington has changed and is no longer a village with mining at its heart. It is a growing town, with new housing estates being built to the south of the town centre. The long terraced streets remain, however, as a legacy of coalmining history.

Bamburgh

The first inhabitants of Bamburgh lived in a fortified village, high on the rock where the castle now stands. Later the Romans left traces of their occupation, but it wasn't until the Anglo-Saxon king, Ida, made Bamburgh his capital in AD 547 that the village became historically important. From this era, archaeologists have recently uncovered a tiny gold animal, which has been named 'the Bamburgh beast' and put on display in the castle.

St Aidan came here from Iona to preach Christianity at the request of King Oswald, and a wooden church was built, probably on the site of the present church. St Aidan died here in AD 651. A beam of wood in St Aidan's church today is reputed to date from that early wooden church and there is a tradition that St Aidan died resting against that very beam.

Little is known of the church in the early days of the Norman Conquest, but a record exists of every priest at Bamburgh from 1121 to the present day. The church, one of the finest in the county, has a square 13th century tower, a very large arched nave which dates from 1200 and a 13th century vaulted crypt beneath the chancel. The beauty of the church itself is enhanced by the setting of green fields and blue sea in the distance.

The village is dominated by the Norman castle which withstood many sieges, finally being defeated by the great guns of Edward IV, thus becoming the first castle in England to fall to artillery fire! In the late 17th century Claudius Forster was Warden of the Marches and based in the castle. He must have been a successful Warden because he was given the castle by the king, and it remained with the Forster family until the 18th century. The castle and its estate was then bought by Lord Crewe, Bishop of Durham, who had married Dorothy Forster,

Old dovecote at Bamburgh

25

aunt of the last Forster owner, Thomas. Lord Crewe, having no direct heirs, left the castle and estate in the form of a charitable trust. It is thanks to the good management of the trustees during the 19th century that Bamburgh village looks the way it does today.

The castle was then bought by Lord Armstrong, the great Victorian inventor and industrialist, who did much to restore and rebuild it. His family still own it and it is open to visitors.

In the past Bamburgh seems to have nurtured brave and stalwart women. Even its name comes from a woman – Queen Bebba, wife of an Anglian king, giving us Bebbanburgh and thus Bamburgh – or so it is said! Then there was Matilda, wife of Robert, Earl of Northumberland, who held out against the enemy besieging the castle and only finally surrendered when they brought her captured husband before the castle walls and threatened to put out his eyes.

In the 18th century, Dorothy Forster, niece of the first Dorothy and sister of Thomas, became another heroine. Her brother Thomas, a notably unsuccessful Jacobite general, was awaiting execution when Dorothy rode all the way to London and either by bribery or subterfuge, rescued him from the Tower.

The most famous heroine of all, Grace Darling, was born in what was probably her grandparents' house opposite the church, in 1815. She was taken as a three week old baby to the lighthouse on Brownsman, one of the Farne Islands, where her father was the lighthouse keeper. In those days the keeper's family was allowed to live in the lighthouse in return for helping to maintain the light. Later the family transferred to the newly built Longstone lighthouse and it was from her bedroom window there that Grace saw the wreck of the steamship *Forfarshire* on 7th September 1838. Grace and her father's epic battle through the storm in their rowing boat to rescue the nine survivors is well known. Soon Grace became a national celebrity and for the rest of her short life she was seldom out of the public eye. A slender and rather frail-looking girl, she developed tuberculosis and died four years later. She is buried in St Aidan's churchyard where her monument is a local landmark. Her story is told in more detail in the Grace Darling museum opposite the church where there are many interesting relics of her life.

In appearance, the village has changed little in the last hundred years. The population has dropped from 450 to 367 permanent inhabitants. In the 1890s most people found work locally on the farms, in domestic employment or in the nearby stone quarries. Today some residents still work locally but others travel further afield for employment. The village school, opened in 1877 and at its peak having 160 pupils, is now closed. There used to be a small gasworks at the beginning of the century. Lamps to light the village were bought and maintained by public subscription. It is said the lamps were removed and stored during the summer months. Presumably people went to bed at sunset then! There is no longer a gas supply in the village.

Visitors are no longer met by pony and trap at the nearest railway station but come by car and coach, attracted not only by the village and castle but by the unspoilt sandy beaches. We have a cricket club, an indoor bowls club, a bird club, an art club, a keep-fit group and, of course, the Women's Institute. A children's Christmas party is held in the village, quoits are played at an annual 'feast Sunday' on the green, tennis is played on temporary grass courts on the castle green, and Bamburgh Castle golf club must have the finest views of any golf course in the land. Truly, Bamburgh deserves its title of 'The jewel in Northumberland's crown' – or so we like to think!

Bardon Mill

Bardon Mill and Henshaw parishes lie between the river South Tyne and the Roman wall, in an area of great beauty.

Bardon Mill's proximity to the famous Roman site of Vindolanda brings many tourists to the area. They usually stop at the Bowes Hotel, the only pub in the village and which has a good reputation for food, or buy their postcards at the only shop in the village, the post office, or view the goods at the pottery, famous all over the northern region for its strawberry pots.

Although coal mining and corn grinding once formed part of the work of the area, they have both disappeared and mixed farming is now the main occupation.

There are many local places of interest, including the Roman wall, Vindolanda, Willimoteswick Castle, Beltingham church, Tow House, Barcombe Longstone, Ridley Woods and Allen Banks. The Roman wall and Vindolanda are very well documented but the others are slightly less known aspects of the area.

Originally, Willimoteswick Castle was built in the 12th or 13th century. It has been pulled down and rebuilt several times, though some of the original structure does remain. It originally belonged to the Ridleys, but was confiscated because of Muchamp Ridley's loyalty to

Charles I. It passed to the Lowes family and then to the current owners, the Blacketts of Hatton who at one time owned most of Northumberland (with its 1982 borders). It is now a private home and visitors are not allowed to tour the castle, mostly for safety reasons.

If you cross the river by the iron footbridge, which was built in 1883 at a cost of £550, and turn left, you will pass the pleasant woods of Ridley, which are designated as a nature reserve by the National Trust. Continue a little further along this road and you will reach the beautiful little village of Beltingham. Its main claim to fame is its gorgeous little church. It had the honour in the 9th century to be a resting place for the body of St Cuthbert as it was borne westward by the monks of Lindisfarne in their flight from the terror of the invading Danes. Originally the domestic chapel of the Ridley family, it was then designated as St Cuthbert's church.

It is the only church in Northumberland built entirely in the Perpendicular style and it has much which should be preserved for future generations. There is a shaft which once belonged to an ancient Saxon cross, which is believed to be a station cross older than the church itself. There are three 900 year old yew trees on the north side of the church. The age is taken from the church guide written by the Rev C. W. Herring. On the east side of the church, on an old blocked doorway, there are deep incisions, reputed to have been made by archers sharpening their arrows in readiness for battle. Inside the church is a hole cut in the direction of the altar, through which the elevation of the host could be seen. It is called a leper squint or hagioscope. There are two stained glass windows given by a Dowager Countess of Strathmore, Lady Bowes Lyon, and by the Honourable F. N. and Lady Anne Bowes Lyon in 1906. They were dedicated to the commemoration of mercies vouchsafed in a car accident which occurred in Bardon Mill parish on 27th August 1904. It must have been one of the first motor car accidents this century.

The martyr Bishop Ridley, born at Willimoteswick Castle in the 16th century, must have been baptised here. He was later burned at the stake for his political beliefs. The private burial ground of the Bowes Lyon family is here, and there is a lychgate presented in 1904 by the Honourable Francis Bowes Lyon. It provides a lovely little entrance gate to the church grounds.

Adjoining the village of Beltingham are the grounds of Ridley Hall, at one time the country seat of the Bowes Lyon family. The hall itself is 300 years old and it stands in 40 acres of grounds. The grounds are extremely well looked after, with large areas of sweeping green pastures, bordered by ranks of tall imposing trees. Closer to the house, the grounds become more colourful with large flower beds rich with riotous colour. When the Bowes Lyon family left Ridley Hall in 1948, it was converted into a private school, the St Nicholas Preparatory School. This school was run by the then vicar of Bardon Mill, Rev Evans. He closed his school in 1966 and Ridley Hall was taken over by Northumberland Education Authority, and it now houses Haydon Bridge high school boarding pupils. Adjoining the grounds of Ridley Hall is the nature reserve of Allen Banks, a popular spot for picnics.

There are many other sites of interest in Bardon Mill and Henshaw. Henshaw village itself is an attractive and peaceful spot and it is here that the Women's Institute hall stands. It was originally a Methodist chapel which closed in 1939.

Henshaw village stands on a steep incline about a hundred yards north of the busy A69 road and can be reached by way of a narrow lane. With two chapels and also All Hallows church standing on the opposite side of the A69, Henshaw was frequently referred to as the 'Celestial City'. All these places of worship were built from stone quarried from the now disused quarry on Bayldon Farm.

The hamlet of Tow House stands to the south of Henshaw on the A69. The name is probably derived from the bastle house which dominated the village green and is called Tower House. Rumour says that a tunnel runs under the river South Tyne from the bastle to Willimoteswick Castle.

Beadnell 🐚

Nothing concerned with the sea stays unchanged for long, and Beadnell is no exception. This community has always had to adapt, given the varying fortunes of fishing and farming; never more so than in the last 50 years. The village lies on a wide sweep of sand, some of the loveliest in Britain. Since the Second World War, tourists, holidaymakers and new residents have streamed here in ever greater numbers, seeking escape from noise and hurry.

But people bring change. In 1920, this was a peaceful fishing village of 49 dwellings. Now there are around 400 houses, and even more caravans. How can a community accept such expansion and still preserve its identity and quiet beauty? This is Beadnell's dilemma.

If you stand at the harbour on a summer afternoon and watch the windsurfers' gaudy sails skimming over the bay, the children playing

Beadnell Harbour

on the beach, and the wild dunes stretching away to the Long Nanny burn, it is easy to forget how the place has evolved. Yet all around lie reminders of its past. The lime-kilns cast a shadow like a fortress, relics of the early 1800s, when Beadnell bustled with quarries, small coal-shafts and the horse-drawn tramway which carted stone to the kilns for burning.

The harbour itself – the only one on the east coast to face west – once clattered with industry. From here, until the First World War, great 50-foot keel boats with brown barked sails pursued the summer herring. Boats from Scotland, Cornwall and Ireland docked here; and local women worked from morning till night, gutting fish and packing them into barrels. At that time, there were 60 or more fishermen in

the village. Now there are only five. The two cobles remaining in the harbour represent the end, not just of an industry, but of a way of life.

Some curious beliefs associated with the fishing still survive. Older Beadnell folk remember a time when, if a fisherman met a vicar on the way to the harbour, he would not go to sea. Even now, some never mention the name of the pink animal with the curly tail; and, when the fishing is poor, some will burn salt on the fire to 'gliff the devil'.

Superstition aside, the village has a strong Christian tradition. Just east of the harbour, at Ebb's Neuk Point, lie the ruins of a 13th century chapel. Legend has it that the original was built by Oswald, King of Northumbria, for his sister, St Ebba, in the 7th century.

Walking north from here along the rocky shore, you come to Benthall

Farm, called 'the Benty' after the rough dune grass. This is the last farm left in the village. Houses have sprung up where the hay pikes used to smell so lovely and where huge, heavy-footed horses used to plod before Dick Kennedy's plough.

Beyond Windmill Steads, the site of fishermen's cottages, and Dell Point – 'delved', as its name implies, for coal – you reach the Haven. Here, children splash and 'doggers' (green crabs) scuttle among rock pools, where, earlier this century, fishing cobles sailed into the sunrise, and women in shawls and barefoot children helped to launch them and haul them up. Until well after the Second World War, in wintertime, women gathered mussels and limpets on these rocks to bait the 'long lines'. 'Sixteen hundred hooks a day,' the fishermen's wives will tell you; 'It was slavery!' In bad weather, they would gather on this same bank-top, gazing anxiously out to sea. Older residents still talk of the terrible blizzard of 1895, when local boats took refuge among the Farne Islands; and of the three men drowned ten years earlier, in sight of their wives and children at Beadnell Square.

It was a hard life. It pared people's values down to what really mattered: caring for one another and for the place. You can still feel that in Beadnell. In the centre of the village, 'the toon', clustered around St Ebba's church, the village shop and The Craster Arms, there's a strong sense of community, into which newcomers are welcomed. The large new estates of Longstone Close and Park, begun in the 1960s, have been rapidly absorbed into village life.

Centres of social activity as various as church, shop, pub and Women's Institute help bind together the layers of old and new. You have only to attend a village wedding to see how well this works. Natives and newcomers alike turn out to see the old customs observed. Bride and groom pay a toll to jump the 'petting stool', symbolizing the beginning of their journey through life together, while guns are fired to scare away bad luck.

All summer, all winter, the wind blows across Beadnell Bay. It combs the bent-grass on the dunes and braes, where Bronze Age skeletons lie curled up beneath the sand. Round the stony ruins of St Ebba's chapel it whistles, and over the ridge and furrow of medieval fields. Up in 'the toon' it shakes the windows of the fishermen's cottages, newly converted into holiday homes. It rattles the sides of the caravans. Nothing escapes it.

And the tides of visitors come and go, and village life quietly continues. In their black huts, the last few fishermen mend their gear. At sea, they haul their crab and lobster pots and, in summer, their salmon nets. One day, perhaps, their boats will be gone from the harbour. What will replace them? Nightclubs and amusement arcades? Most people want a future for Beadnell which draws upon the best of its past. As long as the tides wash onto these shores, this community will keep on accepting the best of changes and resisting the worst.

Beal 🐝

Beal is a farmstead and hamlet near the sea with a station on the main-line North East railway. It lies on the mainland, west of Holy Island.

During and after the Second World War, old Ford cars were bought for £5 by some islanders and used to operate a taxi service between the mainland and Holy Island. The route was a perilous one across the sands and only accessible at low tide. The taxis ferried passengers from the railway station or the Plough Hotel, known locally as the 'Halfway' (halfway between Edinburgh and Newcastle). Nowadays there is a causeway over to the island, but refuges are still provided for those caught by the tide.

Beal was originally named Beehill as the monks kept bees there. Beal also had a school which was built in 1872 for 60 children, though the average number was 40. The school is now used as an expedition centre.

Bebside & Cowpen 🐝

Bebside and Cowpen are suburbs of Blyth Valley, situated in south east Northumberland. The population of both communities is 7,292. Many of these have lived for generations in the area but unfortunately now, because of unemployment and greater inducements elsewhere, the movement of people is greater, miners moving to other coal-fields, others seeking employment abroad. At the same time, the area is expanding rapidly, especially Bebside with its new superstore eventually to be surrounded by new estates.

Records tell us that agriculture was the beginning of the settlements, today a mixture of industry and agriculture prevails with others commuting out of the area for employment.

In the early 20th century mining was of great importance, until 1987 when the last pit was closed. The miners grafted hard for their living, at the end of the day appreciating the warmth of their fireside. They had no running water and not until later in the century was sanitation improved.

The Sidney family of Cowpen opened the first Roman Catholic school in 1843 with the Church of England following in 1858, now there is a fairly large school complex from nursery through to high school.

The war years too affected the communities, as illustrated by the war memorial. There was also an isolation hospital in the area. Maybe because of the trials and tribulations of the time, the people became very closely knit. No need then for locks, bolts or security lights, everyone's doors were left unlocked and a welcome extended to everyone that made their acquaintance.

Notoriety can be seen in the naming of the Kitty Brewster Hotel, road, farm and industrial estate. Kitty, it is said, was a lady who murdered her five children in the bath tub. She is also said to have brewed ale and taken in lodgers, leaving the rest to the imagination! Another explanation, however, is that the word 'kitty' meant a gaol and 'brewster' a man who brewed ale. Who's to tell and who's to know?

The 'Paraffin Man' is remembered, always on a Monday trudging along with his horse and cart selling everything he could get on his cart, very often bartering with his customers – a rabbit or chicken for a few candles. The schoolchildren, too, loved to spend their coppers at Charlie's shop, twopence for a cigarette and a light or a penny gobstopper. Today the shop still caters for the children, with another generation of the same family.

Cobbled streets can still be seen in the old part of Cowpen with its rows of houses close together, surrounded by newer estates. Bebside is losing its identity, merging with Cowpen until eventually it will be linked to Cramlington, no doubt both communities changing with the times.

Bedlington

Thirteen miles from Newcastle upon Tyne, standing on a ridge, is the community of Bedlington. To the south runs the river Blyth, through Plessey Woods, Bayard Woods and the Free Woods. This area has many beautiful woodland walks. To the north, the boundary of the shire is marked by the river Wansbeck with its riverside park. Bedlington folk can look eastwards and see the North Sea, and westward the rolling

St Cuthbert's, Bedlington

Cheviots. It is a lovely spot – within easy reach of city, country market towns, remote moorland and seaside places.

The name Bedlington is of Saxon origin, meaning the place where the tribe called the Baedlingas lived. It is said that about AD 900 the Bishop of Durham bought 'the vill which is called Bedlingtun and its appendages, Nedertun, Grubba, Twisle, Cebbingtun, Sliceburn Gammes'. The bishop chose a prominent site for a church, which even today is a landmark.

The Saxon church would have been made of wattle, daub and thatch, and the only remaining trace is a stone carving depicting two angels, now fixed to the nave at the south east corner. Eilaf, one of the seven monks who fled from Holy Island with St Cuthbert's body, was the first rector of this church. After the Norman Conquest, William the Conqueror's son marched north to quell the rebels. The monks of Chester-le-Street fled with Cuthbert's body. The body rested in Bedlington church on Saturday, 12th December 1069. When it was safe the body was taken to its final resting place in Durham.

The Normans replaced the flimsy Saxon church with a stone building. The original dog-tooth carving of the Norman arch is still discernible.

Around 1120 the south wall of the nave was built and one small Norman window opening survives behind the pulpit.

The stone 'cross' standing in the Market Place, contrary to popular belief, has no religious significance at all. Earlier it stood on the other side of the road until in 1782 it was rebuilt in the Market Place. It is in the shape of an upturned nail. In the days of bargaining and bartering this is where 'paying on the nail' took place.

A different kind of life from farming, weaving and nailmaking began to emerge in the late 18th century. Mining of the rich coal deposits began and the Bedlington ironworks were opened. Bedlington was once well known as a pit village with its rows of colliery houses. There were numerous coal mines in the area. Netherton colliery was sunk in 1818.

The ironworks began in the late 18th century. Situated on the banks of the river Blyth with an abundance of trees, the coal near at hand and water power, it was an ideal spot, and its close proximity to the port of Blyth was very favourable.

The first train to run from King's Cross was pulled by a Bedlington engine, as were Holland and Italy's first trains. Replicas of *De Arend* and *De Snelheid* are in Utrecht Museum and the *Bayard* in Rome. George Stephenson and his son were frequent visitors to the ironworks. Their first locomotive *Blucher* had axles, boiler plates and wheels from the works.

Sir Daniel Gooch DL JP, famous son of Bedlington, born 24th August 1816, had links with the ironworks too. He became Locomotive Superintendent to the Great Western Railway at the age of 21. He was responsible for the laying of the first Atlantic cables in 1865 and 1866 and the French Atlantic cables of 1869. His birth is marked on The King's Arms in Front Street.

Bedlington is the home of the Bedlington terrier. Probably the beginning of the breed was early in the 18th century, a favourite of gipsies on the Borders, who hired them out to the landed gentry to exterminate vermin in ponds and woods. The terrier's lamb-like appearance with its short hair, only one inch long, achieved through proper trimming, belies its active hunter's temperament. With its light springy step it is a very attractive dog. Between 1800 and 1820 this breed was used in badger baiting, fox hunting and cockfighting. These activities were later declared illegal. Nowadays the Bedlington terrier is very popular in the USA.

Bedlington today is very much alive and well. The main street is wide and bordered with flower beds. An 18 hole golf course on the southern outskirts is a valuable amenity developed from an open-cast coal site in 1972. The community centre, run by the local council, hosts varied entertainments, a regular programme of activities and is available for receptions. There are many public houses and eating places. Thursday is market day and this attracts many visitors.

New housing estates have been built, increasing the population to approximately 13,000. A court house consisting of five courts was officially opened by HM Queen Elizabeth II in July 1993. An impressive new Catholic church of St Bede was dedicated in 1992. Next to it is the Salvationist's Citadel.

Sport is important and there are football teams to suit all ages and a long-standing cricket club. There are still plenty of spacious areas left around Bedlington. Walks are still possible through fields, woods and along rivers and they are clearly marked.

Belford 🐏

Belford has existed as a settlement for some 3,000 years. Evidence of habitation can be seen on the brow of the crag overlooking the village. The name is believed to be derived from 'Beol's ford' of Saxon times. Over this period Belford has had a chequered career and suffered severely from the passage of both English and Scottish armies in the long troubled history of the Borders.

It is claimed that the Market Square and its cross originated in the medieval period. At this time Belford was the centre of a sprawling estate which included Middleton, Easington, Lucker, Spindlestone, and parts of Elwick and Ross.

Today Belford is a village of some 1,000 or so inhabitants centred on the church of St Mary. To the west of the church on a site where West Hall Farm now stands, the moat of the Castrum de Beleford can still be seen. The manor house which replaced it was pulled down when Abraham Dixon became Squire of Belford and built the new manor house of Belford Hall in the mid 18th century.

The squire sat downstairs in the church and had his own private door by which he entered. Older members of the community say one didn't quite bow the knee – but almost! At Christmas he would send round a piece of beef and logs for the fire to his tenants.

Once a year the 'hirings' took place in the market place. This was a great day, with roundabouts, swing boats, and hoop-la stalls – also a circus which stayed for two days. These activities came to an end in the 1920s.

If asked 'Why choose to live in Belford?' the short answer would be, 'Because Belford has everything' – three churches, a doctors' surgery and health centre, chemist, post office, community club, baker, butcher, hardware store, craft gallery and information centre, one hotel and two inns, two small supermarkets, a newsagent's, two hairdressers and a village shop which one might call the Harrods of Belford, because if they don't have a certain item in stock they will do their best to get it for you.

Altogether, a happy place to live. The villagers are friendly and there is a good community spirit.

Bellingham 🐾

Bellingham grew up by the side of the Hareshaw burn near its confluence with the river North Tyne. Surrounded by rolling hills and moors, it is approached by a downhill route from almost every direction.

The oldest building, St Cuthbert's church, dates back to the 11th century. Its thick stone walls and stone-slabbed roof bear testimony to the turbulent times of Border wars and family feuds when the church served as a refuge for people and animals. Nearby is St Cuthbert's Well, natural spring water reputed to have miraculous powers and still used for baptisms.

The earliest evidence of the town's name (pronounced Bellinjum) comes from the 13th century when the de Bellingham family lived in their earth and timber castle on the site still known as Castle Hill. No bearers of the family name remain locally but two branches went west and founded Castle Bellingham in Ireland and another Bellingham in Washington state, USA. In the 18th century four main families in control of the district were Charltons, Dodds, Milburns and Robsons. Their descendants and those of other families like Armstrongs and Scotts are happily still with us tending sheep and cattle or pursuing other peaceful occupations.

Bellingham became a small market town serving a large area; a centre for sheep and cattle sales, fairs and hiring days for shepherds and other farm workers. Local craftsmen, cobblers, saddlers, tailors, blacksmiths and many others supplied the essentials for life in this remote area.

In 1840 an iron foundry was established by the burnside and rows of primitive cottages were built higher up to house workers. This boom was short-lived and it closed down after eight years.

The next big change was the arrival of a train service up the North Tyne valley with a station at Bellingham, followed, many years later, by bus services. People chose to go further afield to shop, which, along with wartime restrictions, caused the collapse of several local businesses. In 1956 the train service became a victim of the Beeching axe. Next, Hareshaw coal pit and others ceased production, and several families left Bellingham to work elsewhere. On the brighter side there were new beginnings. Forestry work became available; the damming of the North Tyne above Falstone (to form Kielder Water) and increased tourism have provided some new jobs.

The small town of Bellingham was the administrative capital for the rural district of the same name, one of the largest but most sparsely populated in England. The council offices were in the former workhouse built in 1839 by the Board of Guardians to house the needy (vagrants had to break stones in payment for a night's lodging). Twenty years ago Bellingham became a ward of the new Tynedale District, centred in Hexham. The old workhouse took on another new role. Retaining only one small office for council business, it now houses a branch of the county library, the Tourist Information Centre, tearooms and a hairdressing establishment.

The town hall is used for dances, discos, concerts etc and formerly for regular cinema shows. Smaller events are held in the Reed Hall (former school), the Masonic hall (former shop), and the Methodist hall.

Three council estates built since 1945 adjoin the older stone-built, grey-slated core of the village. They are built of brick covered with rough-cast and many are now owner-occupied. Former shops have been made into houses and several bungalows have sprung up on the outskirts of the village. Nowadays 'village' appears to be a more appropriate description than 'small town'. Special accommodation is provided for the elderly in bungalows, The Shieling and an Abbeyfield house. The new health clinic is a great asset. Purpose-built, it is run by a very efficient and sympathetic team. Even though Bellingham has grown in area, its population has not increased greatly, from about 1,000, since the middle of this century, but overcrowding has gone.

Hesleyside Hall, the biggest house in the parish, was originally a bastle (fortified house), stronghold of the Charlton family. Additions have been made over the years, making it into a fine mansion still occupied by Charltons.

In the Foundry Yard are a new ambulance station, small industrial factories and the Social Institute. Most of the rows of workers' cottages have disappeared. Few signs of the ironworks remain apart from the waste heaps and the Low Dam which harnessed the necessary water power, but heavy floods have washed much of it away.

Being on the Pennine Way and on the edge of Northumberland National Park, Bellingham is a stopping place for walkers, cyclists and other holidaymakers. The youth hostel, local hotels and bed and breakfast establishments are kept busy throughout the season. There are shorter walks along the riverside and a woodland walk up the Hareshaw burn ravine ending at the spectacular 30 foot waterfall – Hareshaw Linn. Last century a village picnic was held annually in a natural amphitheatre a short distance from the waterfall. A few very old photographs remain to tell the tale.

Tennis and bowls courts are available on the school premises, also badminton and football. There is carpet bowling in the town hall during the winter months, and various evening classes in the school. The popular nine hole golf course celebrated its centenary in 1993. The Dramatic Society usually stages one or more plays annually and for the musically inclined there is the Choral Society.

Sheep and cattle sales still attract dealers from far and wide and are busier days in the village; but the busiest day of all is North Tyne and Redesdale Agricultural Society's annual show day, held on a Saturday in late summer for over 150 years.

Daily needs are again well catered for in the village shops and by local workmen, but to visit the dentist, optician or hospital a 17 mile journey to Hexham or further is necessary.

It may have been reduced to village status, nevertheless Bellingham is still thriving and is a very pleasant place in which to live.

Belsay

Belsay, which boasts a very colourful history, has belonged to the Middleton family for some 800 years. Early in the 13th century, about 1226, two brothers John and Richard Middleton, married two daughters of Walter the Scott of Belsay and each inherited half the property. Richard was chancellor of England from 1270–72 and bought John's share of the estate.

Tragedy struck in 1318 when the great grandson of the chancellor

Belsay Castle

forfeited his estates for participation with his cousin Sir Gilbert de Middleton in rebellion. He was involved in kidnapping and raiding during the misrule of Edward II and was hung, drawn and quartered. Belsay estate was given to Sir John Crumbwell, constable of the Tower of London, and Thomas de Bamburgh, King's Clerk, for their lives and later by Edward III to Sir John Strivelyn, one of his military commanders and some-time constable of Edinburgh Castle. Sir John, on his death in 1391, settled Belsay on Sir John Middleton, who is presumed to have been the grandson of the last Middleton possessor of the castle, and is believed to have married Strivelyn's eventual heiress.

In September 1804 Sir Charles Miles Lambert Monck, sixth Baronet, drove away from the Jacobean porch of old Belsay Castle on his honeymoon. He had changed his name from Middleton five years before in accordance with the will of his maternal grandfather, Mr Monck of Caenby, Lincs. The honeymoon lasted two years, during which time his wife Louisa, daughter of Sir George Cooke Bt; gave birth to a son, Charles Atticus Monck, while Sir Charles threw himself into the study of Hellenic architecture with the singular purpose of designing a Grecian-style house to build in Northumberland on his return home. During the period 1810–17 Belsay Hall was built, away from the castle, which still remained habitable. The quarries, from which the stone was hewn to build the hall, were later converted into gardens and the whole area landscaped. These beautiful gardens remain today, having been restored twice over the past 50 years. They fell into neglect during the Second World War when servicemen were in residence and again during the 1970s.

In 1867, Sir Charles Monck died aged 88 years and was succeeded by his grandson, Sir Arthur Middleton. He was a most respected employer and ran a thriving estate with many staff in all departments; farmers, joiners, drainers, masons, foresters and numerous staff in the hall, which must have been a very cosy place with fires in all the rooms. Two men were employed solely to 'lead' coal from Angerton station to the hall. Another two men were employed to saw logs to a specific size to fit the huge grates of the library, dining room and study.

The village, which echoes the Greek theme with its arcaded construction, must have been a very busy place with the many shops centred mainly in the arcade. There were two confectionery shops, Anderson's and Pickering's; Mr William Pickering had a motorcycle repair shop and later moved from the arcade to a purpose-built garage on the opposite side of the road, serving petrol and carrying out repairs for miles around, his being the only garage between Cowgate, Newcastle, and Otterburn. Cuthbert Snowball ran the post office and telephone exchange along with his wife and family, and they also had a saddlery shop adjacent to the post office. Mary Nixon had a tearoom at the Pavilion, now known as Woodbine Cottage, next to the police house where Mr Douglas, the first policeman, took up residence in 1927. Travelling towards the village from the police house we come to Guidepost; here the joiner lived above his workshop and at the corner the blacksmith lived next door to his smithy. In the 1930s a new and imposing blacksmith's shop was built opposite to his residence, as befitted the talent of Edwin Creer, who was reputed to be the finest blacksmith in Northumberland. This shop is now an elegant tearoom.

The village school, built in 1870, replaced the old school house of the 1830s. The council school was purpose-built to accommodate 150 pupils; this must have been a very cramped situation for the pupils, who would be taught in either the hall or the one classroom! Mr Firth was the headmaster and his wife the assistant. He was the proud owner of a motorbike combination. Up to the mid 1950s Sunday services by the vicar of Bolam were held in the school and regular dances and evening classes were well supported by countryfolk from a wide area.

The Women's Institute and Methodists continued to hold their meetings in the old school house until 1960. Numbers in the school have varied over the past 50 years from around 25 pupils to the present 80 and still rising. A larger mobile classroom has been installed to cater for the rising population which is most encouraging for the survival of our idyllic village.

At the west end of the village, there was, during Sir Arthur's time, a tollhouse, or gatehouse as the locals called it. And at this very junction the local RAC man directed the traffic! He was responsible for collecting the toll money and opening the gate to travellers heading towards Otterburn. One local character was known to object to the charge and whipped his steed into a high jump over the gate, much to the annoyance of Mr Riddell no doubt. At the junction of the other two roads, Scotsgap and Whalton, facilities for high finance were catered for by Mr Sutherland, the manager of Lloyds bank.

Sir Arthur died in 1933 at the grand old age of 95 years and was succeeded by his son Sir Arthur Charles Middleton, but owing to ill health the estate was directed by his nephew John Middleton, who unfortunately died in 1939. Stephen, his brother, took over the management of the estate, becoming the ninth Baronet in 1942 when his uncle died.

Sir Stephen was anxious to build up a profitable estate again after the war years. William Atkinson, son of the former estate agent, was appointed agent and he very quickly revitalised the estate by advertising nationally for heads of various departments. The woodlands were cleared and a vast planting programme was put in operation; the building department modernised and repaired property ready for new employees; farming acreage was extended; parklands were let to tenant farmers and the grounds were restored to their former glory. For the first time, the rhododendron gardens and castle grounds were open to the public. Employees were expected to take their turn manning the gate to the hall and castle. The hall became a very busy place both during the day for business, as the office and Sir Stephen's study were here, and in the evenings when there was the Scottish dancing club and the youth club. Private functions were held at the hall, such as the English Speaking Union, the Historical and Antiquarian Society, the Red Cross and many others. Catering for these events was usually from Arcade House Hotel, once the temperance hotel in the village, where Mrs Holms ran a catering and accommodation establishment.

By the 1970s the estate was hit by the economic situation and the number of staff was drastically reduced; much of the work was carried out by contract and eventually the Department of Environment, later English Heritage, restored the grounds once more and again the gardens were open to the public. A variety of functions are held here now as in the 1950s, but of a very different nature. It is a popular place for visitors from both far and near. Today, village trades are much depleted – only the garage and store with post office remain – but all the houses in the village are occupied, with young families who are interested in and part of our village community.

Biddlestone ✿

The small village of Biddlestone was created around Biddlestone Hall, and the surrounding estate of land, farms, stables and kennels. Six cottages for the estate workers were built east of the hall, and are still there today, now privately owned as the estate was split up and the farms sold off in about 1950 to meet death duty claims. Any mature woodland was also felled then, but was replanted and has grown up well again.

In former days the owners were the Selby family, some of whom are buried in a small cemetery south of the village. Although the hall was demolished about 1950 the adjoining and much older Catholic chapel remains and is listed. One or two services are still held there each year. It is known there was an ice house, and also an underground passage believed to go west to Clennell. 'Osbaldistone Hall' in Sir Walter Scott's novel *Rob Roy* was in fact Biddlestone Hall.

It has been a typical country estate, complete with a Catholic priest's house, and a carriage drive leading away down towards Netherton, past Netherton mill. Once or twice a year a toll of one shilling was charged to anyone who happened to travel along the carriage drive that particular day. This was discontinued about 1950.

The hill behind Biddlestone is called Harden, site of the famous redstone quarry, the stone of which has been sold and transported all over the world. In the 1950s it went by lorry down to the goods train at Rothbury station, then down to London, and was used to lay the road surface along The Mall towards Buckingham Palace, amongst others.

Whilst wartime petrol rationing was in force the landlord could only travel by car down Burradon banks as far as Cock-le-Bush, then he had to return to Biddlestone Hall. Later on he bought the Netherton school field and after that he could travel all the way around his estate.

Biddlestone is surrounded by Newton Farm, The Rookland (new in the 1950s), Puncherton, Singmore, Biddlestone Townfoot, and Biddlestone Edge. The source of the Netherton burn is away behind Biddlestone at 'the white stones', yet the name Biddlestone is reputed to have nothing to do with 'smashing stones'!

With the maturing woodlands, neat hedges and good farming the area is very attractive, at any time of the year. The local population is today about 30.

Birtley 🦜

The village of Birtley stands on a high ridge some 700 feet above sea level and is situated five and a half miles south east of Bellingham. It commands superb panoramic views over the North Tyne valley and beyond to the northernmost part of the Pennines, to Wark Forest and to Scotland. The place name of Birtley means 'bright clearing' being derived from the Old English 'beorht' meaning bright. W.W. Tomlinson in his book *Companion Guide to Northumberland* informs us that it used to be called Birkley. This is confirmed by the inscription found on the silver communion cup in the church which reads 'Birkley chalice, given by Mrs Reed of Chipchase, 1743'.

The remains of several British camps encircling the village provide ample proof that the area was inhabited at the time of the Stone Age. Such camps existed at West End, Birtley Shields Dene, Mill Knock, Countess Park and Carry House. In addition to these, many interesting relics have been discovered at Carry House camp including spearheads, daggers, knives, long swords and part of the harness and horse trappings of a British chieftain's war chariot.

Later evidence of man's use of this area can be seen in the cultivation terraces around the village and a little to the west there are vast deposits of iron slag. Relics of medieval metal workers have been discovered nearby. Later on in the village history, limestone was excavated in the area and kilns remain, notably the one on Kiln Bank.

Birtley Hall stands at the top of Kiln Bank. The present property occupies the site of the old castle and was formerly the vicarage. On the opposite side of the road stands the church of St Giles which dates back to the 12th century. The discovery of a significant stone on the site during the last century suggests that there was a Saxon church here, however.

There is a holy well situated to the north of the village. This chalybeate spring issues from a high rock beneath a waterfall. Nearby, above the spring, is a rock standing twelve feet high and known locally as the Devil's Rock. Legend has it that a demon once attempted to leap from this rock to the opposite side of the river North Tyne a mile away. The demon's hoofmarks can still be seen on the top of the rock. To counteract fears of the Devil's influence the well was blessed by a holy man, hence the title Holywell.

Nearby at Mill Knock quarry religious services were held on summer Sunday evenings. Prayer meetings were held at Town Head, previously known as Shepherd's Home.

The population of Birtley parish has decreased considerably over the past 150 years. In 1851 there were 428 people recorded on the parish census. This number was reduced to 134 by 1993.

The old village consisted mainly of thatched cottages. Water was collected from wells and springs until 1921 when two taps were installed in the village. Life was made easier with the arrival of electricity in 1952. Further changes have occurred in the tenure of property over the years. Most of the village and surrounding farms were owned by the Duke of Northumberland but now about half of the dwelling houses are privately owned.

The village of 1831 would have been virtually self-sufficient with 23 traders living here. A stone plaque on the wall of a property known as Manor House reads 'Thomas Robson, Draper, Licensed dealer in tea, coffee, snuff and tobacco'. Now only the post office and The Percy Arms pub remain.

The centre of learning in the village has followed a similar pattern. In 1859 some 71 children paid to attend the village school. In 1971 this school closed and the children were transported elsewhere.

Birtley today is a charming, peaceful village. The gardens and surrounding verges are well tended and there is a profusion of colour during the summer months. In recent years the combined efforts of the villagers have been rewarded with the Best Kept Village awards. The village is much admired by the increasing number of walkers who pass through and who still enjoy the same views as did our ancestors.

Bolton

Bolton lies on a fold of land in the valley of the river Aln. Surrounded by beautiful scenery, there is an abundance of wildlife to be seen in the fields, hedgerows and woods – deer, foxes, hares and the smaller stoats and weasels, with a surfeit of rabbits. A few red squirrels survive in the woods and herons, moorhens and kingfishers delight the eye on the riverside nearby.

To the south Alnwick Moor rises above the farmland, to the north towers Titlington Pike, and to the west and north the impressive range of the Cheviot Hills dominates the skyline, culminating in Cheviot itself, cloud topped in summer and snow capped in winter.

The history of Bolton village goes back to pre-Christian times. A burial cist was found in the churchyard, and a further urn was later found in the grounds of Bolton Hall.

In Saxon times a 'tun' or homestead was formed near a 'bol' or mound – hence the name of Bolton. The mound is probably the site of the present church – it is thought likely that a wooden church occupied this site in the 10th century when Bolton chapel was founded as a chapel of ease to Edlingham. The church itself contains little evidence of its earlier origins, apart from the Norman chancel arch, as it was restored in the 1850s and 1860s.

A leper colony and hospital was founded at Bolton about 1225. This was situated in the Guards field, to the north of the village, on an island surrounded by a bog. The site is still recognisable today. The hospital was occupied until the 16th century, throughout the turbulent years of the Border reivers and the continued warring between the English and the Scots.

The most memorable date in these times is 1513, during the reign of Henry VIII, when the English army of 26,000 men encamped at Bolton. The commander and other nobles 'partook of Holy Communion' in the chapel and 'pledged themselves to defeat the Scots in the field or die'. A few days later James IV of Scotland was slain at Flodden Field with over 9,000 of his men.

In 1553 the lordship of the manor was granted to Robert Collingwood; thence, through several families, it passed to the Burrells.

Little has changed at Bolton in the past centuries. There are two mills – at Bolton and Abberwick – in the area, both on the river Aln. They were working mills until the late 1930s, providing oats to feed the horses on the farms. With the coming of mechanisation the mills ceased to operate. The main occupations in the area are still in farming, but some of the villagers now commute to nearby towns and others are retired.

The village school was built in 1850 by Bryan Burrell. A single classroom with a one-roomed cottage attached, the school was intended to accommodate 80 children. It was a Church of England school to serve the townships of Bolton, Broome Park, Abberwick, and Titlington, and £10 each was given annually by the squire and the vicar for the education of the poorer children. By 1926 the number of pupils on the register was 67. Later a kitchen was added, and electricity installed, to provide hot meals for the children. Since then the rural population has declined, and the number of children dropped to 18 in 1968, when it was decided to close the school. The school was also the centre of local activity until 1929, when the village hall was built on land given by the Burrell family and using money raised by public subscription in memory of those who died in the First World War. It has continued to function as the centre of village life to the present day. Recently villagers raised the funds required to refurbish the hall.

A long established family in Bolton – the Gallons – were first mentioned in the chapel register in the 13th century. Several generations of the family have served the community as blacksmiths, the last having died recently.

There were five large houses with estates surrounding Bolton. East Bolton House was demolished earlier in the century. Shawdon Hall was built on the site of an old pele tower in 1779. Titlington Hall, of the same period, nestles beneath the pike on the side of the hill.

The two wings of Bolton Hall, close to the village, were built in different periods. The north was erected in 1689 on the site of an earlier building, and the south wing was added about 1800, the house to act as a dower house to Shawdon Hall. There is also evidence of a much older building between the wings, possibly a medieval tower. The house at Broome Park was demolished in the 1950s, but a new home was established in other buildings in the park. The estate has remained in the original family – the Burrells – for many generations.

There are five old cottages in the village. In addition the hall was recently divided into two houses and the adjacent outbuildings converted to make a further four homes. Thus the village of Bolton today consists of about a dozen homes, a post office, a village hall, and recently a small garage business. In addition there are several farms and cottages, together with the four large houses, all centred around the chapel surmounting the 'bol'.

Boulmer

The tiny fishing village of Boulmer in summer, lies low and tranquil along the shoreline, but in stormy weather seems to cling tenaciously to the rugged edge of north east Northumberland. Certainly, the village was never planned. It just grew, with a quiet charm, on a gentle curving bay. Whilst there will always have been a small farming community in the area, fishing must be the reason for Boulmer's existence.

In 1300 the village was part of the barony of Alnwick and still today most of the properties are part of the estate of the Duke of Northumberland. When repairs are required, the tenants 'go to the castle'. These may be quite normal repairs, missing slates and the like, but rumour has it that one old lady decided to go to the castle about a ghost in her house!

The thing most folk know about Boulmer is its history of smuggling. In the 1800s casks of spirits were still sometimes dug up on the beach and some of the houses had secret hiding places. One tale told is of the woman who sat on a barrel of brandy with her skirts draped around to conceal it from the searching eyes of the Excise man. Another is of a notorious smuggler who, having been caught and taken before the magistrates, had his sentence revoked after a member of the nobility pleaded his case. It was always supposed that this was done, not out of the goodness of the gentleman's heart, but because he did not wish to lose his supplies of gin from Holland. There is a rhyme which goes 'Jimmy Turner of Ford did not think it a sin, to saddle his horse on a Sunday and ride to Boulmer for gin'. With no coastguards at that time it was probably very worthwhile to run the risk of discovery by the Excise men. The Scottish border would be reasonably easy to cross, even when travelling with packhorses.

In spite of its smuggling record, Boulmer was never a 'wrecking' village. However, over the years a 'ship ashore' sometimes meant a great variety of goods being cast up on the beach; many village children tried their first cigarette when tins of them were washed up. In the 1940s, a small boy tugged at the Customs and Excise man's sleeve saying, in a loud voice, 'You want to see what my granda has up in his attic.' Thankfully an inspection brought to light nothing of interest to the government official!

Boulmer may have been notorious for 'rescuing' contraband, but it is also renowned for its splendid record of sea rescue. The tradition of lifesaving goes back a long way. For as long as men have fished off our lovely but sometimes inhospitable coast they have been willing to risk their lives to rescue others. The Royal National Lifeboat Station was established in 1825 but, before that, the Duke of Northumberland provided a lifeboat in the village. The first boats were of course rowing boats, followed by those with sails as well as oars. The station had been founded over 100 years before the arrival of the first motor boat.

When, in 1967, the RNLI decided to withdraw their boat, it looked like the end of a 150 year tradition of sea rescue in the village. However, local feeling was such that Boulmer Volunteer Rescue Service was established and by early 1970 Boulmer was again in the rescue business. Many are the bravery awards presented over the years, the most recent being the award of silver plate by the Department of Trade and Industry to a BVRS crew for their part in a dramatic rescue involving the vessel *Nordboen* and helicopters of the RAF Search and Rescue Flight stationed at Boulmer.

Before the advent of tractor power, the women helped launch the lifeboat. A magnificent painting of such a feat hangs in the Fishing Boat Inn. The heroic conduct of the women was recognised by the presentation of a vellum by the RNLI, after they pulled the lifeboat for a mile through a blizzard to Seaton Point when a launch from Boulmer was impossible.

Like all fishing villages, superstition and customs, although to a lesser extent, still remain. In the early part of this century some men would turn and go home again if they met a woman on their way to sea. Some villagers still put their thumbs up if the bacon-producing animal's correct name is used; it is known by various names, the guffie, the animal, and, for reasons lost in the mists of time, the minister. In the 1920s a visitor was horrified to learn that 'they were killing the minister'. A wedding custom means that the bride's car on leaving for the church is stopped and guns are fired over it. It is not allowed to proceed until the bride's father hands over what the gunmen decide is a fair amount with which to toast the bride and groom in the Fishing Boat Inn.

Boulmer must be one of the few true fishing villages left in Northumberland and can have changed very little over the last hundred or so years. Even the arrival of the Royal Air Force during the Second World War, although providing very welcome employment locally, has done little to alter the place. Summer brings an influx of caravan dwellers to sites about a mile south of the village. Known collectively by locals as 'swallows', some of these holidaymakers are third generation visitors. The Fishing Boat Inn may be a little more crowded and coffee mornings and the like will have larger attendances while the swallows are in residence but, basically, the village changes little. Perhaps the friendly and uncommercial atmosphere of the place is why many visitors choose to return year after year. Boulmer's lovely natural harbour with its graceful fishing cobles is a sight to remember.

Bowsden 🐚

Bowsden is situated eight miles south west of Berwick upon Tweed and nine miles north of Wooler. The coast is seven miles away and the Scottish border eleven miles. From the village can be seen the Cheviot Hills and the sea.

The village itself comprises three farms, the Black Bull Inn, the post office, which is open three mornings a week, several new bungalows and the older houses set back from the road. These are mostly built of local limestone and roughcast. There are approximately 84 inhabitants, many associated with agriculture; others travel out of the village to work in the neighbouring towns. Many older people have chosen this pleasant, peaceful village for their retirement.

The original settlement is believed to have been situated a little to the south of the present village in an area still known as Bowsden Hollins. From an old tithe map of 1862, it would appear that the present right of way was probably the main thoroughfare connecting several villages and settlements.

In the late 1800s, Bowsden was a busy, industrious community. The quarrying and burning of lime for agricultural purposes was thriving and the four farms within the village employed many men. Records show that there were two blacksmiths and a joiner, four boot and shoe makers, a grocer and poulterer, and a provisions merchant. There was also a postmaster, and Boulmer's Directory of 1887 tells us that 'Letters arrive by mail cart from Beal at 11 am and are despatched at 1.20 pm.' The 1862 tithe map shows two inns, The Black Bull at the west end of the village and The Lamb at the east.

The school, which closed in 1963 and has now been converted into a house, was erected by subscription in 1873, and replaced an older building located on a different site. The schoolmaster lived in the village, but many of his pupils faced a walk of several miles each day to obtain their education. There was a reading room which was supported by contributions from members. This building was used by the villagers as a games room for billiards and darts into the 1940s.

The village hall was built in 1924 and over the years has been the venue for many dances, parties and soirées, as well as the regular meeting place for the Women's Institute which held its first meeting in 1925.

Byrness 🐑

Byrness (pronounced Burrness) is the last village in England on the A68 just before the road winds steeply uphill to cross the Scottish border at Carter Bar. It occupies a sheltered position on the valley floor by the north bank of the river Rede and is protected from the worst of the weather by the forested slopes of the surrounding hills. On the doorstep are Chattlehope Spout, at 75 feet reputedly the highest waterfall in Northumberland but often dry in summer, Catcleugh reservoir which supplies 2.3 million gallons of water daily, mainly to Tyneside, and the dark green expanse of Redesdale Forest.

Situated as it is on a popular tourist route, Byrness offers a number of amenities for holidaymakers – filling station/café, pub/hotel, youth hostel, camping and caravan park – and attractions such as forest trails, the Pennine Way which runs close by, a twelve mile forest drive and an annual Midsummer Madness fair.

Until the 1950s, however, Byrness was merely a district with a scattering of isolated hill farms. Its main claim to fame was that the first sheepdog trial held in England took place here in 1876. But for many centuries before that Byrness was part of the huge parish of Elsdon. In 1793, to cater for the spiritual and educational needs of the community in this remote part of his living, the Rev Louis Dutens provided a chapel. The total cost of £1,750 was raised by voluntary subscription to which he contributed two-thirds. He also provided a school; the resident curate at Byrness was the teacher and had to teach free of charge twelve children of poor parents.

The chapel, now the church of St Francis, stands alongside the A68. It is one of the smallest places of worship in Northumberland and is notable for the fine stained glass window which commemorates the 67 people who died during the construction of Catcleugh reservoir

(1894–1905). This was the first memorial window in the country to be dedicated to the working man. The graveyard contains some interesting headstones, among them a bronze cross erected by the children of Byrness school to the memory of Matthew Carr, aged twelve, who was killed in the stonecrusher at Catcleugh. The Catcleugh workforce was recruited from Newcastle and Gateshead; the labourers and their families were housed, on site, in wooden cabins. Their children went to Byrness school where they weren't very popular because their heads were crawling with lice which, so it was said, fell onto the exercise books of the local children!

The school, now a cottage, was replaced by a more modern building when Byrness village was built by the Forestry Commission in the 1950s. After the First World War, forestry provided much-needed work for rural communities, particularly in the traditional hill farming areas. As planting began to expand in north west Northumberland, Byrness was established as one of three purpose-built villages (the others were Kielder and Stonehaugh), to accommodate foresters and their families. The forest village was a new concept in local housing. It was built to blend in with the landscape, and there were to be good access roads, plenty of safe play areas for children, a community hall and a general store/post office. Byrness had 47 whitewashed houses each with its own back garden for growing flowers and vegetables, grouped round a series of 'greens'.

In the last 20 years, changes in timber production, particularly the increase in mechanisation, have led to a decline in the workforce. Few houses today are occupied by forestry workers; several are holiday homes and the rest belong to commuters who earn their living in a variety of occupations including civil servants, mechanics, oil terminal workers and sales executives. The decline is reflected in the school population. In its heyday there were over 50 pupils on the school roll, now with only eight it is one of the smallest schools in Northumberland.

For all its changing population, Byrness remains a tight-knit but very active little community. The village hall committee endeavours to involve everyone in gatherings which include the annual children's Christmas party, fashion shows, keep-fit club, whist drives and the renowned harvest tea and auction of produce which follows a service in the church of St Francis. The Playing Fields Association has worked tirelessly to provide new play equipment for the children in the village; a thriving playgroup takes place twice a week in the school hall and a baby clinic is held once a month. Links between the school and the village are strengthened by half-termly coffee afternoons when the whole community is invited to go along and see the children's work and activities. Organised family coach excursions to the coast, to theme parks etc are a regular occurrence in summer and in November the village plays host to drivers and supporters taking part in the annual RAC rally.

In this remote area, lacking the cultural facilites available in the towns, villagers have to be largely dependent on their own efforts to hold the community together.

Bywell 🐾

Bywell as we know it today is a tranquil place, situated in lovely parkland on a wide curve of the river Tyne, and is only 13 miles west of the bustling city of Newcastle. It seems remote from the pressures of the 20th century, but it was once a thriving community, resounding with the noise of ironworkers plying their craft. Four hundred years ago, Bywell was famous for its expertise in the making of stirrups, buckles and bits for the horsemen of the unruly Border country. It boasted 15 shops then, but now it is reduced to a light scattering of houses, a 15th century castle, a 'stately home', and two churches. *Two* churches? In a place which never can have had more than a few hundred inhabitants? Inevitably, legend says that they were built by two quarrelsome sisters, but in reality each church was built near the boundary of its own barony, and they are in different parishes.

St Peter's is the larger church, with a Norman tower. On this spot there was an even earlier wooden church, where one Egbert was consecrated bishop in AD 802, at a time when invading Danes had destroyed the priory of his see at Lindisfarne. The river Tyne flows just below the walls of St Peter's, and these same waters once contributed a bizarre incident to the church's history. In 1771, a tremendous flood swept down the Tyne, and to escape the rising waters some valuable horses were taken into the church, where one mare saved her life by climbing on the altar. Priorities were different in the 18th century, because, although the Squire's horses were saved, six villagers were drowned.

Only 200 yards away stands the second church, St Andrew's, which has a splendid Saxon tower and is set in a circular churchyard. The tower is a structure built by Saxon hands long before William the Conqueror and his Norman barons cast acquisitive eyes across the English Channel, and those same Saxon hands were building with stones some of which

Bywell Castle

were fashioned for Hadrian's Wall by Roman soldier-masons nearly a thousand years before that.

Not only are there two ancient churches at Bywell, but a romantic 15th century castle as well. Henry VI fled there for shelter after his defeat at the battle of Hexham in the Wars of the Roses. That unfortunate king, unequal to the demands surrounding kingship in the Middle Ages, did not find much respite at Bywell. His Yorkist enemies were hot on his heels, and Bywell Castle quickly surrendered to them. Henry escaped by the skin of his teeth, and left behind his crown, his sword and his helmet as he fled again.

But places are not just buildings, however ancient or imposing – places derive their real character from the people who live there. In Bywell, in the days of Border warfare, life was uncertain and harsh, as the raiding Scots could swoop down without warning. Winter and summer, all the cattle and sheep were taken into the village street every night. It was the only way that the folk of Bywell knew to protect their livestock. Imagine the practical difficulties of such an operation!

The men of Bywell were doughty fighters in defence of their homes and families. The Royal Commissioners of 1570 reported that they were 'stout and hardy by continual practice against the enemy'. It can't have been an easy life. Today, the action is over for Bywell, 'after life's fitful fever it sleeps well', but its inhabitants in earlier days met the challenges with courage and fortitude.

Callaly

Callaly Castle dates from the early 15th century and lies about 600 yards north east of the site of a motte and bailey castle from three centuries earlier. The original pele tower was incorporated into the west wing and in 1619 Sir John Clavering modernised his house, building a great hall east of the pele tower. In 1679 the new wing was extended southwards. Then in 1707 to balance the west wing a matching three-storey wing to the south east was added.

In the last 1,000 years only three families have owned Callaly Castle – the Callaly family, the Claverings and the Brownes. Major Alexander Browne purchased the estate in 1877 and carried out extensive alterations. Major Simon Browne came into the estate in 1925. In 1986 the castle was sold and divided into many lovely apartments. Major Browne continued to reside in the castle until his death in 1987 and now his grandson Mr Richard Bateson lives in one of the apartments and farms the estate.

Major Browne and his wife were great benefactors to the WI and gave them a secondhand army hut for their meetings at a peppercorn rent of a shilling a year. This was refurbished by members and used for many years. Most of the members had to travel quite a distance on foot or bicycle so for this reason the meetings were held on the third Thursday of the month when there was a moon! The WI was a hive of activity with social events and classes, but the new breed of country dwellers tend to seek their pleasures further afield.

Cambo 🌿

Cambo is an Anglo-Saxon name, so it is likely that there has been some sort of settlement here for a thousand years or more. Its known history, however, stems from 1688 when Sir William Blackett, a wealthy Newcastle merchant, bought the Wallington estate to which Cambo belongs. He and later his grandson Sir Walter carried out the building and development which largely gave us what you see today, with continuous improvement and building going on throughout the 19th and 20th centuries under the Trevelyans and then the National Trust, to whom Sir Charles Trevelyan bequeathed the whole estate.

The oldest building is the post office and village shop, originally a pele tower and thought to be 16th century. The village hall used to be the school, altered and enlarged for its present use in 1911. The school must have been there since the early 1700s, as its most famous pupil, 'Capability' Brown, went there until he was 16, and we have the date of retirement of his teacher, Thomas Castle, in 1739. The present school, just outside the village, was built in 1885.

In 1742 the remains of the original village were demolished, and a new estate village started with the building of a row of ten cottages just south of the pele tower. At one end of this row stood an inn, The Two Queens, which must have been very busy as it was on the coaching road from Newcastle to Jedburgh. It ceased to be an inn about the middle of the next century as the owner of the estate, Sir Walter Trevelyan, was very prominent in the temperance movement. The church was built in 1843; prior to that Cambo had been in the parish of Hartburn. The remaining houses were built in the 1880s, and the space occupied by their kitchen gardens was finally transformed into a village green in the 1950s under the National Trust.

Cambo is a very pretty village – its buildings are all of the same local stone, whatever their age. The gardens are lovely and colourful, partly because the soil has been tended and manured for a hundred years or more and partly because they are all very open to view, and even the non-gardener who becomes a tenant is inevitably shamed into doing something decent with his plot!

The community spirit is very good. This is partly because the inhabitants are nearly all local, many working for the National Trust or for some other local employer, and it is impossible for a new and unsuitable house to be built, or for a cottage to be sold as a holiday home. It is also due to the plan of the village – it is roughly a square, with a small green and a car park in the centre. On the east side, stand the post office and the church; the village hall is in a central position and on the west side is the old smithy, now occupied by a much valued motor mechanic. There are three drying greens as nobody is allowed to hang their washing in their gardens.

This plan means that villagers meet daily as they go about their business. The village hall is also the centre of most of the social activity, and something goes on there almost every day.

Carham 🐾

The border between Scotland and England is far from straight and tucked into a corner, on a sweeping bend of the river Tweed, is the village of Carham, with Scotland to north, west and south. This tiny hamlet of about twelve whitewashed houses is surrounded by lush pastureland which can carry stock for eleven months of the year.

However, today's appearance of idyllic rural peace is quite at odds with the turbulence of the past. A field still bears the name Dunstan, where a battle was fought in AD 833 between the Saxons and Danes. A stone hammer head which was found in a nearby potato field some years ago was identified as being Danish and perhaps up to 2,000 years old. Could there be a connection?

In 1296 the Scottish army under its great leader William Wallace encamped on the high ground immediately to the south of the village, and by 1380 the whole parish was so wasted by war that it could pay no contribution to the clerical subsidy voted that year. By the early 16th century the people were pleading for 'a little tower of defence against the Scots'. This was, presumably, for refuge against sudden attack, because in times of real war everyone and their animals took shelter in Wark Castle about one and a half miles east.

The present parish church – St Cuthbert's, a plain but attractive building, capacity about 150 – was completed in 1798, but was only the latest of several on the same site. To the north of the church is the site of an abbey occupied by an order of black canons, but it was of little importance. Undulations in the large field between the village and Carham Hall are possibly an indication of buildings there also.

The union of the Crowns of Scotland and England in 1603 began the slow process towards a more peaceful life. Carham, its lands and hall, was bought by Anthony Compton in 1754 and remained in that family until 1919. The last remaining heir was killed in the Great War. Carham Hall is pleasantly situated by the river and could be described as a country gentleman's residence; now it is a residential home for the elderly.

In 1798 the common land of Wark, which had extended to some 2,000 acres, was enclosed, and the Comptons along with other members of the local gentry acquired more land to add to their estates. Farming as we now know it began to develop, in that great era of 'improvements'. Land was drained, limed and manured, and that amazingly important vegetable the turnip was introduced. Thorn hedges were set and trees were planted, many of which we still enjoy today.

The turnpike road from Kelso to Berwick came through the village, with a tollhouse on the Border, but it was the coming of the railway in about 1848 which must have made an amazing difference to people's lives. A tile works was established beside the railway by 1851, manufacturing drain tiles, and later bricks. Carham station was a mile and a half from the village, but having once walked there it would be possible to go to absolutely anywhere that also had a station. Needless to say this freedom only lasted till Dr Beeching's reorganisation and today we are totally reliant on the motor car or the bicycle, which is making a considerable come-back.

The most striking change between those days and today is the diminution of population in the countryside. The village and surrounding large farms would have had a population of perhaps 70 to 80 people whereas today it will be more like twelve to 15. Even in the 1960s numbers would be up to and over 30. This has facilitated the growth of the tourist business. Most farms, and particularly the village, have cottages to let to holidaymakers who come to enjoy the beauty and peace of our corner of Northumberland, but peace for the holidaymaker can equal loneliness for the resident, and the young in particular can feel isolated. The primary school is only four miles away, but from the age of nine children go to middle school and then high school in Berwick, 17 miles distant, a long day for a nine year old. There are not, at present, enough youngsters in Carham or Wark to run a youth club, and the village hall has limited use, apart from the WI and the carpet bowling club. We have no pub, no post office or shop nearer than four miles and the vicarage was pulled down when our church was combined with Cornhill and Branxton.

All in all, Carham and district could be described as quiet, beautiful and safe, and for those with transport, a marvellous place to live.

Carrshield & Ninebanks 🦢

Tucked away in the beautiful Northumbrian hills is a lovely unspoilt valley with two villages, Carrshield and Ninebanks. Carrshield is one of the highest villages in the country and nearby Smallburns is one of the highest occupied farmhouses. Coalcleugh, once the site of a productive lead and silver mine in the 18th century now consists of only two occupied houses.

The river Allen has its source here and the road falls steeply down to Carrshield village, consisting of about 100 residents in a mainly farming community and also the home of commuters, retired people and small businesses. Various community events take place during the year, including a summer barbecue, cricket match and whist drives. There are no shops in Carrshield, the small sub post office shop closed 16 years ago. The school bus daily ferries children to Allendale and Haydon Bridge. The small simple chapel built in 1822 has regular services, but the church was demolished in 1957 being no longer able to support a congregation as the population declined with the closure of the mines. The old school in the centre of the village, once an Outward Bound centre, is now a private house, as is also the old temperance hotel and the vicarage.

Ninebanks, the lower of the two villages, in a gentler landscape, has an old tower built facing the Cumbrian fells to guard against marauding Scots and sheepstealers. The old farmhouse was once the home of Parkin Lee, who lost all in his quest for more gold at Ballarat in Australia, including his Ninebanks estate to William Ord of Whitfield. The small post office, once the home of the Ritsons, coffin and furniture makers, is open three days a week. St Mark's church, up the hill, was built in 1764 and the gravestones supply the names of generations of local people who lived and worked here, and the names of young men who died as a result of lead poisoning. The mines, named Wellhope and Mohope, brought prosperity in the 1800s but resulted in a terrible loss of health and life. When they closed in the 1880s there was a mass departure to the Tyne and abroad. The names of some of the places need no explanation – Hard Struggle, Cold Knuckles, Wolf, Cleugh, Appletree Shield, Hesley Well, Birken Peth, Mutton Hall and Gorcock (a site of cock-fighting). Furnace House in Mohope was a bastle house and contains some remarkable features.

The old blends with the new, the old families with the more recent arrivals, to form a strong caring community in the West Allen valley.

Catton 🐾

Catton is situated at the beginning of the East Allen valley, tucked down in a sheltered hollow with fields rising up on both sides, giving way quite soon to heather-covered fells. Catton is said to have earned its name from the vast numbers of wild cats which bred in the valley at one time. The main part of the village comprises a number of old stone cottages clustered round a triangular green. There is a small amount of ribbon development on either side, but Catton has fortunately remained a fairly compact village. If one includes the outlying farms it comprises about 200 households.

The quiet façades of the old cottages with their colourful well-tended gardens hide a multitude of historical secrets.

The old Board school was built in 1879. When it closed, sometime in the 1940s, it became a field study centre which also took over the one-time public house next door. Both of these are now private houses, since the closure of the field study centre. The village children now travel on the school bus into the Allendale schools, and later, to Haydon Bridge.

The last shop, run by Allendale Co-op, is now closed, although the post office still operates from a private house. Those wishing to shop must now travel to Allendale or Hexham by bus or car. In the past, however, several of the cottages round the green operated as grocers, general dealers or butchers. Deliveries were made by pony and trap. There was a dressmaker, tailor and costumier and also a milliner. One shop was known as 'Willy Slips' because of the steps outside which became slippery in wet weather. Shoes were repaired in the village and the blacksmith was kept very busy.

Not so long ago there were three places of worship. St Paul's church at the top of the village and the Wesleyan chapel on the green are now both private houses. Both, however, clearly retain the look of their original purpose. The chapel at Lane Foot is still very much in use, with a small but active and friendly congregation.

In days gone by the thriving railway brought many visitors to Catton. Many of the villagers catered for the bed and breakfast trade or provided refreshments in their gardens. In addition to these facilities the visitor would have found a number of public houses or farms dispensing beverages in jug or bottle.

In a prominent position, just above the village green, is Catton village hall. Not long ago it was under threat of closure since it needed an enormous amount of money spent on it. It was then realised what a strong spirit existed in the community. The money has been raised, the hall refurbished and the danger of losing another facility averted.

Times in Catton have, indeed, changed. However, the visitors who now come by car or bus can be sure of a warm welcome at the last remaining public house. The Crown has an excellent reputation for food and drink. There is a caravan site along part of the old railway line and several places still cater for bed and breakfast accommodation. Moreover, there are many footpaths leaving the village centre which provide excellent walks of varying lengths, either along the river valleys or up on the high fells.

The population of Catton has changed over the years too. In times past most working locally. Now, however, while some are still involved in farming or providing local services, many, thanks to the improved local roads, commute into Hexham or Newcastle. It is, in fact, a thriving mixed community of all ages concerned about preserving its unspoilt village.

Chatton

The village of Chatton is surrounded by the twists and turns of the river Till in a valley between the Cheviot Hills and the sea. The village has a history which stretches back to a time before Edward I, who signed a treaty in or near the village in the 1290s. In the church are remains of Knights Templar gravestones which date from this time. The Knights were, in fact, fighting monks who owned vast areas of land throughout the country. In the early Border wars they fought for Edward I but later supported Robert the Bruce. Over the years the houses and church have moved with the course of the Till but the general village layout has remained more or less the same for the last 200 years.

At the beginning of the century the village and the surrounding land was owned, with a few exceptions, by the Duke of Northumberland. The stone cottages each had an outbuilding where the family pig was fattened and a small field for a house-cow and chickens. There were five shops in the village, including a 'quality tailor's' which made suits for the local gentry, a post office and sweet shops. Nowadays there is one shop consisting of a general store, post office and newsagent, which occupies the building formerly used by the tailor. The village also boasted a reading room, a carpenter and undertaker, and a brewery. The old carpenter's shop can still be seen opposite the school in Old Road and the brewery, long gone, was situated along the same road and has been replaced by a wooden building next to the wall in the animal sanctuary. A blacksmith was a necessity at the beginning of the century and Chatton is still fortunate to have its forge although the blacksmith has just retired. The forge is situated next to the post office and easily recognisable from the disused horseshoes outside. There were also two inns in the village. The Boot Inn no longer exists but accommodation and good food can still be found at The Percy Arms in the main street.

During the first 30 years of this century the school consisted of two rooms which housed anywhere between 60 to 100 pupils aged between five and 14. Since then the building has gained a hall, some offices and a kitchen, with over 20 children attending. The school is also used by other groups in the village and some of the over sixties who were past pupils have told the children now attending about the stove which heated the classroom, bringing cans of tea to drink at lunch time, the cold feet and chilblains from walking to school in the winter and the strap!

The village has gained some new houses, a village green from a converted garden and an animal sanctuary whose larger guests are regularly visited in their field next to Old Road.

Chatton is alive with colour in the summer as a Best Kept Village should be. The river has good fishing, with permission, and the food is good. As a village we are well worth a visit.

Cheswick 🐑

The little hamlet of Cheswick lies approximately five miles south of the border town of Berwick upon Tweed, between the A1 road and the North Sea. From the surrounding area there are marvellous views of the Holy Island of Lindisfarne, the cradle of Christianity. It is also in a designated area of outstanding natural beauty and of special scientific interest.

The land at Cheswick originally belonged to a family named Chesewic. A tower, that no longer exists, was built some time after 1400 on the north side of the village. A chapel dedicated to the Virgin Mary stood on Chapel Hill at the east end of the village and nearby was Our Lady's

Well. There are several ancient burial mounds on Cheswick Links.

Cheswick 60 years ago was a thriving rural community boasting a school with some 80 pupils, a joiner's shop, blacksmith, reading room and library, with the surrounding farms of Cheswick, Goswick, Cheswick Buildings and nearby Broomhouse and Windmill Hill.

Cheswick House dates from 1859 and stands on the site of an older house, date unknown. The flagpole on the house featured on old navigation charts, presumably as a guide to give ships safe passage into the port of Berwick.

Just up the drive from the house stands a cluster of buildings which was once a small farm. Adjoining what was the farmhouse is the West Hall. This hall has been used as a chapel in days gone by. There is a chair left from those days bearing the letters 'IHS – Iesus Hominum Salvator' (Jesus, Saviour of Men). The WI president has the honour of sitting on it nowadays! The hall was also used by the NAAFI during the Second World War.

Along the beach between Scremerston (once a busy mining village) and Cheswick stood three small villages – Sand Banks, Philadelphia and Salt Pan Howe. Except for the lime-kilns, which one presumes provided employment, nothing remains of them today, although they are remembered by many local people.

Nearby stands Ladythorne House. The name is said to be derived from a clump of blackthorns surrounding a well, which may have been dedicated to the Virgin Mary. The house is believed by many to have been built of bricks brought back as ballast from Holland during the 18th century and there is a ceiling with the date 1721 and the initial 'W', probably the first owner and builder of the house whose name was Robert Wilkie. Cromwell was said to have slept in an outhouse here when he was in the vicinity in 1648. Like most old houses it had its ghost – in this case a headless horseman used to come up the drive and knock on the front door. The house has recently been tastefully renovated.

Near the coast is Goswick Farm and from there it was possible to cross the sands via a line of poles, 'The Pilgrims Way', to Holy Island. The children from the Sunday school, in days gone by, used to look forward to their annual picnic by horse and cart, 'the horses bedecked in shining brass and polished harness', over the sand to the island where everyone enjoyed a very happy day. Likewise, tradesmen would come over to the mainland to sell their wares. One of them, whom the schoolchildren nicknamed 'Chocolate Johnny', used to sell sweets and monkey-nuts and made it his business to be at the school at lunch time for the children to spend their weekly penny. At the same time he was able to get his horse shod at the smithy. There is a good causeway over to Holy Island nowadays complete with refuge box for those who don't manage to beat the tide!

Back to the mainland again, and just a short distance from Goswick station is the farm of Windmill Hill. At the beginning of the century there was no Presbyterian church in the area, so the people from round about used to hold services in the farmhouse kitchen until in 1912 a corrugated iron building was erected and used as a church. This was situated at Goswick station, although it was on Windmill Hill land. It was used until the late 1960s and was affectionately known as the 'Tin Tabernacle'.

South from Windmill Hill is Broomhouse Farm. The present house is thought to be as old as Ladythorne but is believed to be on the site of a much older house whose deeds go back to Elizabethan times.

Inland now, and to the west of the A1 road approximately three miles from Cheswick lies the little village of Ancroft, well worth a mention because of its ancient church where the people of Cheswick worship today. It is dedicated to St Anne, mother of the Virgin Mary. The church seems to have been built around 1089 by the monks of Holy Island and many original features survive of the first Norman building. The tower is 13th or 14th century and is a good example of a pele tower, although unusual in that it is attached to the church building. Before a parsonage was built in the early 19th century, the three-storey tower provided the living quarters for the priest who served the parishes of Ancroft and Tweedmouth. Holy Island can be seen from the top of the tower.

In 1667 the plague struck Ancroft. The victims were carried out into the fields where they were covered with shelters made from branches of broom. After death, bodies and shelters were burned. To this day a field to the south of the village is called the Broomie Huts.

Chillingham 🐌

Chillingham lies approximately one mile from Chatton. The land was owned by the Earls of Tankerville who lived in Chillingham Castle. Although the castle ceased to be the family home of the Tankervilles, the present owner is renovating the building and gardens and they are open to the public.

The village itself housed workers at the castle and is quite small, but contains some interesting buildings, such as the old school which is now a private house, and the octagonal lodges to the castle which can be found next to the castle main gate and the church.

The village is justly famous for three things other than the castle building; in spring the grounds of the castle are carpeted with snow-drops, and the church of St Peter contains the magnificent tomb of Sir Ralph Grey, tucked away in a side chapel. The main attraction though is the herd of wild cattle which inhabit the parkland. The cattle are descendants of those that ran wild in these islands from prehistory. The animals are very shy and stay well away from people, unlike their domesticated relatives which can be seen keeping down the grass in the castle grounds. The wild cattle can be found by turning into the village, crossing the ford, passing the church along the road to the warden's cottage. A mile away is a walker's paradise consisting of the Hepburn woods and the famous hill known as Ros Castle.

Christon Bank 🦢

Christon Bank takes its name from the Christon family who, as yeoman farmers and members of the Society of Friends, or Quakers, originally bought the land from Henry Darling.

In 1759 the estate was sold to Henry Taylor of Rock, but the village of today would be unrecognisable to those who lived then. The coming of the railway in 1850 brought many changes, and from being a settlement of farmers, the village became a busy main-line station with not only passenger traffic but a goods depot, dealing also in coal and stone. The coal, transported in early days by horse and cart, was essential fuel to people who lived in an area where trees were not plentiful, though there were a number of small mines operating in the locality. Whinstone from Embleton quarry was conveyed on a narrow gauge railway, known as Johnny's line, which ran alongside the road from Embleton to the main line. From there the stone was taken, as sets or crushed road metal, to all parts of the country.

In 1891 a Primitive Methodist chapel was built to cater for the many residents of that persuasion, and two public houses – The Blinkbonny, named after a horse which won the Derby, and The Rising Sun, no longer in existence. They no doubt did a good trade in the busy days of the latter half of the 19th century. Disused lime-kilns may still be seen to the east of the village. It is said that the limestone quarry there flooded overnight, which probably accounts for the demise of that particular industry.

A laundry, which also did dyeing and cleaning, was set up by Lady Grey of Fallodon to provide employment for some of the local women. Collections and deliveries were made by a horse-drawn cart, which boldly advertised on its sides the facilities available.

To the south of the village is Paddy's Mount, a slight mound bearing a small clump of trees, the last resting place of an Irish labourer who died in a fall from the granary steps at Christon Bank Farm, and is said to have been refused burial in the churchyard, possibly because of his religious convictions. His friends buried him there, planting the trees and placing a stone as a memorial. Tradition has it that the then vicar of Embleton was an extremely stout man who took a weekly walk across Christon Bank Farm land to inspect outlying parts of his glebe. The farmer and former employer of Paddy could not forbid the vicar's use of a right of way, but he could, and did, narrow his stiles to bar the vicar's progress.

An old map of almost a hundred years ago shows only one building, and a shed, on the south side of the road through the village, whilst today houses line both sides, with new estates tucked in behind, and the prospect of further development.

The laundry has gone. The village bakery, which for many years provided freshly baked bread and cakes, closed in the 1970s, and the goods yard and station are no more. The village shop, a long-established family business, a crafts shop, a poultry farm and the other remaining farms provide some employment, but Christon Bank is now much more a residential village than the working settlement it was a century ago.

Colwell & Great Swinburn

As the A68, old Roman Watling Street, travels northwards from Stagshaw Hill beside Corbridge, it passes between two small villages, Colwell and Great Swinburn, which have been closely associated over the ages. From feudal times they have formed a joint township, sharing the same landlord, and more recently the same church, school, post office and Women's Institute. Colwell, a village of Northumbrian linear tradition, stands on the Hexham to Rothbury road. Great Swinburn is a group of homesteads adjoining the parklands of Swinburn Castle, the family seat

The tithe barn at Great Swinburn

of the Riddells since the end of the 17th century. The castle no longer exists but the family still reside in the castle grounds.

The history of Colwell probably begins with the Iron Age settlement of a dozen round stone buildings, whose remains are still visible on the Blue Crag less than a mile to the north of Colwell and Swinburn. Civilisation brought dwellings to the lower ground on the banks of the Coal or Col burn, where Colwell now stands. There were also three springs – Prickie's Well, Robin Hood's Well, and Coley's Well which was almost certainly the most revered of the three. By the Middle Ages a traditional celebration of one of the wells had been established. This celebration, during which the well was blessed and decorated with flowers, was known as The Colwell Bridal and was held around 4th July on St Ulrich's day. It was the object of popular pilgrimage and, on one such day in 1534, the good knight Sir Thomas Dacre seized three of the infamous Charlton clan who had travelled many miles to attend the Bridal. The Charltons had attacked Tarset Castle eight years earlier, burnt it and dispatched Sir Ralph Fenwick with his 80 horsemen out of North Tynedale. Their apprehension at the Colwell Bridal not only created local excitement, but also went down in history.

Much of Colwell's early history lies in the small chapel which stood on the ridge comprising the north line of the village. Its origin is unknown, but after the Scots burned Hexham Priory in 1296, it was put in the possession of Hexham prior and convent. By the late 16th century the chapel was falling into disuse, and is recorded as being ruined in 1770. An excavation in 1887 yielded little further information.

In 1342 Gilbert de Colwell put a certain Roger de Widdrington in possession of Colwell. By 1346 Roger was also in possession of the castle and lands on the banks of the Swin burn, and the Widdringtons held the estate for over 300 years. This time was not uneventful, for we know of one private dispute in 1599 during which Ralph Widdrington leapt from the castle tower to save his skin and was 'almost bruzed to death', after which his father Sir Henry Widdrington was challenged to a duel to settle the affair. During the 17th century the Widdringtons were living in the 'old hall' or manor house at the west end of Colwell. This is the oldest house in the village, although over the years it has been tailored to less than its original size. In 1695 Colwell and Swinburn were purchased by Thomas Riddell, whose son Thomas rebuilt Swinburn Castle. Within the next 150 years the Riddell family had built a tithe barn and private Catholic chapel at Great Swinburn, and a school at Colwell.

Colwell today is still a small village of hardly more than 20 houses. The wells exist but are unused, and the chapel ruin has overgrown in the old joiner's back garden. An aerial photograph shows the buried remains of a row of bothies, built for labourers who came in 1884 to dig nearby Hallington reservoir. Since the turn of the century the manor house has lost its 'fine carved fireplace' and 'dovecote of respectable antiquity', whilst in 1993 we lost our postmistress after 42 years' service. We no longer have the mission rooms where men met to read, chat and play dominoes, where school meals were cooked and people worshipped on Sundays, but the village hall is the venue for today's local events. The empty smithy retains its stone slab roof and the evidence of a layperson's chapel is well preserved in one of the farm granaries. Old Mrs Gray, who reached her century, would be proud to know that her blackleaded range is being cared for and is, as she left it, in working order.

Great Swinburn stands quietly sheltered by the parkland trees and the private church is well attended. The tithe barn towers solemnly nearby on a rocky outcrop of the open fell, a Class II listed building whose 200 year history seems to be lost without trace.

Many of the villagers can recount the days when the school bustled with pupils and grannies told of clogs hanging in the clogger's shop; when the Swinburn Castle bell would be heard ringing out for the evening meal; when the locals danced at the village ball on a Friday night (for five shillings including supper); and when people picnicked annually on Bore Well Sunday, by the sulphurated spa waters of the Bore Well near Well House to the east. The technology in the kitchens and on the farms of Colwell and Great Swinburn is as up-to-date as any you may find today, but underneath we are only a small step away from all our yesterdays.

Corbridge

Snug in the Tyne valley, where the A68 north to Scotland crosses the river and the A69 between Newcastle and Carlisle, lies Corbridge. A natural junction and ford, Corbridge became a place of some importance in Roman times, not as a military stronghold, but as a supply depot and administrative centre for the various forts and camps on the Roman wall which stretches across the open moors and fells a mile or two north of the village. The foundations of a substantial complex, known as Corstopitum, are now a tourist attraction on the fringe of the village, much visited by school parties and foreign visitors.

Until recently a blacksmith's forge operated on the north bank of the Tyne at the end of the bridge, the traditional site for smithies at well frequented crossings. After some years of idleness the forge now has new life as a craft shop and art gallery.

Northumbria was one of the earliest centres of Christianity and the building of Hexham Abbey, three miles away, meant that Corbridge too has had a church since about AD 674. Viking and Pictish invasions led to the more secure location of Durham becoming the bishopric after battles at Heavenfield and Corbridge, but Christianity was strongly established in the area, and even now St Andrew's church lies at the very heart of the village.

Under King John, Corbridge became a borough and burgesses had entitlements to grazing, firewood and turf in exchange for keeping watch each night. A weekly market drew people from as far as 30 miles away (a long distance in those days), possibly to buy specialist ironwork such as stirrups, spurs, buckles and nails, so this was a time of prosperity and peace when the population reached around 1,500. Renewed invasions from Scotland and the Black Death brought this period to an end, Corbridge was ransacked and devastated and the population did not reach this level again until the 19th century.

Two pele towers are evidence of troubled times. One, known as the Vicar's Pele, was the home of the vicar from about 1310 until the 18th century when a large vicarage was built about half a mile from the church. For a while this pele was the local tourist office. The other tower was incorporated into a fine house known now as Pele House, but formerly as Low Hall. Opposite this stands Monksholme, one of the oldest dwellings in the village, which was originally the New Inn.

The enclosure acts of the 18th century, though improving agriculture, led to a different distribution of land – the Duke of Northumberland's holding becoming 1,125 acres, the vicar of Corbridge's 43 acres, and the poor of Corbridge's 29 acres. One of the small post-war housing developments next to the vicarage is known as Glebelands, attesting to the fact that this was part of the church holding. Many walls, hedges, trees and houses date back to this period, and the old Roman wall was raided for many of its stones.

Though Corbridge was once very rural, the Tyne valley railway line brought Newcastle, 15 miles to the east, within easy reach. Since the war, new estates, both council and private, have grown up around the village and the roads have been vastly improved so that many people now commute into Newcastle to work, whereas previously employment was on the land, or in local trades. Though this detracts in some ways from the village atmosphere, it means that the growing population can support both a first and middle school, though the older children travel to Hexham at the secondary stage.

It has become a popular retirement area also, with a subsequent boom in the provision of sheltered housing and residential and nursing care. A great community effort has taken place over the last few years to rescue from closure and renovate the local cottage hospital, known affectionately as the 'Charlotte Straker' after the benefactress who endowed it. The many events organised for the hospital fund involved all sections of the community and all the village organisations.

One generous donor was authoress Catherine Cookson, who for some years made her home in Corbridge, just opposite the hospital.

There are many springs and wells around Corbridge, so small 'pants' or watering troughs are to be found tucked away in odd corners. One of these, on Spoutwell Lane, runs through a stone horse trough, through the water garden of Byethorne, the home of Sir Lawrie Barratt, and eventually into the Tyne just beyond. The Red Cross benefits greatly each year when these beautiful gardens are opened to the public.

Another major annual event is the County Agricultural Show held on the rugby fields, which attracts thousands of visitors to see everything from tractors and prize cattle to home-baking and stick dressing.

Rugby and cricket both continue to flourish as well as activities in the parish hall such as carpet bowls, badminton, a flourishing bridge club and drama group productions. This is also the location for a day centre and lunch club for senior citizens, so Corbridge is not a place where anyone could complain of nothing to do – except perhaps the teenagers, who find most of their social and sporting life in Hexham.

Cornhill on Tweed 🦢

Cornhill, in the fertile Tweed valley, is shown on the old records as Cornhall, or Cornaul. One of the first written records of Cornhill occurred when the Scottish king Malcolm won a small skirmish against the forces of the Saxon Earl of Northumberland, south east of the village, in 1018.

The church of St Helen was a chapel of ease for Norham, under the bishopric of Durham, in 1082, and may also have been a burial ground for earlier people. Possible Saxon remains were found here in the 19th century. In 1750 the church was rebuilt but it seems to have left the locals unimpressed. In 1842 the Rev J. Raine wrote, 'It became so delapidated that it was replaced by the modern building now there.'

In 1385 the Earl of Fife, commanding a group of French soldiers, burned down the pele tower to the west of Cornhill. This is now the site of Cornhill House. One of the attackers, a Gilbert de Swinhoe, stayed here and married Marie Grey. He rebuilt the tower and extended it into a more barn-like building. In 1542 the border survey described it as 'Newe and embattled, covered and put in good reparacion (with stout barnekin about) by one Gilbert Swinhoe, gentleman, and owner of the inheritor of the said town of Cornhill.' There is some evidence today of this. Another source says it was 'Well finished and great succour and releffe in times of warre as well for the inhabitants of the said town as for other nevbours [neighbours].' In 1549 a group of Scots under the French general D'Esse took the tower, finding it well provisioned, particularly with salted salmon. The pele was still standing in 1560.

The village school was founded in 1837 to accommodate 60 to 70 children. It was built on a site donated by H. J. W. Collingwood, followed by a master's house in 1868. This building was in use until 1965, then it was replaced by a modern building and in 1993 another school replaced that one.

The mid 19th century village may not have differed much in appearance but its function and its inhabitants were significantly different. The houses, or most of them, were thatched. It supported, as well as a schoolmaster, the railway personnel, based at the station called 'Coldstream' but in the village. There were farmers, a miller, a weaver's shop, a boot and shoe repairer, a cartwright, a joiner, a tailor, a grocer/baker, a cooper and a village shop and two pubs. The nearest post office was in Coldstream.

Many of the older residents remember the village of 60 to 70 years ago with nostalgia, a thatched cottage seeming in retrospect to be preferable to a council bungalow. The railway is sadly missed, particularly by those who do not drive. In the years after the last war the local doctor, who was based in Coldstream as he is now, served patients on a 70 mile stretch by train or bike, depending on the wind – train out and bike back or bike out and train back in. Gradually, with the advent of the car, public transport has dwindled to a bus service from Berwick to Kelso.

The village can no longer keep many traders in occupation. We are served by a splendid shop for most needs, a part-time post office, a school, a church, the hotel called The Collingwood Arms, and the social centre of the village, a lovely hall which was opened in 1961. The work available in the area is limited to agriculture and seasonal work. Those who are in employment as a rule travel to the towns.

The environs are rich in history and you will have a long way to travel to find more appealing surroundings. The river Tweed looping the village is rich in fish, its banks full of wildlife, and is very beautiful in its own right. The Cheviot Hills, only a short drive away, provide a splendid backdrop to the south. It is a very pleasant place to live.

Cramlington 🌿

Right in the middle of what is now a major town in Northumberland, population approximately 29,123 and still growing, you will find the original pretty little village of Cramlington. It still retains its character and is very much a part of the community. The village existed for many hundreds of years as an agricultural settlement and in the last 200 years as one of the coal mining communities in south east Northumberland. It has kept its charm and is steeped in history and legend.

The church dominates the village, its tower looking down over forest, hills and sea. It has recently turned over part of its ground to local schoolchildren and conservation groups, who have planted wild flowers and trees to encourage wildlife. It is sad that visitors pass us by as they speed along the busy coast road on their way to the Borders and Scotland. The village looks its best in spring and summer when flowers bloom and trees some 100 years old are lush with new growth.

The Blagdon Inn, once a coaching inn, is a blaze of colour as they put out tubs on the forecourt. In fact, it is not hard to imagine it looking as it did when the stagecoach stopped to let its passengers off. Every week there is an outdoor market in Smithy Square which is very popular. The travelling fair sets out its rides and stalls on the green just outside the village, and everywhere is a hive of activity as everyone enjoys themselves.

There have been many changes in village life. One lady remembers she used to stop on her way home from school and watch as sheep had their throats cut. A bucket beneath the bench caught the blood which was then used to make black puddings. This was at the 'killing shop' beside the post office. She still shudders just thinking about it today. Mr Jack Raffles also used to stop on his way home from school and watch the pit ponies being washed down. He is very well known in the village for his great collection of black and white photos of the old village and surrounding areas, which he displays in the shopping mall.

Craster 🌿

In medieval times, Craster was situated in the grass field just below and to the east of Craster Tower. There were twelve cottages, six facing six, with a road running between them to the sea. Traces of the original village can still be seen today. The villagers sought the protection of the fortified pele tower of the Craster family. The Crasters have lived at the site for almost a millennium. The existing tower was built in 1450 with a much later Georgian addition.

The exact date of the exodus of the fishing community down to the 'haven' is uncertain, probably about 1700. The haven, being a perfect natural harbour with two limestone islets (Muckle Carr and Little Carr) acting as breakwaters, provided safe anchorage for the fishing cobles. The first houses were built where the gardens are today, just below Dunstanburgh Road. By 1801 there were 19 houses in 'Craster Seahouses' as it was called, and in 1828 a population of 100. The old Square or 'curtain' was constructed in 1822 and the gardens for the houses of the Square were at the site now occupied by Robson's yard.

The village was naturally divided between the haven hills by the stream known as the Craster Letch. Prior to 1847 a public house of sorts was kept by Ralph and Eliza Archbold. 'Ralph the Briton' as he was known, was often in the hands of the press-gang and shortly after his death the pub was transferred to Charles Archbold's house, the present day Jolly Fisherman. There were at one time four herring yards. Robson's yard is dated 1856 and was the first smokehouse, and is now the only yard operating, smoking the famous Craster kippers.

In 1863 there were 33 herring boats and 17 line fishing boats operating from Craster. Before the harbour was built in 1906 the area was very rocky, and small boats brought the catches ashore. Fishing family names were Archbold, Smailes, Dawson and Simpson. Fishermen's wives had a hard life. From October until March lines were baited, with about 700 hooks to each line, and each fisherman baited two lines. The wife was involved in 'skenning' the mussels out of the shells and limpets were used as well to bait the hooks. This work went on when the boats came ashore and if the boats were late ashore, it could mean she would be busy until late evening. Summer months, crabs and lobsters were caught, and most wives spent their time in the herring yards, splitting or gutting and packing them in barrels.

In 1906 the piers were built in memory of Captain Craster, killed on active service in India. As well as fishing, Craster also developed a prosperous quarrying business, shipping stone by sea on lighters to be taken to London and Roker Pier. The stone was taken down from the quarry by an overhead rail system of wires and buckets, to be tipped into bins on top of the south pier. The bins were made of wood with steel bands around them. These bins were taken down at the beginning of the Second World War, as they thought they could be used as landmarks for enemy planes. There was a POW camp situated on the North Hills which was first occupied by Italian prisoners and later Germans, who were very talented artists and decorated their huts with paintings.

Cresswell 🎋

Druridge Bay is a five mile sweep of golden sands on the Northumberland coast where even on the sunniest Bank Holiday the beach remains uncrowded. So imagine the feeling of privilege and peace one experiences being in sole ownership of this beach on a fine 'out of season' day when the tide is out and there is no other person in sight.

Set on the southern end of Druridge Bay lies the village of Cresswell, normal population approximately 200 which, as the village is host to two caravan sites, can increase tenfold during the summer months. Originally a fishing village, the fishermen forsook one perilous occupation for another, equally dangerous, when the coal mine opened in the nearby village of Ellington. Nowadays there are only two part-time local fishermen.

Although the fishing industry declined drastically at the beginning of this century, the lifeboat, which came into the village in 1875, one year after a father and his three sons were drowned in a fishing accident, remained until 1944, crewed mainly by the Brown family who occupied most of the fishermen's cottages over that period of time. A lifeboat house was built adjacent to the beach.

Cresswell can also boast a 12th century pele tower. Scenically set in a belt of trees, it still stands gazing out over the bay waiting once more to provide refuge for the villagers and their cattle from the Danes who used to pillage this coastline. It comes complete with a resident ghost, the White Lady. She was the daughter of the Cresswell family who resided at Cresswell Hall and she fell in love with a Danish prince whom she used to meet on the beach. Her two brothers ambushed and killed him and, heartbroken, she is supposed to have committed suicide by either throwing herself from the roof of the pele tower, or locking herself in and starving to death, thereafter assuming the form of a white owl forever flying over the links seeking her lover. The latter part of the story probably arose because owls did roost in an old shed beside the pele tower and at dusk on a summer evening could be seen flying over the links.

No longer though, because with the growth of the caravan sites and the attendant vandalism over the last three decades, the shed no longer exists and the door to the tower had to be bricked up. In fact the high sand dunes are no more as vandalism has many faces, one of them being the removal of our coastline for profit. The proposal to site a power station about two miles north of Cresswell is now in abeyance, but not cancelled, and now British Coal has plans for opencast mining-cum-colliery waste disposal half a mile south of the village.

Of the aforementioned Cresswell Hall only the disused stable block remains, slowly crumbling and taking with it the secret of the underground passage leading from the stable yard to the quarry beside the coastguard house. When the estate was sold Cresswell Hall was bought by Ashington Coal Company – now British Coal – and subsequently demolished to enable them to access the coal beneath it. St Bartholomew's church also exists due to the largesse of the Cresswell family; before it was built the villagers had to walk to Woodhorn to attend church.

Although Cresswell is now in England, it obviously wasn't always thus as the village lies approximately 30 miles north of Hadrian's Wall, placing Cresswell in southern Scotland during the Roman occupation. Now, however, the village is approximately 50 miles south of the Scottish border, making its occupants true sassenachs. Apart from the coastal erosion, the passage of time seems to have dealt lightly with Cresswell. Old houses have been demolished or altered, and new houses built, but if the current planning policy of allowing no new development to the north of the Crows Nest continues in force in the future, the overall structure of the village should remain constant.

The saying about familiarity breeding contempt can be very true. Being born and bred in a place tends to accentuate the drawbacks, but these pale into insignificance when, driving down past the church, the unfolding vista of Cresswell framed by the sea appears, bringing home how fortunate we Cresswellers are to live here.

Crookham

Crookham, from Crucum and Crokome, is derived from the Old English for 'farmstead in the crook of a river' – in this case, the river Till.

The medieval history of Crookham was largely determined by warfare and the relatively loose hold lords had over their scattered manors in the north. Crookham was laid waste by Robert Bruce in 1314, and several times over the next two centuries Crookham, along with Ford and Kimmerston, had its taxes either reduced substantially or cancelled because of the extreme devastation of war. The 16th century saw the rise of the Anglo-Scottish border raids and Crookham was the favourite meeting place for the English gathering for a foray into Scotland or to repulse Scots venturing down the Till. Thefts of cattle, the burning of cottages and barns and even the killing of villagers and rape of women were not uncommon.

In Edward I's assessment for subsidy in 1296, Crookham is listed as having a population of 13, with Ford and Kimmerston having seven each. By 1429, Crookham had three messuages (houses with outbuildings and land), four cottages, 300 acres of arable land and 200 acres of pasture.

Crookham displayed an independent and lawless nature, a very northern trait! In the Assize Rolls of 1293, for example, there are two manslaughters, two burglaries and one murder recorded for the village – from a population of 13! Records also show Crookham being fined at regular intervals from 1256 to 1838 for not responding to Hue and Cry (ie refusing to pursue wrongdoers) and for not keeping the stocks in good repair.

Following the preaching tours of John Knox, Crookham became a great Presbyterian centre. In 1678, there was an 'affray' between the Covenanters under Robert Morley and English troops under Colonel Strother. To the anger of the Colonel, not only did the villagers refuse to respond to his call for Hue and Cry, they also entertained the Covenanters to dinner and lodgings before the fight and supplied them with weapons and refreshment during the battle. Crookham held a famous conventicle in 1725, founded a church in 1732 and their first church was built in 1745. The fourth minister, Thomas Hall (1809–44), was regarded as the original of Matthew Paxton in John Mackay Wilson's novel of the same name.

After 1760, the open land began to be enclosed and more intensely cultivated. Land was divided up into manageable farms, ending the village field system. Crookham, having no 'live in' squire, developed into a thriving commercial centre. In 1828, it had 44 houses, a school and chapel. There were two mole catchers, a saddler, a violin maker, two blacksmiths, three grocers, a gardener, a millwright, two joiners, two shoemakers, three stonemasons and a carrier. Many people rented rooms to the packmen who plied their trade in the area. There were three inns – The Red Lion, The Wheatsheaf and The Blue Bell. Two coaches, two carriers and a horse post called daily at The Blue Bell, which had always been an important stopping point.

By the turn of the last century, like many villages, Crookham's population and commercial viability had been depleted due to the industrial and agricultural revolutions taking place in Britain. Under the direction of Lady Waterford of Ford, the old layout of the village was altered to its detriment. The wide square at the centre of the village was lost and many cottages and shops pulled down. The Red Lion and The Wheatsheaf were closed, as was the case in Ford village. In their place, a few Victorian cottages were built along the line of the road. Now, only The Blue Bell, a market garden and a part-time post office remain but the village is still well populated, robust and with a strong integrity of its own.

Darras Hall 🖋️

The Darras Hall Estate, adjacent to the old village of Ponteland, consists of about 2,500 private residences and is unique in inception and method of administration. Apart from a small shopping area, a garage, a church and a first school, there are no public services; no industry is permitted on the estate other than a few market gardens.

Historically the name Darras probably derived from D'Arreynes, believed to be a Norman family who held land here in the 12th century. The present Darras Hall is a typical Northumbrian farmhouse dating from 1830. 'Hall' is a very common name for a farm in the county and does not necessarily imply a large mansion.

In 1890, when many people lived in towns and cities in houses without gardens, Joseph Whiteside Wakinshaw and a few friends formed the Northern Allotment Society, with the object of leasing or buying land on the outskirts of Newcastle, to be sold on to its members who paid a nominal sum to join the society. The first purchase was Red Cow Farm, situated in the area now known as Westerhope. This land was split into plots on which the members could build houses and grow produce to sell in the city and thus provide an income. Market gardening and farming were the only commercial activities allowed on the estate. Joseph Wakinshaw's own house (which later became a public house) was called Runnymede.

Similar developments took place in subsequent years, culminating in the largest in 1907 when three farms, Darras Hall, Little Callerton and

Little Callerton Moor, a total of 1,025 acres, were purchased.

The new Darras Hall Estate, as it was named, was split up into 197 lots of about five acres each, and sold by auction to members. The sale realised some £20,000 more than the original cost, sufficient to cover the cost of roads, fencing, water supply and sewerage. One of the original nine roads, laid out on a grid pattern, was named Runnymede Road. Drainage of the heavy clay land presented problems and a call was made to the owners for extra funding. (This old problem is still with us in the Ponteland area.)

Plots ranged in price from £35 to £150, and were soon to be broken down into building sites, mainly on road frontages, where services were available. Lack of public transport meant that progress was initially slow, but, the railway line to Ponteland having been opened in 1905, the trustees offered a stretch of land through the estate enabling the North Eastern Railway Company to build a branch line to a terminus in the centre of the estate, where a station was built close to the area earmarked for shops etc in Broadway. However, insufficient passengers led to the closure of the line, together with the Ponteland line, to passenger traffic in 1929. The trackbed reverted to the Darras Hall Estate Committee and has been designated a public bridleway. The station building, last used by the United Reformed church, was demolished in 1993 to allow for the erection of 20 bungalows for elderly residents of Darras Hall.

The arrival of buses after the First World War, and a greater number of people owning motor cars, assisted development of the estate, but it was the 1950s before full development took place. Remaining frontages and 'back-lands' were developed, often by big building firms with the resources to lay roads and utilities, splitting up the costs over a number of properties. By 1990 development had filled up nearly all available land and now only rarely does a building site come onto the market, with a price tag which may be some 10,000 times its original cost.

The estate is run by the Darras Hall Estate Committee, whose members are elected at the annual general meeting of owners, from an office in Broadway. Trustees have been appointed since the inception of the estate and they hold in trust several blocks of land, including the freehold of the shopping centre and of the United Reformed church, the recreation ground behind Middle Drive and the Bridleway, on behalf of those owners who have signed the deed of accession to the trust deed. All plans for new building, alterations or additions have to be placed before the committee for approval, regardless of whether approved by the local planning authority, to ensure that all is in compliance with the conditions of the trust deed. This sets out all that may or may not be done on the estate, and must be signed by every owner before he or she can vote at the annual general meeting of owners held every March. A small annual charge is made on all owners in order to cover the running costs of the estate and necessary maintenance work.

Tree-lined roads and large attractive gardens surrounding well-spaced houses present a very pleasant outlook. This is borne out by the demand for property 'on Darras Hall', with often above-average values. It is a very popular location for people whose work involves moving into the area.

With all the facilities of Ponteland; easy access to the International Airport, only two miles away; the great and historic city of Newcastle, eight miles away; the huge shopping and leisure facilities of the Metro Centre only minutes away by car; to say nothing of the beautiful scenery of Northumberland, of which it is part, then Darras Hall has indeed much to commend it.

Joseph Wakinshaw was a very forward thinking man of his time, and to him lies the credit for the existence of the Darras Hall Estate.

Denwick 🌿

Just a stone's throw from the busy A1 and about halfway between Newcastle upon Tyne and Berwick upon Tweed, a curious traveller would find the sleepy little village of Denwick and pass through it in a trice, noting perhaps its attractive stone cottages and flower-filled gardens. It is overlooked from one end by the tiny church, built about 1880 and standing on a wooded knoll, which in early spring is carpeted with aconites and snowdrops.

The village is recorded as a settlement as early as the 8th century, bearing the same name but with various spellings eg Denewicke, Denwycke. One of the early meanings of the name is 'farm in the valley', and indeed the village stands in the midst of beautiful farmland. Three of the main holdings are attractively named Goldenmoor, Silvermoor and Peppermoor, the last said to be named after a local piper who lived there, rather than the colour of its fields. Denwick remained a small farming community for centuries and was eventually incorporated into the estates of the first Duke of Northumberland, to whose family it still belongs.

The village was mostly rebuilt in its present style in 1830. The cottages were further modernised this century, when at the same time a schoolroom and a village hall were built. The two oldest houses in the village, Laburnum House 1806 and Denwick House 1808, are still occupied. The latter was built as the factor's house by Northumberland Estates. At one time the entrance to the village was graced by a rather beautiful stone archway. Sadly this was demolished in recent years to make way for improved access to the A1 Alnwick bypass. Quite near to the site of the archway lie the remains of a stone cross, put up to commemorate the many villagers who succumbed to plague in 1665.

Denwick was the home, last century, of the Common (though un-common) family. Most famous of these was John Common who in 1818 invented a double-drill turnip sower, a great step in those labour-intensive days. In recognition of this he was presented with a silver medal and ten guineas by the Society of Arts in London, and with 20 guineas by the Highland Society of Scotland. Also, in conjunction with one Henry Ogle from the nearby village of Rennington, he built a reaping machine which was extensively adopted in America. It must have been an important contribution to the Agricultural Revolution. John Common laments in his memoirs that he derived no fortune from his inventions. Other members of this unique family achieved fame in different ways, being reputed to have lived to great ages and to have performed feats of strength and agility. One of them is said to have grown a new set of teeth some years before his death at the age of 110. Another lived to be 115, and in his youth entertained the populace by standing on his head on church steeples or handy local towers!

The more usual occupations of the villagers have been farming and estate work, and, for a time, quarrying. A seam of fine sandstone lies just east of Denwick and fine-grained stone was much prized by masons for carving work. The quarry ceased operating early this century. The area was then used as a training ground for young recruits during the First World War, and a great many soldiers were housed in wooden huts on the edge of the quarry. After the war, these huts were converted into dwellings and served as cosy homes for a good many years. Even in that unlikely area, the local love of gardens prevailed, and there are still traces today of the gloriously colourful plots which were tended by the inhabitants of these temporary homes.

The shop, post office, public house and blacksmith's shop which were a feature of Denwick village life 100 years ago have long gone. Only a joiner's shop remains, in spite of the fact that the number of households recorded then is virtually unchanged. The population now numbers under 60 souls. Their needs are met by mobile shops and library and by the busy market town of Alnwick which lies just a mile and a half away. A twice weekly bus takes passengers as far as Newcastle, but most villagers now enjoy retirement and tend their gardens in the picturesque surroundings where they have spent most of their lives.

Dilston 🕸

The parish of Dilston lies to the south of the river Tyne at Corbridge. It is a limited residential area in agricultural surroundings, the land being owned by Lord Allendale. The actual village of Dilston no longer exists, though records show that there was a thriving township from the 13th to the 18th centuries on the eastern boundary of Dilston Castle.

The castle has had various owners, the most notable being the Radcliffes, later becoming the Earls of Derwentwater. During their occupation of approximately 200 years the castle was added to and altered many times. Following the demise of the Earls of Derwentwater the property fell into disrepair and was finally demolished in 1765, leaving only the ruined tower, the chapel and archway entrance to the forecourt.

A new hall was built in 1835 after the estates had been passed to Greenwich Hospital. Some years later the estates were sold and Dilston was bought by Lord Allendale. In 1878 Dilston House was built, a short distance east of the hall, and this is now occupied by one of the present Lord Allendale's sons.

Dilston High Town is a hamlet of cottages and farm buildings, one of which was converted to an institute for estate workers. In 1926 Dilston WI was formed by Lady Allendale. After meeting at Dilston Hall for one year, the WI ladies then shared the use of the institute with the men, finally taking it over completely in 1936.

At Dilston Haugh Farm adjacent to Devil's Water, the farm buildings have been converted to a group of houses. The mill house and cottages are now in private ownership and other conversions are in the pipeline for farm buildings and cottages at Dilston New Town.

After he moved to Bywell in 1942, Lord Allendale granted the hall for use as a maternity refuge for Newcastle hospitals. The Dilston maternity home became established and remained until 1965 when it was transferred to a new unit at Hexham General hospital. After this the hall was used for the education of mentally handicapped children and in 1971 MENCAP became the owners of Dilston Hall, including the church and ruined castle. It is now known as Dilston College for the education of teenagers with learning difficulties.

The small church of St Mary Magdalene was built by the Radcliffe family as a Catholic church. Thanks to the initiative of Canon Malden and several local people the church was refurbished and used for Anglican worship. It was much used by the staff and patients of the maternity home, several babies being christened there. Sadly in recent years the church has again been closed, although the students still use it for Christmas worship. Plans are in hand for the restoration of the castle tower, church and Earl's Bridge. Dilston has had a very colourful history, well documented by various historians and novelists. One well known book is Anya Seton's romantic novel *Devil Water*.

Devil's Water meanders below the castle and hall, passing a permanent Scout camp by Earl's Bridge, the mill house and cottages before joining the river Tyne. It is an area rich in woodland, wildlife and agriculture, yet within easy reach of Corbridge, Hexham and Newcastle.

Doddington 🌿

Doddington is a small village in the fertile valley of the river Till about three miles from Wooler on the Berwick road. At the beginning of the century, Doddington was the town and Wooler the village. It would have been a very busy place, boasting a market, alehouse, tailor's shop, blacksmith, undertaker and miller – remains of the corn mill may still be seen. There are now two large farms with rows of cottages, a church and village hall.

The church of St Mary and St Michael has the unusual feature of having a west end chancel and is built on the site of a 12th century church. Restored in 1838, it is well cared for and used each Sunday for worship. The large vicarage was sold in 1970, the vicar now residing in Wooler and being responsible for the parishes of Doddington and Kirknewton.

In the south east corner of the churchyard is the watch tower, built in 1826 when there was alarm about body-snatchers' activities on behalf of Scottish surgeons. So we had the church taking care of the souls and the townsfolk guarding the bodies.

The school and house were sold in 1955, there being only eleven pupils and one teacher at that time. In 1937 there had been two teachers and

37 pupils. The closure brought the school to an end after 104 years. The schoolmaster and his wife were the leaders of village life and when they left, many social activities ceased.

The reading room, now called the village hall, was originally a small hut. A new hall was gifted by farmers Mr J. G. Rae and Mr Richard Harvey and other subscribers; this was modernised in 1956, proved a great asset and was regularly used for dances, parties, billiards, indoor bowling and the annual show. It is used now on fewer occasions, although the local WI use it as their headquarters.

The Dod Well, in the shape of a cross, stands at the south side of the village. Originally fed by a spring, it supplied the entire village with pure sparkling water. Due to flood damage in 1947, the flow from the spouts ceased, but still hundreds of gallons pour from a channel under the well. A special fern known as a 'Yea' grew from the bowl of the well, kept in the memory of the villagers by an old song beginning 'The Bonny Dod Well and the Yea pointed fern'.

The toll cottage opposite the well was restored in 1984, it being the oldest dwelling in the village and which once housed the post office. Other cottages are now housing people from all walks of life although few are now needed for farmworkers, due to mechanisation. A great change in population is evident since the war years when the 22 cottages would have been filled with farmworkers and their families. Much has changed in farm life since 1945 and it is sad to see the rich farmland being 'set aside'. It is remarkable, when looking through the visitor's book in church, how many people come from far and wide to visit the birthplace of their ancestors. Some of the old rows of cottages had names such as 'The Cat Row', 'The Market Place' and 'The Police Station'. The whole of Doddington and hundreds of acres surrounding it was owned by the Chillingham estate until the 1930s when it was sold off to meet the needs of the Tankerville family.

The bastle house or pele tower which stands in South Doddington steading was built by Sir Thomas Grey in 1584. Time has destroyed the building, which the Scottish raiders failed to do. The remains are still a good example of one of the most recently built fortified houses.

On Dod Law there is a quarry, noted for its fine pink sandstone, once worked by local craftsmen and now occasionally by men travelling from Durham. Also on Dod Law are the rock mark symbols carved by the Ancient Britons and over the front of the hill is a cave known as 'Cuddy's Cave', probably so named from the traditional connection with the wanderings of St Cuthbert, the Northumbrian saint. From

Dod Law are some of the finest views of Northumberland, overlooking the winding river Till, the Cheviots in the background, while to the east lies Holy Island and, on a clear day, the eye may see well into Scotland. Of recent construction is the thriving, well laid out golf course, growing in popularity.

Edlingham 🌿

Eadulfingham, the 'ham' of Eadwulf, was one of four Northumbrian royal villages given to the Church in AD 737 by King Coelwulf, who resigned his throne to become a monk on Lindisfarne. A village of several hundred people surrounded the castle and church.

The village today is on the sloping south side of the Edlingham valley above the church and from most houses in the village the occupants have a superb but slightly differing view of the opposite side of the valley, a view of heather and bracken-clad moorland interspersed with rocky outcrops and conifer plantations. The large field in front of the houses is a splendid example of medieval rigg and furrow ploughing. In the winter after the sheep have closely cropped the grass, and when the sun is low in the south west, the riggs cast a shadow which accentuates the furrows. Snow melts first off the riggs and the field then becomes striped green and white. Below this field runs the Edlingham burn where alder and hawthorn grow. Here in early summer the cuckoo calls incessantly and from the heather moorland above comes the cry of the curlew.

Beyond the burn is the road from Rothbury to Alnwick. This bypasses the village and was first built in 1753–54 at a cost of £90 per mile. The entire road from Hexham to Alnmouth was built by public subscription in order that surplus corn could be transported to the port of Alnmouth for export. This Corn Road was a toll road. As examples of the tolls, at each gate along it, every cart drawn by three horses was charged twopence and every horse was one penny.

Horses were used extensively in the area for transport and agriculture until the 1930s. The cottage now called Moorview was the smithy. The vicar used to drive a pony and trap from Edlingham vicarage to Bolton for services at the chapel there. The views from the Bolton road across Whittingham vale to Cheviot are stunning. Today the vicar lives in Whittingham and comes along the same road by car to conduct the twice monthly services. Horses are still regularly ridden along the village roads but they are now kept for recreation, eventing and racing.

The church of St John the Baptist is a predominantly Norman church on the site of an earlier Anglo-Saxon building which was consecrated in AD 840. The present building was begun about 1050. The west wall of the nave retains the original west doorway into the church. The massive tower was added in the 14th century and was a place of defence and security for the villagers during the Border raids. In the same period, about 1340, the defensive solar tower, gate tower and curtain walls were added to Edlingham castle.

The castle was originally a two-storey moated hall-house built in the mid 12th century by John de Edlingham. All the principal rooms, including the hall, were at first floor level with service and storage rooms below. When the tower was added it was built over part of the moat, so parts of it collapsed in 1650 and the whole castle was abandoned. The foundations of the hall-house and the courtyard were excavated by English Heritage in 1983 and the remaining stonework of the tower was made safe. The castle and the church attract visitors from many parts of the world.

The other eyecatching architectural feature of the village is the five-arched viaduct near the castle. This carried the railway from Alnwick to Cornhill. The line was opened on 5th September 1887 and the last passenger train ran 43 years later on 22nd September 1930. Goods trains and, during the last war, troop trains continued to run.

One local farmer recalls potato picking, when a boy, in a field adjacent to the line. He remembers throwing potatoes at the driver who retaliated with well aimed pieces of coal. Severe flooding in 1949 destroyed a bridge south of Wooler and the line was finally closed in 1953. The station and the stationmaster's house were sold and are now private dwellings. In the same year the village school, having only three remaining pupils, was closed.

A relic of a much earlier transport system can be found in the village. The Roman road known as the Devil's Causeway ran from Corbridge to Berwick. The Corn Road crosses the Causeway to the west of the village. From here the Causeway heads towards the west of Edlingham Demesne Farm. The present footpath more or less follows the Roman road.

There have been two important trials associated with Edlingham. In 1682/3 Margaret Stothard was accused before Justice Henry Ogle of witchcraft. She was acquitted. In 1879 two poachers, Michael Branaghan and Peter Murphy, accused of armed burglary at the vicarage were not so lucky. They were convicted and sent to Dartmoor prison. Later two different men were convicted of the crime. The Home Secretary gave the poachers a free pardon and financial compensation in 1888. Four policemen were accused of giving false evidence but the jury found them not guilty. The Home Secretary answered questions on the case in the House of Commons.

Today Edlingham is a settlement of only 18 houses, with outlying farms and cottages in addition. There is a strong sense of community here and with our nearest village of Bolton. Most people see Edlingham from the Corn Road as they drive between Alnwick and Rothbury. Some stop at Corby Craggs to admire the magnificent view over the village and farms. The residents are fortunate, they see the beautiful, unspoilt countryside from their own homes.

Eglingham

From a farmer's house among the hills, a little west of Eglingham, Sir Walter Scott wrote to a friend, 'We are most delightfully situated amidst places renowned by the feats of former days; each hill is crowned with a tower, camp or cairn.'

The Rev Anthony Hedley said the name of Eglingham was probably derived from the British 'eglys' signifying a church, with the Saxon term 'ham' – dwelling; the combination would mean a village with a church.

The village church of St Maurice celebrates its patronal saint on the 22nd September. In bygone days a service was held in church, and following an established custom the 'gentry' of the parish supplied a table each for the party, eg the Collingwoods, Milvains, Carr-Ellisons, Baker-Cresswells and other local gentry. Today it is celebrated on the Sunday nearest the 22nd September with a service in church and light refreshments served afterwards – how things have changed.

Until 1980 the Archdeacon of Lindisfarne was the vicar of Eglingham and was assisted by a curate who lived in Memorial House. In the time of Archbishop Geoffrey Fisher, the parish was fortunate to have Archdeacon Foreman. The archbishop and archdeacon were brothers-in-law and the archbishop spent a number of holidays at the vicarage. He was a very friendly 'down-to-earth' person and enjoyed having chats with the local shepherds and tradespeople.

The parish has a Franciscan brother living in retreat at Shepherd's Law. Brother Harold lived in a caravan whilst he was building the hermitage. On completion Archbishop Runcie visited the hermitage and villagers were invited to the dedication service.

The church is associated with the village school – the present school being built in 1867 with the land given by the Ogle family of Eglingham Hall. The school opened in January 1868 and at the end of January the number of pupils attending was 80. Today there are 42 pupils aged up to nine years attending the school.

At one time Eglingham had two public houses: The Ogle Arms – coach stop for Alnwick and the Wooler coach – and the Tankerville Arms. The publicity for The Ogle Arms included the words, 'This old established Family and Commercial Hotel is situated amidst lovely scenery and the centre of excellent fishing strains.' The Tankerville Arms included in its publicity, 'Horse and Conveyance on Hire'. Other occupations for the villagers in past decades included blacksmiths – and the forge is still in existence near Ogle House (formerly The Ogle Arms) – and tailors (there was a 'drapery and tailoring establishment' owned by Robert Coxon who also sold tobacco, pipes and pouches). There was a village shop and post office and of course the staff employed at Eglingham Hall, eg butler, cook, sewing maid, kitchenmaids, gardeners, hunts-man and others.

The head gardener lived in the lodge and there is a beautiful topiary of a pheasant at the lodge gates. This is quite a focal point of the village. The topiary originated during the occupation of Eglingham Hall by the Ogle family from 1568 until the late 1800s. Oliver Cromwell visited the hall and legend has it that Cromwell and Henry Ogle fought a duel there. The poem *Cromwell's Visit* by James Hall is subtitled 'An Eglingham Legend' and tells the story of the visit.

Amongst other occupations in the area was coal mining. There is still a shaft at Tarry, which derived its name from the coal which contained 60–65% tar. There is now only one house at Tarry where there used to be about a dozen. The owner of the remaining house is the daughter of Colonel Milvain who lived in Eglingham Hall at the beginning of the 20th century. When Colonel Milvain moved to Eglingham Hall the Duke of Northumberland gave him a piece of land on the understanding that he started the Milvain Hunt. The Hunt is now located at Beanley Kennels – a short distance to the west of Eglingham. Colonel Milvain created another topiary up Eglingham Drive. This is appropriately of a fox and hounds and can still be seen by anyone visiting Eglingham Hall.

Sadly today there is only one public house, no village shop, no blacksmith, joiner or tailor. The post office is open for about five hours on two days of the week.

There are more houses in the village, but the old lifestyle is gone. A few people try to keep the community life going, but it is very difficult as people travel away to work – a few going to Newcastle or further afield.

The focal point for community life is the village hall, which was originally a water mill. When the mill was burned down the village hall was rebuilt on the site and opened by Lady Milvain in 1914. It is used for carpet bowls, a youth club, toddler group activities, WI meetings and their fundraising efforts, the occasional dance, whist drive and the annual leek show. These activities are supported mainly by people living outside the village.

Elsdon 🪶

Anyone visiting the village of Elsdon now would be surprised to learn that it was once the capital of Redesdale. It looks like a typical moorland village, with its green, church, shop-cum-post office, pub and a cluster of stone houses. But dig a little deeper and it is bursting with history.

Once it was the home of the Warden of the Middle Marches, the king's representative in the lawless territory between England and Scotland. Later it became an important centre on the main drovers' road to Scotland, with its own court, gallows and no fewer than four inns. Now there is only one pub and the coaches whizz past through Otterburn on the A696. Yet only 150 years ago the *Chevy Chase* stagecoach from Newcastle to Edinburgh stopped at Elsdon before the 'New Line' turnpike road over the Ottercaps was built.

The body of St Cuthbert rested here in AD 875 on its wanderings towards Durham, and the ancient church is named after him. Visitors from more 'civilised' places are amazed to find that it is never locked and they are free to enjoy its peace and tranquillity. The church has seen its share of history and many of the fallen of the battle of Otterburn in 1388 are buried here in a mass grave.

The key to all this ancient history is the pele tower which dominates the village. Built in the 14th or 15th century with stone walls several feet thick, it replaced the original motte and bailey castle near the present village hall. For 500 years it was the fortified home of the rectors of Elsdon before becoming a private home in 1962. It is now a listed building and is open to the public on request.

As it always has, Elsdon is slowly adapting to change. Even within living memory there has been change a-plenty, yet tradition is jealously guarded, and though extremely law abiding by present day standards (vandalism and graffiti are non-existent), even the children retain a sturdy independence.

The greatest loss to the village in recent years has undoubtedly been the closure of the village school, founded in 1832, when the three-tier education system was introduced in 1975. At that time there were barely sufficient children to sustain it and in spite of fierce opposition the children were destined to be bussed out of the village and the school became a diocesan youth centre, only to be sold a few years later. It is now a thriving recording studio. No longer, except in the holidays, can the joyous sound of children playing on the village green be heard, and the village seems dead and deserted during the day. Yet ironically, there are now more than enough children to sustain a school.

Fortunately many of the traditional children's activities have carried on, thanks to the villagers. The bonfire on Guy Fawkes night, trick or treat at Halloween and the Christmas party are all immensely popular, whilst the youth club is flourishing and arranges an annual sports day, outings to the seaside and other exciting venues. Most of the children can show visitors the pinfold, where stray sheep and cattle were impounded, and the site of the cock-fighting pit and the bull-baiting stone on the village green. (Fortunately these dubious practices ceased many years ago.) Other traditions kept alive are the fair granted by Edward I in 1281 for St Bartholomew's Day (now Elsdon Fete on August Bank Holiday Monday), and cheese-making, once a thriving industry and recently revived at Soppitt Farm.

Apart from farming, traditional industries have all but died out. In 1858 there were in Elsdon four grocers and shopkeepers, three tailors, three cloggers and boot and shoe makers, two dressmakers, a straw hat maker, a butcher, a joiner and undertaker, and a cartwright. Now there is one village shop-cum-community post office and many local people who are not involved in agriculture either work in local hotels, forestry or on the Army range at Otterburn.

The coal mine, opened about 1900, escaped nationalisation in 1947, but closed in 1972 when coal became too difficult and too expensive to extract. The site still flourishes as a coal distribution depot and employs a dozen or so men.

Blaxter quarry nearby, which used to train and employ local stone-masons, has recently been reopened on a small scale, but the old skills are dying out, and the local stonemason who used the former blacksmith's shop has recently retired. The premises have been sold for a holiday cottage. Fortunately, within the last few years, some extremely pleasant council houses have been built which have given the village a new lease of life.

Mention Elsdon and most people immediately think of the gibbet. This is the grisly memorial to a murderer hanged in Newcastle in 1792 for the murder of a woman near Elsdon. William Winter's body was displayed on what was then the main road, within sight of the farm where his crime was committed, in an attempt to deter others. A replica of the gibbet stands there today.

Embleton

Viewed from the sea, the undulating whinstone ridge which shelters much of the village from the east winds resembles a caterpillar, hence the old name Emeldune, meaning the hill of the caterpillar. Many of the houses are built of whinstone, and the bare face of that rock can be seen in several places.

The history of Embleton stretches back to beyond medieval days, when the village was inherited by the lady Rametta of the Viscount family. The land was owned at different periods by Simon de Montfort, and by the Earl of Lancaster, who built a gallows there and a prison which was in frequent use. The Earl of Leicester granted a market every Tuesday, and a yearly fair on the eve of the feast of St Matthew.

Embleton suffered much during the Wars of the Roses, and from the ravages of Scottish invaders. Farms and mills were frequently burnt, but if sufficient warning was received, roofs and house timbers were removed to a place of safety, to lessen the effects of conflagration. Money, too, was hidden away and in the 1800s a hoard of coins (94 groats from the reigns of Edward III and Edward IV) was discovered in the churchyard. In the time of Elizabeth I the bailiff was permitted to keep a sleuth hound to track down cattle thieves. Local farmers, for many years, paid an annual fee of sixpence for permission to drive their stock into Dunstanburgh Castle for safety. It is said that their first action on waking was for inhabitants to feel their throats, to see if their heads were still attached to their bodies.

No one was allowed to hunt or hawk without permission, and anyone digging coal without the king's authority was heavily fined. The manorial court which met in the moot hall oversaw the use of common lands,

which have now diminished to a few square yards of village green. The
building where the court met no longer stands, but the Old Hall was
erected on the site, and there the bailiff collected rents from the tenants.
In the area now known as Spitalford a leper hospital once stood.

The tower of the parish church, visible from many points around the
village, dates mainly from the 14th century though the lower stages
have traces from the 11th century. The first known rector was one
Adam, and the medieval south porch has a niche which possibly held a
statue of the Virgin Mary, to whom the church was originally dedicated.
It was probably during the Reformation that the church received its
present dedication to the Holy Trinity. The chancel was rebuilt in 1867
at the expense of Merton College, whose warden and fellows hold
the patronage of the living. The strength of the lower tower seems
to indicate that the building was used as a place of sanctuary during
troubled times. The carvings on the wooden pulpit bear evidence of the
humour of the carvers, since several of the floral embellishments have
been replaced with caricatures of human and dogs' heads.

The east window, by Kempe, portraying the saints, was erected in
memory of Sir George Grey in the 1880s. For hundreds of years the

Medieval dovecote at Embleton

home of the vicars of Embleton was a pele tower built in 1395 at a cost of £40, a later vicar being licensed by Edward IV to crenellate and fortify his dwelling. In the early 1800s extensive additions were made to the vicarage by John Dobson.

In 1833 a Presbyterian church was built to meet the needs of members of that church who had settled in the area. The old manse was the birthplace in 1849 of W. T. Stead, the public spirited journalist and reformer who perished in the sinking of the *Titanic*.

In the 1700s a group of Quakers met in a house on the site of the Dunstanburgh Castle Hotel, and Quakers' Row commemorates a burial ground once used by the Friends. Of the many vicars of Embleton who were authors and essayists, the most famous is Mandell Creighton, in whose memory the village hall, one of the largest in the north of the county, was erected. When first built it included a reading room for the use of working men and a snooker and billiards room. At about that time Lady Grey started a women's club, and since the club is still in existence today, it must be one of the oldest non-denominational organisations for women in the country.

For a hundred years the main occupation of the men was the quarrying of whinstone for use as sets and road metal, conveyed by a narrow gauge railway, known locally as Johnny's line, which connected with the main line at Christon Bank. The working out of the quarry and the mechanisation of the farms has brought about a lack of employment in Embleton, which has become a residential village, with a general dealer's and post office, a greengrocer's shop, a garage and a small dairy farm all being run as family businesses. The early 1970s saw the closing down of the Howick Co-operative Society which supplied groceries, drapery and butchery. Embleton still boasts a village school, founded by the Rev Vincent Edwards in 1688, and during mid Victorian times a girls school was held in what is now the parish church room.

Two dovecotes, a medieval one of stone and a later brick-built cote can still be seen. Many of the old cottages have either been demolished and replaced by modern houses, or renovated to suit modern requirements, and new developments provide accommodation for holidaymakers and others drawn to Embleton by its situation in an outstandingly beautiful area. During the summer the population is increased by visitors spending days on the golf course or on the wonderful sandy beach. A curiosity on the shore is Andrew Barton's rock, which can only be seen during exceptional tides. Sir Andrew Barton, whose name is inscribed on the rock, was a famous Scottish sea captain and pirate who was killed in a naval engagement with the English. It is thought that this was partly the cause of the battle of Flodden, as James of Scotland insisted on satisfaction for the death of Captain Barton and the capture of his ships.

Falstone

Part of a Saxon stone cross was found at Hawkhope Hill in the 19th century, praying for the soul of Rob(ert) – an original Robson? – from the 7th or 8th century. Little is known about the early Saxon inhabitants but names recur over the centuries, such as Robson, Charlton, Dodds, Elliot and Armstrong. For instance, Robsons lived for over 300 years at Emmethaugh and Charltons lived at Charlton and Hesleyside after living in Falstone parish. The last Robsons left Emmethaugh in 1936 and it is now under Kielder Water.

There is no record of a Saxon church, although there is likely to have been one at Hawkhope Hill. The medieval church was on the site of the present United Reformed church. During the Commonwealth the church was Presbyterian and at the Restoration in 1660 the Presbyterians retained the building, although altering and rebuilding it through the succeeding centuries. The Church of England parish church of St Peter was built in 1725, and rebuilt in 1824 and 1890–92. Kielder Presbyterian church was also established at the beginning of the 18th century and held as a joint pastorate with Falstone. The first minister was Alexander Feden.

The lawlessness of the area, with many forays across the Border, is witnessed by numerous peles and bastle houses at Falstone, Ridge End and Hawkhope, being near to the last coal mine.

There have been numerous mines, such as two in Falstone, Shilburnhaugh, Plashetts and latterly at Hawkhope burn at Falstone. They were drift mines. The coal from Shilburnhaugh was reputed to be the best in Northumberland and the second best in England.

Much of the parish was, in the old days, beyond the arm of the law. The Excise men made forays to stamp out the manufacture and trade in whisky on which duty had not been paid; there were remains of stills at Shilburnhaugh until the coming of Kielder Water. There is a place near Smale called Smugglers Leap where a smuggler escaped being captured by jumping over the wide gulley.

Until the introduction of extensive sheep farming in the late 18th century much of the land was covered with scrub oak and silver birch, with alders beside the running water. The large flocks of sheep and use of wood for building and fuel quickly cleared the area, to be succeeded after 1926 by large tracts of softwood forest.

Falstone was almost entirely self-sufficient in the small-scale production of clothes, farm implements, iron and tin ware. There was a blacksmith, shoemaker, tinsmith, tailor, joiner and linen man. The railway up the North Tyne valley was opened in 1871 and was closed to passengers in 1956. It did much to open the valley to trade and farming.

Very little of the area is suitable for arable farming, but herds and flocks abounded throughout the 19th century and had to be driven on the hoof for sale in the heavily populated areas of the Midlands and London. The drovers' road that was used also allowed the conveyance of salt and coal on pack animals. A small piece of drovers' road still remains from Stannersburn to the Shilling Pot, now part of the main road. On it is Peggy's Rest where a horse of this name always decided to stop.

Most of the population until 1914 was engaged in farming (hinds and shepherds). Farming declined rapidly with the introduction of forestry, and with the rapid mechanisation of forestry from the 1980s the working population has considerably decreased. Much of the work since the building of Kielder Water for leisure activities is seasonal, although more visitors come to the valley throughout the year.

The area has a school at Kielder (17 pupils) but the old school in Falstone is now a café and craft shop. The kitchen was converted from the common stable, where horses were kept both for the pupils and for rail travellers. At its peak Falstone school had over 70 pupils. The children now travel to Kielder, Thorneyburn, Bellingham, Hexham and Haydon Bridge.

Roads were either unmetalled or rough stone tracks until the advent of motor transport. Many bridges were built in the valley, especially by the Swinburne estates in the 19th century. Falstone bridge was built in 1843 from stone of Steele's quarry, also Lewisburn, Forks, Akenshawburn and others up to Bloody Bush.

The Forestry Commission have built numerous roads and bridges to service forest industries but they are not public roads. The new road from Yarrow Moor to Kielder is more scenic and much wider than the old road it replaced, which is now under Kielder Water. The area now looks forward to even more change in the National Park with the opening of further leisure activities.

Featherstone 🦚

Featherstone is situated about two miles south of Haltwhistle on the
Alston road. It consists of two small hamlets – Park Village and
Rowfoot – about a mile apart. Park Village has about 20 dwellings
lining a curving narrow street, now thankfully bypassed. It is a pleasant
jumble of terraced cottages, larger houses and pretty gardens. There is
a Methodist chapel, built in 1850 and still very much in use, but no
shop. Rowfoot sports rather fewer cottages but has an old school which
is now the village hall, a pub called The Wallace Arms, the old forge,
and the old station and stationmaster's house of what was Featherstone
Park station.

Both villages are made up of traditional 18th and early 19th century
stone cottages, some with dates carved above the front doors. Apart
from three new bungalows and a large house on the outskirts of Park
Village, and a few new porches and windows here and there, it must
look much the same as it did in 1852 when the branch line from
Haltwhistle to Alston was built, sadly axed in 1976. Most of us can
remember it well; now we walk our dogs along the old track where
wild flowers flourish, and if you are lucky you can see red squirrels in
the larch trees and even a deer or two may cross your path.

During the last war Featherstone became a very important place for
one hot summer night in 1942. George VI and Queen Elizabeth (now
the Queen Mother) were visiting munitions factories 'somewhere in
England'. The Royal train was put into a siding at Featherstone station,
certainly a safe place for their Majesties to stay, as the Luftwaffe would
hardly bomb an area where several thousand German officers were in
a prisoner of war camp nearby. The King and Queen went for a walk
on that warm evening and called in at Featherstone Castle, the war-time
home of a boys' prep school from Rugby.

The story goes that the headmaster opened the imposing studded door
armed with a carving knife – he had been helping in the kitchen! Imagine
his astonishment at being introduced to their Majesties. He showed them
round the castle and out onto the lawn beside the boys' dormitories.
Rumour had spread amongst the boys that the visitors were special,
and as they hung out of the windows on the ground floor they stared
in disbelief as the King and Queen came over to talk to them. The King
asked them to come out and meet him, so dressing gowns were hastily
put on and they clambered out. One boy in his haste had put his dressing

Featherstone Castle

gown on inside out. 'How wise,' the King said to him, 'you are making sure it doesn't wear out and saving your mother's coupons!' Although the school is no longer at Featherstone Castle, parties of schoolchildren spend holidays there and they still climb in and out of those same windows.

In the 12th century the castle was a bastle house. It was the stone building (a rarity in those days) where the 'feu' duties were paid in kind, being a contribution to the valley defence force, thus the name Feuderstone which in time became Featherstone. In the 14th century a pele tower was built, and in the 17th century the two buildings were joined by a manor house; this is now the west front with the main entrance. After the Civil War the castle and estate were confiscated from the Featherstonehaughs who were Roman Catholic and on the 'wrong side'. Recently a priest's hole was uncovered in the chimney of the main hall during repair work. Eventually a Protestant Featherstonehaugh bought back the estate, but on inheriting Uppark House in Sussex the castle was sold to the Wallace family, who altered and extended it with great flair and imagination, so that it has the reputation of being one of the most beautiful castles in Northumberland.

Like all such romantic places it has its ghost story – this one is definitely founded on fact, however much it has been embellished through the ages. In the 16th century the daughter of the house, Roman Catholic Abigail fell in love with Protestant Dick Ridley from nearby Hardriding. One of the Featherstonehaughs, Matthew, had been Catherine of Aragon's chaplain and was beheaded for his loyalty to that unfortunate queen – so Albany, Abigail's father was determined that she should not marry a Ridley, and married her off to Thomas Blenkinsopp against her will.

After the ceremony in Haltwhistle, the wedding party rode out to 'beat the bounds' of Featherstone common which was Abigail's dowry. As they were riding through Pinkin's Cleugh they were ambushed by the Ridleys. During the skirmish Abigail threw herself between her husband and her former lover and was killed. Meanwhile, back at the castle, Albany Featherstonehaugh was waiting anxiously for the wedding party to return. At midnight he heard the horses' hooves in the courtyard; those horses that had survived had found their way home riderless. Unaware, Albany sent the servants to fetch the food from the kitchens below. The door of the Stone Hall opened, and through the fog and smoke a terrible sight met his eyes. A silent procession filed in and took their seats at the table, each with his head under his arm. Albany fell to the floor and died of shock. It is said that on a certain night each year the ghostly party can be seen . . .

Felton & Thirston

Felton and Thirston villages sit astride the river Coquet, joined by a medieval bridge, now an ancient monument. They are situated nine miles south of Alnwick, Felton to the north of the river, Thirston to the south. Earlier this century a second bridge was erected and the old bridge is no longer open to traffic. The A1 passed through Felton, but in recent years a new bypass was constructed and Felton is once again a peaceful place to live.

Felton has seen much history. Situated on the Great North Road, main coaching route from London to Edinburgh, coaches would stop here to rest and change horses. Many notable characters passed this way – Edward I, Edward II, the Duke of Cumberland on his way to Culloden, to name but a few. Oliver Cromwell stayed the night at 'Ye Olde Angel', now a private residence, on his way to the battle of Dunbar in 1650. This occasion was recently marked by a brass plaque placed on the building by the WI, celebrating its 75th anniversary.

The beautiful 13th century church of St Michael and All Angels stands above the main part of the village, an unusual and interesting building, with an entrance porch both massive and rugged dated about 1400. During the Border wars the Scottish reivers rode this way and, during church restorations in 1870, 70 skulls were found lying together, sad relics of a long-ago raid or battle. Of unusual interest in the churchyard is the grave of Elizabeth Hogg, who was the victim of body-snatchers, or resurrectionists, shortly after burial. They were well on their way to Edinburgh before being apprehended at Berwick by the local constabulary. After the arrest of the miscreants the body was returned and reburied.

During the 19th century Felton must have been much busier than today, with many more shops and inns, and several very large country houses employing large numbers of servants. With an abundance of skilful craftsmen it seems that everyone's needs were catered for in the village. In recent years the village population has increased slightly due to two small developments and the 'new villagers' have integrated well into their new environment. Today Felton boasts a post office, two shops and one public house, and a village school. The Methodist chapel and Roman Catholic school are both now closed. The mill, in a picturesque setting by the river, is residential. To the west of the village is the estate of Felton Park, the hall built on the site of an earlier castle. In 1857 the then lord of the manor, Thomas Riddell, had the Roman Catholic church of St Mary built within the park. To the north of the village is the Nelson obelisk erected by Alexander Davison, Nelson's prize-agent, dedicated to Nelson's heroic achievements and his private friendship with Mr Davison.

The village is still surrounded by fields for sheep, dairy and arable farming. Many residents now commute to occupations outside the area, since there is no industry within the village envelope. The river Coquet, the dividing line between the two villages, is the longest river in Northumberland, meandering its way down from the hills to pass through Felton. It is a salmon and trout river, a popular venue for fishermen, where the wildlife and bird life is prolific.

Thirston lies south of the river and is split into East and West Thirston, the main population of the village living in the latter, a much smaller community than Felton. A Presbyterian church was built here in 1820, followed by a new church in 1920 now the United Reformed church. There was a village school here, now closed. The grocers, joiner shop and blacksmith who plied their trades in the 19th century no longer exist. The hostelry by the river, The Northumberland Arms, still thrives and the old water cornmill by the side of Thirston burn is now a private residence. Thirston is a quiet and pretty little village which uses the amenities in Felton, its close neighbour. The two communities jog along happily together.

Fenwick 🦢

Fenwick in its early days was part of the Haggerston estate, which covered several miles. It consisted of 18 houses, a school, blacksmith's shop, bothy and reading room, sweet shop and general dealer's. Two residents each had two cows and supplied the villagers with milk. The occupants of the houses were estate workers from the Haggerston estate, which was owned by Captain C. I. Leyland. The workers were all tradesmen, joiners, plumbers, gamekeepers and foresters, or carters (horse-drawn, of course).

The men spent winter evenings in the reading room where billiards, bagatelle and newspapers were supplied and daily goings on discussed. The reading room was gifted by Captain Leyland to the people of Fenwick. The building was formerly a granary and the upper floor is reached by outside stone steps. This building is now the village hall and serves the community.

A school was built in 1876 for 80 children, and average attendance was 66. Over the years the village has increased to 42 houses, but shops have disappeared. The village policeman, who occupied No 12, is no longer required (a matter of some regret) and the school is also closed, leaving today's children to travel to Belford by minibus. Since 1969 there has been a sub post office here.

The place of worship, known as Kyloe church, was rebuilt in 1792 with a chancel added in 1862. Kyloe was one of five chapelries carved out of the extensive Saxon parish of Holy Island. Kyloe church is now redundant and is in the process of being converted into a craft and work shop, with living quarters. It is still a landmark for fishermen, as years ago it was used by sailors and airmen.

Ford & Etal 🦢

Ford and Etal villages were first mentioned in the 13th century as separate communities and now exist as an estate, though each village retains its own character. They nestle just north of the Cheviots, roughly ten miles from Wooler, Berwick and Coldstream and two miles apart.

Etal, overshadowed by the ruined castle, consists of sleepy-looking thatched cottages beside traditional tiled houses. The Black Bull Inn is the only thatched pub in Northumberland and has changed little in the last hundred years. Etal Manor lies at the opposite end from the castle and opens its gardens during Sundays in the season in aid of the Red Cross. The river Till meanders its deceptively lazy way around the bottom of Etal, where picnics abound in the summertime and paddling across the ford gives excitement to the little ones, a healthy appetite to the parents and memories to the grandparents – old pit cottages stood nearby, small, cramped, uncomfortable, but still home.

Many visitors to Etal come by train from Heatherslaw, where the old mill stands. This large building, midway between Ford and Etal, produces over ten tons of flour each year on a site over 1,000 years old. The site also houses a café, a biscuit and cake bakery and a bicycle business with a difference. Here you can hire a bicycle, a tricycle, a tandem or nearly any other shape you wish.

Between the mill and Ford, the Till twists again and the bridge is the ideal place for watching the fish and anglers or gazing at the pit ponies on the pillars which marked the south entrance to Ford Castle years ago. Looking to Ford from the bridge the first sight of Ford Castle is spectacular. Lady Louisa Waterford, widowed in 1859, settled in Ford and restored the castle, living in it until her death in 1891. James IV stayed here in 1513 before the battle of Flodden and many royal friends of Lady Waterford visited 355 years later. Now it houses children and adults on courses run by Northumberland Education Authority. The church of St Michael and All Angels lies in front of the castle. With a Harrison & Harrison organ which attracts organists countrywide, it is a place of peace and rest where the ancient walls give of their strength to weary travellers.

Ford, described as a 'model' village, is quite beautiful with stone buildings, well tended gardens and grounds and friendly people. The Lady Waterford Hall, in the centre of the village and open to the public, was built by Lady Waterford as a school. She then spent 21 years decorating it with watercolour murals depicting biblical scenes and using local people as her models. The first Lord Joicey built the Memorial Hall as a tribute to his wife; it is now used as a home for the billiard club. An old walled garden, once belonging to the castle, now houses Northumbria Nurseries and part of the estate house is a craft shop. At the top of the main street, which once had dozens of small thatched cottages on the green, lies Jubilee Cottage which is next to The Smiddy. This has a most unusual entrance in the shape of a stone horseshoe designed by Lady Waterford.

Many people feel that they have stepped back in time when they come to Ford and Etal, but both villages are alive with hardworking people and over 800 years of history.

Fourstones 🍃

Lying four miles west of Hexham the village of Fourstones stands proudly overlooking the South Tyne valley. It adjoins Newbrough at Butt Bank and extends about one mile to East Fourstones Farm. Although in a different parish to its neighbour, the twin villages take part in most activities on a combined basis and share the same facilities.

There are records of this place-name from the 13th century, with varied spelling such as Fourstayns, Forstanes and Fourestanes, then finally in 1536 Fourstones. According to historians the place derives its name from the four stones which marked its boundaries, and these four stones are said to have been Roman altars. One of these was made the receptacle of secret correspondence between the Jacobite leaders just before the ill-fated rising of 1715. Butt Bank is derived from the Norse word meaning boundary.

On passing through the village in spring or summer you will notice the colour in the beautiful gardens by the roadside, showing a keen local interest in gardening. In the early 1900s a leek club was formed which led the way in showing how to grow famous leeks. One of the founder members, Mr Robert Brown, had many notable successes, including the winning of three challenge cups at the North East Coast Exhibition in 1929. In the same year he had the distinction of being the only leek grower to win the *News of the World* challenge cup three years in succession. Another achievement was the growing of the biggest single pot leek yet recorded, which swept the board at the Hexham Chrysanthemum Show shortly before the Second World War. The annual show was one of **the** events in the district and the added attractions at this show were classes for pigs, and the industrial section which showed some superb specimens of traditional quilts. Yet another feature of the show was competitions in Cumberland and Westmorland style wrestling. This famous leek club ceased its activities in the year 1937 but a leek club based at the Railway Hotel is once again flourishing, when each year there is friendly rivalry to produce the winning leek.

Former industries in the area included Fourstones colliery. The coal seam cropped out near Fourstones station and was first mentioned in

1671 when a rent of £5 was paid to the Derwentwater estate. After the 1745 rebellion these coal seams passed into the hands of the Greenwich Hospital, Mr William Benson finally succeeding as tenant. In about 1900 a cart passing between East Fourstones and Broadfield just escaped falling through an unexpected hole in the road which proved to be an old pit shaft. It was found that a thin crust of road material was all that covered a yawning abyss. The closing of the colliery after the General Strike in 1926 brought an end to the ancient industry.

The quarries worked at Frankham, producing limestone and freestone, provided employment for many local inhabitants. The freestone was of first rate quality and became the most celebrated product of the parish. A large portion of Princes Street, Edinburgh is built of this stone including the Waverley Hotel and the North British railway station. It also figures in part of the Houses of Parliament. The limestone was used for burning to make lime for agricultural purposes. The lime-kilns were situated at Fourstones station some distance away from the quarries but a waggon-way was used to transport the stone.

A local landmark is the large mass of waste from these quarries. Known locally as the 'Blue Heap' it commands an elevated position with distant views. The slopes are mostly covered in fir trees. Today the main source of employment is the paper mill which produces hospital requisites.

In 1883 the annual regatta organised by the rowing club was held in the presence of a considerable number of spectators and some exciting races took place. A cycling club was also held during the period of the penny farthing bicycle. The Fourstones Cyclists won three silver bugles for being the largest group in the district, as well as a number of cups for track racing. When the club ceased its activities the funds were given to the County Nursing Association in order to purchase a new bicycle for the Newbrough district nurse.

In 1836 the portion of railway between Hexham and Haydon Bridge was opened, and the inhabitants of Fourstones waved flags as the first train went by. In 1880 the railway station was opened to the public but it closed in 1967.

Centrally situated is what is locally known as 'the mission' or St Aidan's church, erected in 1892 by the Rev George Cruddas at his own expense, the site being rented from Mr Benson at a nominal sum of one shilling a year. St Aidan's is a cosy establishment and serves the community well.

Opposite St Aidan's is the post office and general store combined, providing an excellent service, now the only shop in both parishes. Fourstones has greatly increased in population in recent years. In 1926 to relieve overcrowding a council estate of 28 houses was commenced, then completed after the Second World War. Recently two private estates have sprung up and a sensitive farm conversion has taken place. Modern-day Fourstones is proving to be a very popular place to reside; quiet, friendly, and within easy commuting distance of Newcastle.

Glanton ✣

Set against a backcloth of Northumbrian hills and overlooking the beautiful Vale of Whittingham stands the village of Glanton. It is notable neither for historic grandeur nor for picturesque quaintness, but, having grown up according to the needs of its inhabitants over the generations, seems to reflect their hardworking lives and rugged environment in its simple, solid character. What we see today are handsome farmhouses with the more functional dwellings of other villagers close by. The easy juxtaposition of the plain and the elegant gives the village an almost hotchpotch charm. No rigid planning governed its growth. Brick blends in beside stone; slate roofs neighbour pantiles and stone flags; very often, brick chimney pots surmount stone buildings; and constant change in the heights and the slope of roofs lends a pleasing irregularity. This great variety of styles and sizes is a result of the fascinating history of the village.

Glanton's origins lie in agriculture. For centuries, it was characterised by poverty with cottages of mud or timber walls roofed by thatch or green sods. Gradually, from among the peasant farmers who worked their strips of the arable fields and grazed their stints of meadow or common land, there emerged a few more successful yeomen farmers, whose fortunes improved still further once enclosure of land enabled better farming practices.

The earliest and most elegant houses in the village were built by these men. Glanton House and The Villa date from the late 17th century and were followed in the early 18th century by Town Farm House and The Mansion. The rest of the 18th century was a time of expansion. Cottages, built by local stonemasons from stone quarried nearby, and roofed with pantiles or stone flags, were being erected to house farmworkers and those supporting the agricultural community – the blacksmiths, joiners, weavers, coopers, butchers and more. Inns provided for the needs of both local people and travellers on the turnpike road upon which Glanton was situated. A Presbyterian church and manse were built and a school was set up for the children's education.

Strangely, growth also came about as a result of adversity rather than success. Around the 1820s farming went through a time of depression and some of the founders of the village became bankrupt and had to sell their land and property. One of the wealthier purchasers had new ideas for the place. Seeing its situation, he developed a firm intention that the village should be based on trade and commerce rather than solely on agriculture. So he began to build good quality, two-storey 'town houses' with shops and workrooms attached, rather than single-storey cottages. It was a significant change. In 1801 there were 50 people working in agriculture compared with 31 in trade. By 1831 the balance had changed. There were now 26 families in agriculture and 47 in trade. The population had risen from 279 to 534 and the number of houses from 59 to 106.

Glanton reached the zenith of its population by 1861. By this time

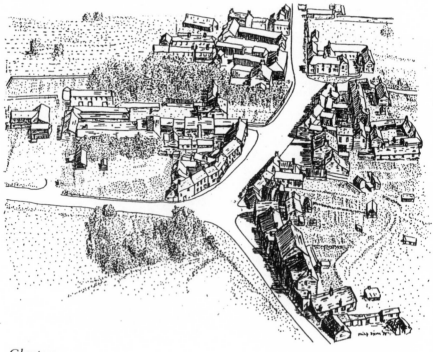

Glanton

houses, farms, cottages, shops, inns and churches appeared randomly alongside each other giving the village its present day, unplanned effect. And still there was constant change with transformation of dwellings to shops or workshops and the building of extensions wherever the need arose. Here was a thriving country business centre with a lively community spirit. Although agriculture was still its bedrock, it had shops, including bakers, butchers, drapers and grocers; light trades such as tailors and dressmakers, boot and shoe makers and cloggers, milliners, saddlers and watchmakers; and heavier trades, some employing large numbers of men, including masons, cartwrights, slaters, joiners, painters, blacksmiths, a cooper and a millwright. There were professional people too – doctors, teachers and clergymen – and many people were employed in personal service.

In the second half of the 19th century, the population declined to about 500 but the overall picture remained one of industry and activity. It was in the present century that all this changed. Greater mechanisation on farms led to a decline in employment opportunities. The great depression of the 1930s meant that the wealthy landed estates could no longer maintain their former lifestyle and a vast source of employment was lost. Two world wars had their effect also.

By the 1970s the population had shrunk to less than 200 people yet the sense of activity and purposefulness persisted. Glanton still had a school, an active parish council, a well used village hall and four churches. There were four shops, a sub post office, petrol pumps, a branch of a major bank and a hairdresser. Two hotels provided accommodation and meals and some private houses offered bed and breakfast. A large number of tradesmen were based in the village. Being centrally located between Alnwick, Rothbury and Wooler, and being conveniently close to a number of other villages and hamlets, Glanton was still a thriving business centre. The width of its main street and the variety of its retailers made it a good place to stop and shop. Twice it was a winner in the Best Kept Village competition and it was awarded a certificate in Britain in Bloom. Its World Bird Research Station, housed in The Mansion, attracted several thousand visitors to the village each year, the beauty of the countryside no doubt being an added attraction. Nevertheless, no one would have denied that there were signs of deterioration in places and that improvements were possible. The old buildings of the South Farm steading were an all too obvious example.

In the last dozen years, change has inevitably continued and further loss of amenities has occurred. The school, built in 1875, finally closed its doors in 1981. The butcher is gone, along with the grocer's and draper's shops; one hotel is closed and there is no bank. Yet, such is the determination and spirit of the community that the village has not been allowed to die. Clear evidence that it is alive and well may be found in the thriving Women's Institute and in the annual show which is regarded as a model of its kind and draws attendance from far and wide.

Glanton has been designated a conservation area, not only to preserve what is best in the existing fabric of the village but to attract grants and other investment. The once derelict buildings at South Farm have been imaginatively converted to provide residential accommodation and workshops. North Housing, in partnership with the Development Commission and Alnwick District Council, has built eight new houses and private builders have matched that figure. The county council, with the support of the Development Commission, has bought the old village school and school house and has leased these to a small high-technology firm.

Greenhead

The name Greenhead is said to mean 'the green places between the headstreams', namely the Tipall burn and Irthing stream.

The youth hostel here was originally a Methodist chapel, built in 1806 but replaced by a Primitive Methodist chapel in 1885. It is a very busy hostel, welcoming many visitors to Hadrian's Wall and the Pennine Way.

The church of St Cuthbert was built in 1828 and designed by architect John Dobson. In 1900 a chancel was built, the nave restored and a spire added to the tower. The village school was built in 1898 at a cost of £1,500. Over this time pupil attendance has been as high as 300, down to the present 26. The vicarage closed in 1981 when church services were transferred to the supervision of the Haltwhistle vicar. The house is now well established bed and breakfast accommodation.

Glenwhelt Farmhouse was built in 1757 as a coaching inn. You can see the fine classical doorway headed by a dial with the face of the flaming sun.

Thirlway is so named because it was reputed to be the weakest part of the wall and the place where the Caledonians first 'thirled' or threw down the wall. Thirlwell Castle dates back to the 13th century and Edward I slept here in September 1306.

Byron was the name of the pit opened in 1867 and situated at Bankfoot. Between 1905 and 1906 the pit produced 41,716 tons of coal but in 1908 a disaster flooded the drifts and the pit closed. The Byron was named as a compliment to Mrs Coulson, daughter of Lord Byron.

Blenkinsopp Castle was built in 1340 by Thomas de Blenkinsopp and by 1542 the castle had fallen into decay. In 1785 the castle was transferred by marriage to the Coulson family and fully restored in 1880, later to be bought by the Joicey family in 1885. Captain Edward Joicey and his lovely actress wife Violet Lorraine lived here for quite a number of years but on the death of his father he moved to Blenkinsopp Hall. The estate cottages, the hall grounds and gardens are well worth visiting, situated in such peaceful and beautiful surroundings.

Guyzance 🦢

Lying to the north west of Acklington is the hamlet of Guyzance. The area is one of outstanding natural beauty with the river Coquet forming a prominent feature.

The actual hamlet comprises a long main road with several cottages on either side, and Guyzance Hall and estate owned by Sir Anthony Milburn and his family. There are also several other dwellings and farms in the surrounding area. There is no church (the parish church is in Acklington), no pub and no shop, but all amenities are within a short drive.

Settlement in the area dates back to AD 737 and the name Guyzance, which is Norman, comes from Guines, near Calais. Along the banks of the river Coquet are several landmarks. A disused mill stands opposite Whirley Shaws hill. There has been a mill on this site since 1336 and the weir on this stretch of the river dates back to 1350. The weir can be seen today, although its main use now is to provide a fishing spot for the herons that visit this part of the river.

The remains of Guyzance nunnery and its Norman architecture can be found beside the river at Brainshaugh. It was established before 1147. During the 19th century it was occasionally used for marriage ceremonies and before the last war open air services were held at the nunnery. Today, apart from being a local landmark, it is used as a family burial ground.

Across the river from the nunnery lies the 'dye works', now a row of handsome town houses. The building was initially a foundry for tin and iron but it was converted into a woollen mill in 1791 and remained in use as such until 1884. The derelict building was taken over by Ellwood Homes of Newcastle in 1915 to make hydrate of alumina, a white pigment previously obtained from Germany. During this period it became one of the first premises in the area to be lit by electric light, provided by hydro-electric power. After a change in ownership in the late 1920s there was a fall in the quality of production and the pollution in the river increased, and as a result the Duke of Northumberland refused to renew the lease and production ceased in 1930.

The weir on this stretch of the river, which was so important throughout all the manufacturing activities, is still in good condition. It has a very attractive curved design and an excellent covered salmon ladder.

The artist Wilson Hepple (1853–1937) lived in a cottage further along the river from the 'dye works'. He is famous for his horse, dog and kitten paintings. He and his son are buried in Acklington cemetery.

When Guyzance Hall was built at the end of the 19th century and the estate developed, it created new jobs and brought more people to the area. In those days, there was a schoolroom (dating back to 1852), a joiner's shop and a blacksmith's at West House. During the war the schoolroom was used regularly for whist drives, to raise money for the Red Cross, and the occasional dance complete with squeeze box and fiddle. How did they manage with so little room?

Today, only the schoolroom remains, but its educational use has long since past. Local children now attend the village school in Acklington. Once a month the schoolroom is used for an evensong service.

Although the area remains mainly agricultural, tourism is increasing and Guyzance has become a popular holiday spot. Some of the houses on the estate have become holiday homes and people come from all over the country to enjoy this beautiful part of Northumberland, with its scenery which has changed little in 1,200 years.

Haltwhistle 🦥

There has probably been a settlement here for over a thousand years, but by 1086 Haltwhistle was officially on the map, registered in the Domesday Book. During the Middle Ages it established itself as a small market town for the area and there are still one or two buildings remaining from that period. The church of the Holy Cross was built in the 13th century though its origins date to the 9th century. The blacksmith's in the Market Square is probably the oldest commercial building in the town. In 1719 the first school was built at the bottom of the Comb Hill. The money to build the school came from Lady Capel and it still stands and is used by the Haltwhistle brass band as a practice room.

The boom years for Haltwhistle were 1837 to 1914 with the coming of the railway, when industry developed along the Haltwhistle burn. Mines, mills, breweries, brickworks, lime-kilns, a quarry and a gasworks were all connected to the railway line by a horse-drawn waggon-way. The main employers today are Crown Berger (paint manufacturers), BP Chemicals (plastic bottle producers) and Kilfrost (specialists in anti-freeze).

Today, Haltwhistle caters for tourists, who enjoy the beauty of the countryside with many fine walks around the district and easy access to the Roman wall with its museums at Carvoran, Housesteads and Vindolanda. The area is also well served by tourist accommodation with small friendly hotels, family run guest houses and self catering cottages.

The large variety of shops cater for all needs with market day on a Thursday. Haltwhistle is served by a regular bus and train service and there is a special 'Roman Wall' bus service operating during the summer months. Sports activities are also well catered for – a recently completed all weather tennis court, an open air heated swimming pool, football pitches, outdoor bowls, cricket, squash courts, badminton and many more. A warm and friendly welcome awaits all visitors to Haltwhistle.

Harbottle ✤

Harbottle lies within the Northumberland National Park on the fringe of the Ministry of Defence training area. It lies in a hollow of heather covered hills, which are capped by rocks, and the river Coquet winds its way down the valley towards Rothbury some ten miles away. The name 'Her-botl' denotes in Anglo-Saxon, the 'botl' or building of the 'her', or army, indicating that the village originated from the castle or from an earlier earthwork erected by Saxon or Danish armies on the same site.

The ruins of the castle can still be seen. Built in 1160 by the united efforts of Henry II and the Bishop of Durham, at one time it was the most distant outpost on the Border. It was soon sacked by the Scots, but was then rebuilt more strongly. One hundred years later they besieged it in vain. It was partly destroyed again after Bannockburn, but by 1515 it had been more or less restored to receive Margaret Tudor for her confinement. She was the sister of Henry VIII and had been the widow of James IV of Scotland, and it was here at the castle that she gave birth to a daughter also named Margaret, who was later to become the mother-in-law of Mary, Queen of Scots. When the stronghold fell into ruin, some of the stone was used to build the Harbottle Castle which stands at the other end of the village. This has now been turned into flats.

The population of Harbottle is 120, but much goes on. There is an annual show, over 125 years old, held on the first Saturday in September, with classes in cookery, flowers, vegetables, children's work, walking sticks, sheepdog trials, various sports and a clay pigeon shoot. When the day's events are over, the marquee is cleared and everyone gathers in the evening at the ceilidh. There are village activities to suit everyone, with both junior and senior cricket teams and junior football, and bowls are played in the village hall where there is also an art class which holds an exhibition of work every year. Darts, pool and quiz nights are held in the Star Inn and the Girl Guides meet once a week in the cricket hut. In days gone by Harbottle had a weekly market and annual fair and the lord of the manor held court in the Unicorn Inn, which is now the Star Inn. There are no shops in the village now that the shop/post office has recently closed and the post office has been moved to within the Star Inn.

Harbottle is flanked by two villages. One is Holystone, on the south side, where in the 7th century in the time of King Edwin, St Paulinus baptised 3,000 Northumbrians at the Lady's Well, a most beautiful, peaceful spot which can be found just behind the Salmon Inn in the village. On the north side lies the village of Alwinton with its beautiful church of St Michael and All Angels. One distinguished visitor who came to the village was Sir Walter Scott, who came to gather material for *Rob Roy* and stayed at the Rose and Thistle Inn.

Hartburn 🐝

Hartburn – where the deer still come down to the stream. The village is picturesquely situated above the river Hart and its wooded ravines.

The first place to attract visitors is the parish church of St Andrew, and, reading through the excellent guide book there, they discover that the church's origins go back to the 10th and 11th centuries – probably as a tower for sheltering in, and for visiting monks from Tynemouth Priory. Much of the land in and around the village belonged to the church, rather than to the landed gentry. The mysterious Devil's Causeway crosses the river at the west end of the village, and there is much evidence of the Romans being in the area. In the churchyard is buried Thomas Whittle, who died in 1731. He was an eccentric poet who wrote the ballad *The Mitford Galloway*. The author of the great *History of Northumberland*, John Hodgson, who was the vicar here from 1833 to 1845, was also buried here.

The beautiful vicarage no longer houses a vicar – five churches are looked after by one vicar who lives in Whalton. One end of the vicarage was once a 'vicar's pele'.

Clustered near the church are Beehive Cottage – once an inn – the Old Smithy and Glebe Farm. Another cottage was converted into a parish room for the use of villagers. A group of spinners meet here monthly, but the clinic has now moved to the nearest surgery.

The school, which closed in 1973, is now converted into two houses – one is aptly named Book End. Another house now stands on the site of the old school canteen. The old school house was built by Dr Sharpe, vicar of Hartburn from 1749 to 1792, and his parishioners. The schoolmaster lived above the parish stable. There is a wonderful view over the river and its wooded banks.

Until recently the village builder (and his 20 or so 'merry men' as customers called them) worked from an old cottage converted into a workshop. He previously worked from the old smithy. The skills learnt here are now being practised further afield, but traditionally designed and built stone and slate houses are a tribute to their workmanship.

Walking along the road, leaving behind the traditional dry-stone walling which encloses the fields with the ancient breed of Jacob sheep grazing to the left, start counting the different varieties of trees along the edge of the woods to the right. You should be able to name at least a dozen different species, taking us way back into history, possibly to

Saxon days – if we follow the theory that in order to 'date' a hedge, we add a century for each species of tree. This brings history to life, as we can imagine the Tynemouth monks exchanging their knowledge about remedies concocted from the herbs and flowers gathered along the hedgerows. The hedgerow is the source of medieval folklore and medicine. The edible plants and fruits were gathered. The various woods were used by the villagers for baskets, fencing, tool handles, crooks, furniture, kindling, whittling and carving, the leaves used to stuff mattresses and pillows, oak tannin used for ink – each tree and shrub had a different use, and some were believed to have magical qualities.

Watch out for the traffic passing by, as you wander along. This busy road is the direct route for many heavy vehicles, both local and long distant.

The names of some of the houses at this west end of the village reflect the rich folklore abounding in this area – Dragon's Den, Baker's Chest. One cottage, ideal for a retired couple today, was once two cottages, lived in by large families and supporting a little shop. The post office was once here too, but after changing hands is now closed.

Don't miss the woodland walk along the riverside path. The woods once belonged to the church, but are now managed by the Woodland Trust. They abound with flora and fauna. A grotto, hewn into the rock, is an unexpected sight.

In 1993 the population of Hartburn was 24 adults and eleven children and young people, with a changing number of lodgers and holidaymakers. The census in 1851 reveals that 24 adults and 13 children lived here. One hundred years ago the jobs included domestic work, masons and labourers, gardening, grooms, joiners, shoemaker, schoolmaster and vicar. Two lodgers in the village were Irish labourers.

Nowadays, working people travel to Newcastle or Morpeth, but there is still domestic work, gardening and work with horses available. A small business in the village produces water pumps for the Third World.

Old glebe land – once the school garden – is now supplying four households with produce from allotments (not to mention leeks for Middleton Leek Show). Gardening is a popular pastime for all the villagers, and the village fares well in the Northumbria in Bloom and Best Kept Village competitions. Judges comment on the good community spirit shown in keeping the village looking beautiful.

Public transport to Morpeth runs at times geared for the school-children, so everyone is dependent on travelling by car. The nearest garage, shops and surgery are three miles away at Scots Gap, the post office is five miles away at Cambo. Twenty years ago the village was served by travelling tradesmen – a butcher, grocery vans, a fishmonger, a baker and a greengrocer. Now only the mobile library comes into the village, every fortnight. Walking is now for recreation, and once again the hedgerows are scoured for fruits and kindling. Interest in wild flowers and herbs is increasing, and conservation and looking after our beautiful countryside is becoming increasingly important.

Haydon Bridge 🌿

Haydon Bridge is situated on the A69 halfway between Newcastle and Carlisle and stands on both banks of the river South Tyne. The population has grown to 3,000.

The earliest known settlement of Haydon, a word believed to be of Saxon origin and meaning 'enclosure', is situated on the steep valley side one mile north east of the river crossing. All that now remains is the chancel of the 12th century church, built in part with stone which had given witness to the earlier Roman occupation. In 1796 many of those same stones were used to build the new parish church of St Cuthbert. The latter, whilst not a building of great architectural promise, does have some small measure of individual identity by reason of the pagoda-style capping to the square tower. Reflecting perhaps the seriousness Victorians gave to Christian understanding, three other places of worship were also built and continue in use today.

As the village name implies, there must be a bridge. Two bridges in fact, but the modern concrete structure erected in 1967 must be left to be appreciated by latter day travellers. Of greater interest is the now pedestrianised narrow, six-arched stone bridge which was last rebuilt after the great flood of 1773. Although suffering further dilapidation some 30 years later it still affords a pleasing aspect of the South Tyne and its verdant and tree-lined banks with encroaching local stone-faced Victorian dwellings.

Some of the events and people that have added colour to the story of the village over many troubled decades can now be identified from some of the street names. Radcliffe Road sparks thoughts of the Earls of Derwentwater and the anguish caused by reason of their Jacobite tendency. John Martin Street reflects the birthplace of the internationally recognised early 19th century painter who used local landscapes as background to many of his epic pictures, a small number of which are frequently on exhibition in Newcastle's Laing Art Gallery. John Martin lived in a cottage at East Lands End where there is placed in the gable wall a plaque to his memory. His brother achieved fame of a different sort. He is said to have walked up and down the parapet of the bridge at midnight playing the violin behind his back, and preached to imaginary congregations from the pulpit of the old church. His madness led to him attempting to burn down York Minster.

Of more parochial interest are the events which John Shaftoe Street commemorate. The Rev John Shaftoe was the third son of a long-serving Northumbrian vicar. After his death in 1695 and by reason of his will, a trust was set up to grant his wishes that a grammar school be provided and further funds allocated for both the education of the children and care of the elderly within the chapelry of Haydon Bridge. Over the years, and up to the present, the benefactor is well remembered through the name of the schools and the provision of grants in the interests of education. The present senior school, an offshoot from those earlier provisions, now educates many pupils from west and north Northumberland. Almshouses which also bear his name can be seen today on the south side of the river, shielded from the north by a crenellated wall.

Within the immediate vicinity of the village, manufacturing and commerce have had but a small and unsustained part to play. The dominating activity has always been and remains agriculture. At one time or another metal ore, coal and limestone were extracted but even the advent of the railway and the one-time promise of a canal to ship out lead concentrates failed to promote the village beyond that of a small dormitory centre surrounded by arable and animal farming.

Alas, Haydon Bridge may simply be remembered by many as some-where they hurriedly passed through. But for those who stop, it is not without its clutch of interesting and rewarding hostelries in which to rest, refresh and perhaps plan the next stage of their excursion to possibly more well known archaeological and historical pickings to be found only minutes away.

Hebron 🌿

The small, quiet village of Hebron (or Hebburn) lies at the junction of the road from Ulgham with a minor road from the A1 leading to Longhirst village and the town of Morpeth. There are a few stone cottages and a small development of modern bungalows to the south, most of which have pretty gardens.

A small, well kept church stands on the north side of the village. In the late 17th century, this church dedicated to St Cuthbert was in a ruinous state and was rebuilt late the following century, the present chancel arch being the only reminder of the old building. A blacksmith's shop is situated at the junction of the road from Ulgham with the Morpeth and Longhirst road, while the West Farm buildings are now occupied by a road haulage firm.

For schooling, shopping and other services, the village people are dependent on the nearby town of Morpeth. North of Hebron is Cockle Park, the centre for the Newcastle University's Department of Agriculture experimental station. The farm buildings include the Cockle Park Tower, built in Tudor times and restored in the 18th century.

Heddon 🌿

Two thousand years ago it was here – the Roman wall at Heddon. In AD 54, soldiers from the sunny climes of Italy marched along the wall. They must have gazed long and often into the bleak distance – to Durham Moor in the south, Cheviot and Simonside to the north, and the Pennines in the west; all were clearly visible from their grey outpost, the Twelve Mile Castle on the now famous Hadrian's Wall. The wall is still walked on, but now it is by visitors from all over the world. They can also stop and buy souvenirs at the little craft shop built over the actual site of the Twelve Mile Castle.

The village of Heddon clusters around the church of St Andrew. There has been a place of worship on the hilltop site for at least 1,300 years, with some evidence of the original Saxon building still visible. St Andrew was a favourite saint of Wilfred, Bishop of Hexham, circa AD 680. The small Saxon church has evolved into today's sturdy parish church with bell tower and single chime. The Methodist chapel was built (almost next door) in 1877 and both church services and church functions are well supported by villagers.

There has been a small settlement at Heddon since time immemorial. It was always surrounded by farms and smallholdings and in the 19th century there was some coal mining. The only evidence of the mining is a couple of rows of pit cottages, but the farms still remain. However, alongside the traditional agricultural establishments have been added a popular plant nursery centre, and that new phenomenon, a 'pick-it-yourself' fruit farm.

In the past Heddon provided a watering hole for both man and beast on their way from Hexham to Newcastle. Perhaps the drovers stopped at The Three Tuns, which still stands on the main road, and directly opposite this inn was the village pond. The pond was filled in long ago, to be replaced by a small flower garden, seats and a war memorial. Ironically, next to this garden is the modern watering hole – a petrol filling station. There is a good bus service into Newcastle, some eight miles away to the east, or Hexham, twelve miles west. With the building of the A69 motorway in the 1960s, there is now much less traffic through the village. At the turn of the century there was also a train service from Heddon, but this line was closed several years ago and the track made into a lovely walk alongside the river.

Over 100 species of birds have been recorded within the parish, and a rare pair of kingfishers are nesting in the bank of the Tyne. Foxes are common, both around and in the village itself. There are several badger setts and roe deer are regularly seen. There is also a growing population of the rare red squirrel. The village has its own nature reserve, Heddon Common, owned by the borough but managed by the parish council. The common supports a varied flora, with oak, beech and rowan trees. Many of the indigenous species of birds can be seen there.

During the last part of the 19th century there was an upsurge of building within the village – a school and school house, a reading room, The Swan pub, with the smithy next door, and the old vicarage. In 1922, the WI 'hut' was erected. In 1936 the Knott Hall was built, named after Sir James and Lady Knott who were local landowners and benefactors. The hall is widely used by the villagers for a variety of meetings and functions.

At the end of the 1950s the hamlet of Heddon began to change and evolve into the village that it is today. Some of the pit cottages were demolished to make way for a small council development and farmland was sold to allow the building of two private estates. The cottage-shops were superseded by a shopping precinct with a grocer, post office and newsagent. The old school was replaced by a modern single-storeyed building with playing fields, flower beds and inside toilets. The blacksmith moved in 1971 to new purpose-built premises, and the original smithy became The Swan's dining room – the enormous internal chimney, however, still remains as a reminder of the past. The reading room is now a private dwelling and a glass building houses the library.

Amongst the new, however, still lurks the old – the carter's cottages, the joiner's/undertaker's cottages (with the stables behind), the first church house with the hearse house next door, the depot where coal was stored before being taken downriver to Newcastle and beyond. The village is now an amalgam of old and new, but totally homogeneous in character.

It is people that make a village community, and despite the changes of brick and mortar, the character of the village has not changed. There is personal service in the shops from the owners; 'neighbourhood watch' means keeping a concerned eye on your neighbour, as well as their property; the parish council are actively concerned with village matters; and the flower tubs and hanging baskets around the village (inspired by the 'Heddon in Bloom' committee) have certainly enhanced its appearance.

Hedley on the Hill ෴

Hedley on the Hill stands on the western end of a high ridge, close to the Durham border, which divides the valleys of the Tyne and the Derwent. In the past if you had asked an inhabitant of Hedley what the weather was like there, he would have said, 'If it's clear enough for you to see Muckle Cheviot it is going to rain and if you can't, it's already raining.' However, if you do manage to visit Hedley in between the showers you will be amazed at the outstanding views that you get from this tiny village set in south east Northumberland. The view before you extends westward to the Pennines and north to the Cheviots and is laid out like an aerial photograph. The road that runs through the village, part of 'The Old Lead Road' was used in the past for carrying lead from Allendale to Blaydon where it was loaded onto ships bound for London.

The name Hedley is derived from two old words 'hed' and 'lea' meaning heather and clearing. The heather which may have once covered the original clearing seems to have disappeared but some of the houses, with parts dating from the 17th and 18th centuries, still remain. We know that the old houses in Hedley were not built before the 17th century because of its past history. At one time Hedley was situated further down the hill. The Black Death reached the village in 1666, and those who managed to survive it, left and founded a new village at the top of the hill. In agricultural terms the land was very good and was lying on tons of high quality coal, so farming and mining were very important.

Also belonging to the past is the legend of the Hedley Kow, which was an evil goblin or bogle living in Hedley in the 18th century. He teased the servant girls by imitating the voices of their sweethearts, unravelled knitting, upset pots and pans, put spinning wheels out of action and gave cream to the farmhouse cat. Travellers too were bothered by the goblin, who tormented them and then made them lose their way. The mischievous bogle was capable of changing his appearance and he could become an old lady who would walk into the inn and put sticks on the fire so that it would flare up and burn the chimney.

One man who has lived in the village for 75 years can remember when things were very different. There was a school, built in 1846, which he attended until he was 14. A general dealer's shop and a post office provided some of the necessities of life, although most villagers had their own allotments and grew their own vegetables. As a boy he went regularly to the Wesleyan chapel which had been built in 1837. After the First World War the village wanted to commemorate those who had lost their lives and as a result of various fund-raising activities a village hall was built, commonly called 'The Institute'. Many activities took place there. There were dances, concerts, billiards, whist drives, dominoes and card games. It could be used as a library, and as it had fires at either end of the hall, older people could use it during the day. Apparently, the postman who walked from Stocksfield with newspapers as well as post, had his sandwiches there before collecting the post and walking all the way back to Stocksfield.

Three buses every day travelled to Chopwell, Greenside and other local places. Hedley had a thriving football team and other sporting activities were organised as well. They played quoits and when their play churned up the village green they were asked to stop and their game continued at Currock Hill Farm just out of the village. They played pitch and toss with someone keeping an eye open for the law! At this time many people earned their living as farmers, farmworkers and miners in

Hedley but others remembered were a policeman who walked his beat, a blacksmith, a pub manager, a joiner who kept about 200 white rabbits and sold their fur, and 'midnight mechanics' who were kept busy and what they carried, mixed with ash, was thrown onto the fields!

Today, Hedley has much better sanitation but unfortunately has lost most of its community activities. The school closed and now houses two families, the shop has long gone, the post office has more recently gone, the chapel is now a dwelling place and the village hall is no longer there. The plaque listing the names of those who died in the war, taken from The Institute, can now be found in St George's, Mickley, which is the parish church for Hedley. There is a bus which travels to Hexham once a week, picking up from other villages on the way.

Numbers in the farming community have decreased and no coal mining activities take place now. There are 182 people living in the village and there are 75 houses with more being built. Most people who are of a working age commute and the children are bussed to and from school. The Feathers Inn provides the only meeting place in the village. A leek club is organised from there as well as domino evenings, occasional quiz nights, Easter egg and bonnet competitions and a barrel race. A small committee of villagers runs a summer fair and barbecue to raise funds for the provision of fireworks on Guy Fawkes night.

Holywell

Holywell got its name from the well just below the manor house in the village. This house is the oldest in the village and was built by Sir Ralph Bates with stone from a quarry in the field beside the old bridge. The quarry has now, of course, been filled in.

Monks used to live on the site of the manor house and 'holy water' from the well was used to bathe people's eyes in the belief that it would restore their sight. (It is also said that there is a tunnel going from the manor house to Delaval Hall, also used by the monks.) The blacksmith (he was also the local undertaker) used to live opposite the manor house.

The road passing over the old bridge – still under the present bridge – was used by travellers going from Blyth to Newcastle, often stopping at Holywell for a rest and to water their horses. Mary, Queen of Scots stayed at the manor house on her way from England to Scotland and the present Mortimer family have the letter of thanks, sent at the time, thanking them for their hospitality.

The main industries were farming and mining. Some of the land is still farmed but the colliery and colliery houses have all gone and in their place are new housing estates.

Holywell Dene was much visited in bygone days by people from North Shields and surrounding districts arriving on bicycles for picnics, fun and games and to pick bluebells, to return home tired but happy after a day in the country. The Dene is still enjoyed by many people today, visiting the nature reserve where there are many different species of birds to be seen.

Although there have been many changes Holywell still retains the feeling of being a village, having the post office, shop and The Fat Ox, an old coaching inn built in the 16th century. There is also a Veterans' Hut, purpose-built, for the senior members of the community. Here, people can meet and relax and reminisce about bygone days, read, play pool, listen to music or have lively discussions about current affairs.

Horncliffe

About five miles inland from Berwick, along the curving, gracious banks of the tidal river Tweed, the chain-bridge heralds that particular bend in the river where, perched on the high red cliffs just beyond it, sits the small village of Horncliffe. Or Horckley, as it used to be called. If you stand in the haughs (expansive level fields on the banks) on the Scottish side, only the odd roof can be seen, and this was where the armies of Charles I and Oliver Cromwell camped in the 1600s. In those times the ford was the attraction, but since 1820 this point has been spanned by the chain-bridge built by Sir Samuel Browne, who used it as a prototype for his later design of the Menai Bridge in Wales. One foot leads to leafy Scotland, the other remains securely locked into the cliff face which welcomes the traveller into Northumberland. Just one tarmac road leads into and out of the village, thus it retains a strangely remote quality full of surprises.

Its heart for many years has been the river, though it is hidden and many visitors come and go and never know the existence of it. To take a walk down one of the network of paths to the river and watch the silver salmon leap on a summer evening is beautiful. Now we see only solitary, expensively-clad fly fishermen, but a few years ago the river was alive with boats, fishermen and ghillies netting the salmon for sale all over the country. They lived in butts and benns, mostly now demolished in favour of more spacious dwellings, and the bothies on the river bank have been renovated and make excellent holiday cottages. In the 1930s James Strothers, 'Old Pluck', had a good business making leather waders for the fishermen. Photographs of the fishing industry can be seen at the only pub in the village, The Fisher's Arms.

There are no shops now but there have been several; Loosie Lyle sold all sorts but is remembered particularly by the pensioners because she went specially to Berwick on a Saturday morning to bring back their childhood supplies of aniseed balls and liquorice, and 'Cadger Robertson' delivered by pony and trap and presumably cadged honourably. Milk and eggs could be collected from the pub as the publican's brother was a farmer. In those days the only other shop, though there were other businesses, was a tailor's shop started in 1907 by Adam Robertson and through the good and lean years it managed to survive till 1958. In an upper room above the shop the tailor and his assistants toiled making suits and trousers, a good tweed suit in 1908 costing £2 12s 6d. He also delivered by pony and trap and went as far afield as Ashington, 60 miles away, for business. Poor pony!

There were hard times in the 1920s and 1930s but most of the villagers kept a pig in the garden and killed at different times and gave portions to friends and relations to spread the bounty. There was no electricity at that time so the sides of bacon were kept on hooks and salted down, not a scrap was ever wasted. The publican was no exception and his pig was a source of great delight to the children because it was given all the slops from the glasses as well as scraps, so it was frequently tiddly, snored loudly and could be poked unmercifully.

Most folk had orchards and vegetable patches and again the bounty was spread and no doubt fellowship and feuds abounded. Barter was the name of the game. The soil is rich and friable in Horncliffe if well tended and the present day gardens prove it; the onion show and the spring bulb show are still highlights of the village year. In the 1940s market gardener Jock Chalmers had a flourishing business providing local produce which he sold in Berwick, his tomatoes small and sweet were renowned. Now we have a honey farm which produces not only wonderful natural honey but cosmetics, creams and polishes. There used to be a blacksmith kept busy with work from the surrounding farms, and even a horn-maker. Now there are only a few farmworkers, but builders, joiners and carpenters have sprung up in their place.

The church was the mainspring of many village activities and on high days and holidays there were outings for the children in August to Spittal, services at harvest time and garden fetes at Allenby House where Captain Allenby lived. On Remembrance Day, always the 11th November no matter whether it was Sunday or weekday, the workers would come in from the fields or workshop to remember, hats off, tools down, their dead in the First World War, all together around the memorial.

The church was built in 1858, which was about the same time as the school. Sixty local children attended, each subscribing threepence a week for tuition; it was otherwise supported by charity. They had a halfpenny in the bank in 1863, but possessed the beginnings of a library though every acquisition was closely scrutinised by the school committee and any of an immoral nature were firmly rejected. In 1874 £1 was set aside to buy oranges to be given to the children on the afternoon before Good Friday and in 1883 the school was closed for six weeks for a whooping cough epidemic. We still have a school, now accommodated in a modern building set in pleasant playing fields.

After much hard work, village spirit and jollity the present Memorial Hall, opened in 1957, remains the centre of the community and houses all the meetings, hops and get-togethers that typify village life. The village post office, surely the smallest, least stable building in the British Isles, measuring three feet square, is now the hub of Horncliffe every weekday morn. Resilient to the winds of change, it has traded uninterrupted for the past 60 years.

Horsley 🦢

Horsley on the Hill, or Horsley on Tyne, is first mentioned in 1245 as part of the estate of Gilbert de Umfraville. Originally on the main Newcastle to Hexham road, the village has been bypassed by the new A69 and remains a very quiet, rural settlement.

Horsley Wood forms the southern boundary of the village on the bank of the Tyne, divided from Wylam by the Howdean burn and from Ovingham, by the Kitty's burn, where the ruins of Horsley colliery remain. The Roman wall crosses the village near the boundary on the north side, between Horsley and Whitchester.

From the early 17th to the late 19th century mining provided the main employment. Horsley Wood mine lay under the Tyne and during its later history the shaft by which miners descended was on the south side of the river, causing Horsley miners to have to walk round by Wylam Bridge and cross by ferry, or as sometimes happened in winter, walk across on the frozen river. Towards the end of the 19th century increasing water in the working led to the closure of the colliery.

There was also a mine at Horsley North Farm, near the present reservoir of the Newcastle and Gateshead Water Company. Traces of this mine remain in Horsley Wood in the form of the permanent way along which ponies dragged wooden tubs. The coal produced here was first class quality and much sought after.

Farming has always been to the forefront in the village. Around the 17th century there were 20 farms of varying sizes, 15 leased by the Earl of Northumberland and five privately owned – all based upon the strip farming method. Eventually the Percys made what today would be termed a 'take over bid' and became, and still are, the chief landowners in the area.

Great changes took place during the period of the agricultural revolution and by the 19th century there were five compact farms remaining. Living conditions of the farmworkers were improved and cottages were built in short rows, three-sided squares or integrated in new farm buildings. The estate attached small plots of land to the cottages in an effort to encourage a degree of self-sufficiency among the tenants. Today, three working farms remain. Farm building conversions and new housing, whilst providing lovely new homes, also blend into the landscape and retain the character of the village.

The chapel was founded by Charles Wesley in 1742 and on his return to London, his brother John made a second visit to the North. The association with Horsley lasted until 1774, during which time he paid nine visits to the village. John Wesley preached from the steps of the Coaching House, dated 1700. The initials worked in the stone belong to the Richards family, who purchased the house for Wesley to preach in. However, it was never large enough and the meetings had to be held outside. What remained of the pulpit Wesley used was eventually taken to London for safekeeping – rather a pity.

Thomas Trevant, vicar of Ovingham, used the manse as a refuge for nonconformists, where they used to meet in the attic to escape persecution, until the law was relaxed. An original wattle and daub wall is still standing and whilst most has been covered, a small glass panel gives a view of this old craft. Probably the two inns, North Farm, the manse and the Old House – which now has a kitchen-centre attached – are the only buildings likely to have been known to the Wesleys.

The friendly Crown and Anchor now provides a meeting place for villagers to play darts and dominoes, hold shows and chat; whilst The Lion and Lamb (1718) has developed into a cosy licensed restaurant, which attracts many visitors to the village.

Traditions and celebrations were mostly centred around the school and churches, with some people going to the latter three times a day, and not always to the same church. Hence along with their disappearance so too has some of the old village life.

Howick

The village today is set several hundred yards from the Longhoughton to Craster road that runs close to the sandstone and whinstone cliffs. The cottages are spread round the Copley Hall. There is a post office and a sweet shop, and the bus still regularly calls. But once upon a time, and right back to Domesday, Howick was on the south side of the Hall, by the church, almost a mile away. The third Earl Grey, the resident of Howick Hall in the mid 19th century, felt it spoilt his view, so he had all the cottages moved.

Howick is an estate village. Most of the tenants are in some way connected with the estate. The population is 35, but together with the surrounding farms, houses, Little Houghton and the Hall, it rises to 151.

Geologically the parish can boast a fault, known as the Howick Fault. From the cliffs at Howick Sea Houses, looking north, the two rock types of whinstone and sandstone can be seen lying at right angles to each other. The Whin Sill which runs through Howick is quarried for use as a road surface, providing a valuable source of revenue for the trustees which helps in the running of the estate.

The Howick burn runs through the hall gardens, and accompanies walkers who take the Long Walk from Silverwood to the sea (one and a half miles). The hill to the north as the path reaches the sea is known as Camp Hill. The circular markings of the ancient Celtic settlement can still be clearly seen. This was possibly the original Howick, or 'high farm'. *The Times* recently published photographs and a report of the oldest existing footprints in Britain, 300 million years old, found in the sandstone layers on the beach at Howick, near Camp Hill. The prints had been made by the four-legged temnospondyl which roamed the land 100 million years before dinosaurs.

126

The bathing house at Howick

The Grey family has owned the parish of Howick since the 14th century (a thank-you present from Edward II). There was a chapel at Howick from the early 12th century but this was demolished in 1746 by Sir Henry Grey to make way for the first modern church, which Sir Henry had built in the style of a Greek temple. This was fortunately (some say) gutted by fire, and the present, conventional, church built in 1846. The marble tomb of the second Earl Grey, Prime Minister, is opposite the pulpit, on the south wall. The tomb once had a marble canopy which the fifth Earl demolished with hammer and chisel: history does not record the reason. In the churchyard, to the right of the gate, is the grave of five French sailors who were shipwrecked on the rocks by the boathouse in 1913. The people of the village purchased a gravestone, and the grave is still regularly tended by a local family.

Travel before the railways came was by sea. Howick folk would go down to the boathouse at Howick Haven and be rowed out to the big boat anchored offshore. They would then go to Newcastle, or even London. The railway arrived in 1847. It was originally planned to run beside the sea, but Lord Grey, an MP at the time, fought the proposed siting and managed to have the line laid further inland, unseen by any on the estate. There was also much debate in Westminster as to the type of railway system for the Newcastle to Berwick line. Lord Grey favoured atmospheric traction but George Hudson preferred steam, and it was steam that won the day. The nearest station for the village was Little Mill until 1965. Alnmouth, five miles south, is now our station, direct to London in three and a half hours.

The first residence of the Grey family in Howick was a pele tower (where the lawn south west of the hall now is). This was demolished in 1782 by Sir Henry Grey to make way for the hall. Sir Henry had no heir, and left the estate to his nephew, the son of the first Earl Grey, who lived at Falloden.

So the second Earl Grey, the famous Whig, came to Howick Hall. This is the Earl Grey of the Reform Bill of 1832. This is the Earl Grey on top of the Monument in Newcastle, and this is the Earl Grey who frequently entertained the Chinese Ambassador at Howick Hall, and for whom this Chinese gentleman had a tea blended by Jackson's of London specially for the water here, and called it after his host.

Down by the sea, and so close as to be spectacular, is the Bathing House. It was built by the second Earl Grey for the family to use when they went to the beach. As this Earl had 16 children it no doubt was put to good use! Now it is a very desirable 'holiday let'.

The third Earl Grey, known affectionately as Uncle Henry, is purported to haunt the hall. He asked a workman quite recently what he was doing with the staircase! The third Earl was at one time Colonial Secretary; he married a Yorkshire lady called Miss Maria Copley, and together they greatly improved the lot of the locals by building a National village school in 1860, and a reading room in 1883, called Copley Hall. The school was closed in 1961, and is now used by Kings School, Tynemouth, as a field study centre. The sixth and present Earl Grey does not live here.

The soil type of the area tends towards lime, and keen gardeners will be wondering how Howick can grow such fine rhododendrons and azaleas. Lady Mary Howick can remember her father, the fifth Earl, walking round the estate with a phial of spirit of salts in his pocket after there had been rain. He would pour a few drops on the wet soil. If the salts fizzed, there was lime present; no good for rhododendrons. But to the east of the hall there was no fizzing, and Silverwood was created in 1931 to commemorate his silver wedding anniversary. Silverwood flourishes to this day and is open to the public, Easter to autumn, 1 pm till 6 pm.

Howick Hall was inherited by Lady Mary. Her husband, Sir Evelyn

Baring, had a distinguished career in the Colonial Service, and was created Lord Howick of Glendale upon his retirement in 1959. The present Lord Howick, her son, is developing various arboretums on the estate. As a researcher for botanical gardens he travels the world for seed of tree varieties, and Howick is rapidly becoming a place of special scientific interest for tree lovers.

Humshaugh 🌿

Humshaugh lies in a bend of the North Tyne river, six miles from Hexham, protected from heavy traffic to Kielder by the 'new' road, completed in 1947. The hamlets of Chollerford, Lincoln Hill, Walwick and Haughton with its castle, are usually considered part of the village. There is a reference to the village as early as 1279 in the Court Rolls of Alexander, King of Scots. The name's derivation is not clear. 'Haugh' means low-lying fertile ground by a river; 'Hum' may be a corruption of a proper name eg Hugh.

The original village was centred at Haughton and had a population of 267 in 1801. In 1816 when Haughton became 'a gentleman's residence' the village was dismantled to enlarge the parkland, and villagers were moved to Humshaugh. By 1911 the population was 519. Now after many changes the population is almost the same at 529.

There is one main street and many unexpected lanes and some lovely old houses. Smoke still rises from some village chimneys in spite of 'mod cons'. The village is surrounded by trees and fields and is registered as a conservation area.

Farming has always been an important industry here, which together with three nearby quarries gave employment to many. Kielder Forest now provides job opportunities with some villagers driving the great log-carrying lorries.

Humshaugh has been influenced by the same changes as other Northumbrian villages, from the early Border raids, through the mechanisation of farming and the exodus of villagers to jobs in Hexham and Newcastle some 25 miles away.

The North Tyne railway line to Scotland was axed in the 1960s but roads provide reasonably easy access to Newcastle. Life is easier if you own a car, but a bus service operates up the valley between Hexham and Bellingham.

In 1947 the village boasted a tailor's shop, draper, butcher, grocer/

baker, joinery and a post office. All have gone except for the post office which is also a general store, and a small shop open part time. There is a good mix of ages in the village with young families as well as retired people. During the last 30 years new enclaves of housing have been built, some labelled 'executive'. The welfare of the villagers is well catered for by a new health centre and dispensary at the heart of the village. There has been a school here since 1833. During the Second World War children evacuated from Newcastle attended the school whilst Brunton House became a branch of the Newcastle Eye Hospital.

An attractive village, Humshaugh's main claim to fame is its proximity to Hadrian's Wall and Chesters Fort with its Roman bath house. The mansion of Chesters built in 1771 was bought by John Clayton (1792–1890). John Clayton did much to preserve the wall and its forts, by buying whatever portions came on the market and saving them from despoilers. A fine museum at Chesters contains a remarkable collection of Roman antiquities.

While the wall was patrolled the supporting roads were maintained but after the Romans left the roads fell into decay and were so poor that when General Wade went to intercept the Jacobites in 1745 he could not proceed and the Jacobites captured Carlisle. Later a better road was built, part of the wall being demolished for stones. This provoked angry letters to *The Times* of those days. This road is the one known today as the 'Military Road'.

On the other side of the village stands Haughton Castle, given its name in 1373. The castle had a ghost which was eventually exorcised! During the Napoleonic Wars the castle was used as a store for Volunteers' equipment. A nearby paper mill was used to make paper for forged notes intended to depreciate the enemy's currency. The castle was later converted into a residence.

Until recently a ferry operated between Haughton and Barrasford and quarry workers were among the main users. There is a story – unsubstantiated – that this is the place referred to in the Northumbrian song *Waters of Tyne*.

About 1100 a chapel was built at Haughton but the present church of St Peter, in the centre of the village, was built in 1818. At that time Greenwich Hospital had the right of clergy nomination and its officials were anxious to appoint those who had been chaplains in the Royal Navy. The Methodist chapel was built in 1862 after public subscription. The site was donated by John Clayton.

In addition to the customary war memorial, Humshaugh also built a village hall in memory of those who died in the First World War. It was officially opened in 1928 and is constantly used by the various village groups.

Kielder 🦋

Until 1929 the main source of employment at Kielder was farming. The farms were mostly isolated and with very few cars around, people wishing to attend church or any functions in the area, travelled on horseback or walked. Children travelled to school at Kielder on horseback. The LNER operated the branch line between Hexham and Riccarton Junction from 1872 till the Beeching axe closed it in 1956. This was a blow to the sparsely populated North Tyne valley, but still change goes on. Today nearly everybody has a car and children are transported to school by bus – at the age of nine to Bellingham middle school, 18 miles away, and at 13 to Haydon Bridge high school which is 34 miles away.

In 1927 the Forestry Commission acquired land belonging to the Duke of Northumberland in lieu of death duties, and the largest man-made forest was created. This brought employment to the area and houses were built for the forestry workers. Families came from Tyneside and further afield to get work and a home. It was hard work planting trees, and men worked in all weather conditions five and a half days per week. Technology has now taken over, very few workers are employed and the original forestry houses are being sold to private buyers.

Kielder Castle, at one time the shooting lodge for the Duke of Northumberland, was for a number of years the Forestry Commission offices. Today it is a visitors' centre, café and craft shop, which is very well presented and well worth a visit.

In the past there were several pits producing coal in the area, operating from the 1800s up to 1934. Plashetts restarted production after the Second World War and ran until 1989.

In the 1970s the Northumberland Water Authority created the largest man-made reservoir in Europe, drowning a number of farms and hamlets in the process. Kielder Water, as it is known, was opened by HM Queen Elizabeth in 1982 and, although somewhat controversial at the time, has become a popular recreation centre and attraction for tourists, and appears to be a large natural lake. A ferry sails the reservoir in the summer months, and people come from all over to enjoy the many leisure facilities available and the beauty of Kielder.

Kirkheaton ✤

Kirkheaton is best approached from the A696 Newcastle to Otterburn road. Heading north the traveller takes the first left north of Belsay village and, after negotiating a series of S-bends, proceeds almost due west for about four miles, ending in the village of Kirkheaton where the road peters out.

Kirkheaton is still a working village with two farms, a transport company and several houses set around the village green. There are four outlying farms. At the west end of the village are the manor house and the church of St Bartholomew. At one time the village could boast a public house, a shop, a school and even a Methodist chapel but in the 1990s public amenities consist of a phone box and a Victorian letter-box.

The parish of Kirkheaton is bordered to the north by the first three miles of the river Blyth, which rises at the west end. From north to south, the parish measures about one mile. In 1992 the population was 51, compared to 170 in 1881.

The first mention of Kirkheaton is in the subsidy roll of 1296 and the 'inspeximus' of the possessions of Hexham Priory in 1298.

Kirkheaton was originally a detached chapelry of the parish of Chollerton, but at the Reformation it became extra-parochial. There was an ancient chapel which was rebuilt by Dorothy Windsor in 1755. The most notable feature of the church is the bellcote. In 1863 the chancel was enlarged and the vestry added by the Rev Thomas Harris. The interior is entirely of this period. Rev Harris kept a notebook (now held in the Northumberland County Archives) which gives an insight into the village in the mid 1800s. He started a choir for the 'first time for many a year' and had to 'speak seriously to the whole choir about spitting etc in church'. In the 1970s it became a parish in its own right and shortly afterwards it was included in the united benefice of Cambo, Kirkwhelpington, Kirkharle and Kirkheaton. Thanks to a number of benefactors and the love of many people, including some from far outside the parish boundary, services can still be held and there are at least two a month. A plated paten and silver communion cup are used which bear the crests of the Craster and Bewick (of Close House) families, who shared the ownership of Kirkheaton from the mid 1700s to the end of the 19th century.

The Grade II listed manor house is thought to have been built for a Heron of Chipchase about 1580 but there may have been a bastle or stronghouse already on the site. It was refronted in the early 17th century, with hood-moulded windows and doorway. The other walls are about five feet thick. There are several 17th century stone fireplaces, both upstairs and down. A square addition in 1740 gave rise in later times to the probably false assumption that it was built on the remains of a pele tower. From 1900 to 1928 the house stood empty and part of the roof fell in. When it was rebuilt the rooms were heightened and a kitchen wing was added. A priest's hole was discovered during the rebuilding. There is a tradition that Oliver Cromwell once stayed in the manor house and may have used it as his headquarters.

Coal was worked at Kirkheaton for more than 200 years, the first mention being in 1605, when a grant of coal mines was made by James I to two local men. The mines had previously belonged to the dissolved monastery of Hexham. There are signs of the old type of bell-pit, particularly on either side of the old Roman road called the Devil's Causeway which crossed the eastern end of the parish. In the 17th century a drift mine was opened at Boghall, which closed before the First World War. A modern fiasco was another drift mine opened in the 1920s, which only had one train-load of coal hauled out, along the specially constructed line to Ponteland. Nearby Wallridge has its origins as miners' cottages, specially built for this mine!

The transport business started with a horse and cart going every week to Hexham market, along a route now broken by a large limestone quarry. The business has increased over the years and now has large waggons, but its chief trade is still the transport of farm animals. The farms are mixed but are mostly grazing, with cows and calves, fattening bullocks and a great many sheep. Much silage is made and some roots and hay are harvested. The quarry is not at present within the parish boundary but a current planning application will bring it within 400 metres of the south east corner of the village if permission is granted.

Today, the village is well known for its annual show on the third Saturday in June. It started as pony sports just after the war, and profits go to local charities. As many as 1,000 people have been known to enjoy the beautiful setting in the tree-lined field alongside the approach road.

Ingoe and Ryal are respectively a small village and a hamlet to the south of Kirkheaton. Ryal has a very old church and is mentioned several times in the history of Northumberland in connection with Kirkheaton. Ingoe has no church but does have a rock with cup and ring marks, so habitation there may well go back much further than in Kirkheaton.

Kirkley 🦢

The parish of Kirkley has no village centre. It is the location of Kirkley Hall and surrounding farms and lies three miles north of Ponteland. The name was originally Cricklaw, derived from Celtic and Old English meaning 'hill'.

In 1612 Mark Ogle became the owner of the house of Kirkley township, and nearly 1,000 acres of land. Later, Cuthbert Ogle built the first manor house on a site south of the present hall, and had his and his wife's initials cut in the stone lintels. When the manor house was pulled down and the hall built around the Cedar of Lebanon tree in 1764, the initialed lintels were placed above the main porch and windows. This beautiful cedar tree is now over 300 years old.

The Ogle family began as tenant farmers, but succeeded in owning the hall and a large estate as well as serving their country. Captain Chaloner Ogle captured three pirate ships off the African coast and became a national hero, was knighted and had the title of Admiral of the Fleet conferred on him. Nathaniel Ogle was a doctor, joined the Forces and was made Physician to the Army. His brother Rev Newton Ogle governed the estate and purchased almost all the surrounding land. He was later given the title of Deacon of Westminster. It was he who had the obelisk erected on the hill west of the hall to commemorate the centenary of the landing in this country of William of Orange.

Agriculture was always the main occupation of the area. Farms either had a cottage for a married worker or hind, or the worker lived in the farmhouse. Horses played an important part on the farm, ploughing and working the land. This necessitated a blacksmith, and he had his shop at Eastgate near the gate to the hall. At Westgate on the Belsay road there was a joiner's ship and post office. Next to this is the Waggon Inn, which was a farm as well as a tavern, and, although on the western boundary of the township, was the only inn on the estate.

In 1861 a school was built west of the hall to which children walked from the farms and cottages in the area. As mechanisation took over farms didn't employ so many workers, the country population dropped and numbers at school fell resulting in closure of the school in the 1930s, the school now being a house.

In the 18th and 19th centuries corn grown by the farmers was ground locally for the farmers' use, and the corn mill was built at Kirkley. The river Pont was dammed upstream and a race or small stream from it brought the supply of water to drive the wheels, returning to the river lower down. The mill has been out of use all this century and has been converted into a house in recent years. Early in the 1900s a sawmill was opened which gave employment to a number of men. Horses worked in the woods and pulled the heavily loaded waggons back to the mill. Another industry of earlier times was the tilemaking at the Tilery. Men and women worked here and produced, among other things, six-sided tiles nine inches across, which were used in Kirkley church.

On the east side of Kirkley a hog-back bridge took the road from Ponteland to Morpeth past the small church of St Barnabas built by the Ogle family in the 1830s, later given by deed of gift to the parish of Ponteland. Services were held there by the vicar of Ponteland once a month on Sunday afternoons but in 1962 it was closed. Before the church was built the cottage opposite was used as a Friends' meeting house. As with the school and blacksmith's shop, the church was sold and is now an attractive house.

In 1922 the greater part of the estate was sold, in all 21 farms, and Sir William Noble, a shipping magnate, bought the hall and parklands. Seven years later a fire destroyed part of the hall and the following year it was rebuilt and the date recorded on the drainpipes on the south face. Sir William had his coat of arms carved above the door and worked into the stained glass window on the staircase. In 1930 he took the title Lord Kirkley. On his death in 1935 the estate passed to his daughter who sold it in 1948 to Northumberland County Council, and it became Northumberland College of Agriculture, later changing its name to Kirkley Hall College.

In times past entertainment was very simple. People would visit neighbours and play cards. Quoits used to be played in the evenings, and sometimes a dance would be held in a farmer's barn. A tin whistle or concertina would make the music and the dancers would either walk there or come by pony and trap. The barn would be lit by hurricane lamps. It was said that when one smart young lady was alighting from her trap she fell in the mud in the dark.

Lord Kirkley, who was a Presbyterian, used to invite ministers from other churches to hold services in the church and sometimes he had well known soloists and actors to sing and give readings. He had disagreements with the vicar of Ponteland and was known to have a bus parked outside the parish church on Sunday evenings to tempt parishioners to his church. The relationship became so bad that Lord

Kirkley had his wife's body exhumed from Ponteland churchyard and moved to the unconsecrated church at Kirkley.

With the established college, Kirkley now has a centre of great value. The college has courses and classes for all ages and a wide range of subjects and indeed the whole county of Northumberland benefits from it. The large landscaped gardens are another feature of interest and the recently built sports complex will provide a new amenity for the area.

Kirknewton ✤

Visitors travelling along the road to Kirknewton from Wooler will see a sign reminding them that on invitation from King Edwin, St Paulinus baptised the people in the river Glen nearby. This sign also marks the perimeter of a site which contained the royal palace and rare wedge-shaped council chamber, both timber built. It was the centre of the Anglo-Saxon kingdom of Northumbria.

The surrounding Cheviot Hills yield evidence of settlements long before that time. People had been slowly forced by circumstances of climatic change, increased population and cultivation to leave the once fertile and wooded Milfield Plain. Today this road to the Scottish border is a haven of tranquillity and forms the boundary of the Northumberland National Park.

The bastle house at Akeld marks a time of 'hot trod' (pursuit) when raid succeeded raid and slaughter followed slaughter of men, women, children and livestock. Little wonder that around Kirknewton there are no remains of any antiquity save those on the hilltops and the church.

Even in the last quarter of the 18th century when agricultural reforms were well under way and Copeland Castle was owned by the great agricultural reformer Matthew Culley, W. Hutchinson could deplore the lack of fences, the 'abject countenance' of the inhabitants, 'miserably clothed', and their 'deplorable' cottages.

A prosperous time during the late 18th and 19th century brought a pattern of big house and cluster of stone-built cottages every few miles to the Border. Each township was self-contained for the most part, close knit communities of souls dependent on each other and a host of seasonal practices which persisted at least to the Second World War. For example, each household had a pig, one day killed, next day 'cooked' and six weeks pickled, everyone lending a hand (some villagers remember playing with the pig's bladder as a football); the pleasure of the 'Kirn', a party held on each place at the end of harvest; and of course, the special drink provided by the farmer after the last waggon came home at harvest.

The 'hirings' must have caused anxiety. Each labourer was employed only on a yearly basis and if you were not 'spoken to' by 13th May you knew you were sacked.

Josephine Butler, the social reformer, was born and bred in these parts and is buried in St Gregory's churchyard. No doubt she was well aware of the problems of living in a rural community as well as having knowledge of an urban one.

The children looked forward to extra holidays such as St Gregory's Day, Ascension Day and Ash Wednesday when they would be out of school after church. Those were days of big families with three full schools and two churches plus a once a month service in the College Valley school for the shepherds. Now only St Gregory's remains and its school with 15 pupils.

The last few years have seen the disappearance of the shepherds' traditional way of life, each his own flock, each flock its own ground or hirsel. Gamekeepers, trees and birds for sport are slowly taking their place. Instead of employees in farm cottages there are now tenants glad to enjoy small community life and country living as long as they are fit enough to drive. Once there was a railway, now one is dependent in the main on the motor car.

Otherwise holidaymakers come to the cottages, many of which are self-catering and at Akeld there is an entire complex of these dwellings where once there were farm buildings. There are many B & Bs around, including Kirknewton which only lacks a pub. Most leisure pursuits are available without too much travel, especially gliding, hang-gliding, caravanning and walking (plenty of National Park guided walks provided).

Old customs die out but new ones take their place and Kirknewton Show in August is the place where the community shows its spirit and enterprise with sheep dog trials, flower show, craft show and sports including quoits.

Langley 🦎

Langley is a small village situated in beautiful countryside two miles south west of Haydon Bridge. Its present population is under 300.

The village hall reflects the changing face of Langley. It started life as the United Methodist Free church in 1849, then in 1877 a schoolroom was added. After this it was converted into a house and then was used as offices for Langley Barony. In 1953 the offices were bought with money raised before the Second World War and, with a great deal of voluntary labour organised by the village hall committee, the present village hall was completed.

Farming is the main occupation in Langley nowadays, but this was not always the case. The two main sources of employment were the lead mines and Langley Barony Fireclay Co Ltd. The lead mills were first owned by the Earls of Derwentwater, then by the Greenwich Hospital Commissioners and finally by the Dinning family. The lead ore was brought initially from Alston Moor by donkey. The Hexham and Allendale Railway was somewhat diverted in order to enable Langley Smelt Mills to convey the finished lead by means of the railway to the market at Newcastle. Extensive smelting mills flourished from 1805 for over a century until work was discontinued.

In 1888 work was started on the buildings for Langley Barony Fireclay which produced high grade sanitary ware and also firebricks and red shale bricks. The buildings were situated near Langley dam, thus ensuring a good supply of water. Clay was discovered a short distance from the works and at the time experts stated the fireclay was of superior quality and likely to last some time. Their prediction proved correct as production continued until the late 1950s and gave employment to about 150 men.

The most notable building in Langley is of course Langley Castle, which was built at the beginning of the 14th century as protection against marauders. It had a chequered history – including being burnt down in the early 15th century. After the rising of 1715 it was forfeited to the Crown and then settled on the Governors of Greenwich Hospital in 1749. It was bought in 1882 by Cadwallader Bates who began restoring it to its former splendour. The castle remained in the Bates family and in recent times has been put to a number of uses. During the Second World War troops were housed there, later it became a girls school, then a medieval banqueting hall and most recently a hotel and restaurant.

The cross at Langley on Tyne

Situated on the road leading from Haydon Bridge to Langley is Langley Cross, which was erected by Cadwallader Bates in 1883 – 'To the memory of James and Charles, Viscounts Langley, Earls of Derwentwater, beheaded on Tower Hill, London, 24th February 1716 and 8th December 1746 for loyalty to their lawful sovereign.'

Despite coal mining, lead mining and the brickworks, Langley is a place of great natural beauty which has not been destroyed by these former activities. The scenery of the valley of the river Allen is dramatic and picturesque. Nearby Plankey Mill is now the property of the National Trust and draws ramblers, campers and picnickers from far afield.

Village life has changed considerably over the last century. The once extensive lead mills, coal mines and fireclay works, which gave employment to so many, are now closed – although the sawmill is still being worked part time. The railway lines have been removed and the station buildings are now in use as a post office/shop. The school has met a similar fate. Despite this, Langley is still a thriving rural community, whose activities now centre around the chapel and village hall.

Lesbury 🌿

About a mile inland from the North Sea, on the banks of the river Aln, lies the village of Lesbury, its parish including the hamlets of Hipsburn and Bilton. Situated in a valley, and sheltered from the sea and the prevailing winds from the Cheviot Hills, it is approached from the south over a beautiful medieval bridge, a twisting trial of skill for many a lorry driver.

A settlement was established in about the 7th century and in due course came to be known as 'Laeces Byrig' – the fortified dwelling of the leech or physician. In 1296 it was recorded as having 13 inhabitants who paid tax, and the blacksmith was the only person entitled to provide food and entertainment for travellers. Today there are 737 voters on the electoral register and the Coach Inn is ready to cater for residents and visitors alike. The village grew quietly, having little or no wealth to attract invaders, and its 'criminals' were restricted to such as Cuthbert Dickinson who, in 1607, was accused of playing football in the churchyard, and Marina Moor who was recorded in 1659 as having stripped all the lead from the church roof.

Although there is nothing more than a dowser survey to go on, we can reasonably assume that the present church of St Mary, first mentioned in records in 1147, was built on the site of a former Anglo-Saxon structure and it was originally the mother church of Alnwick, Alnmouth and Longhoughton. After it had fallen into disrepair in the 17th and 18th centuries it was restored at the expense of the Duke of Northumberland who employed the architect Salvin, the restorer of Alnwick Castle. However the chancel roof and the eight-sided font are more than 500 years old, local tradition having it that the font was buried for safekeeping by the parishioners during the Puritan period. In the graveyard can be seen graves of seafarers as the inhabitants of Alnmouth were forced to use Lesbury church and graveyard when their own church collapsed after the river altered its course.

There was a working water mill near the bridge in Lesbury for over

600 years until it was closed in 1925 and was burnt down nearly 40 years later. All that remain now are two arches and a low wall.

Lesbury House belongs to the Percy family and was originally the home of the millers. After the closure of the mill the house became the northern dower house for the Percy family and during the last war (and until her death in 1965) the Duchess Helen lived there and frequently attended the church and village events.

A few years previously a strange tragedy had taken place on the narrow bridge when a bus crashed there. An Amble man was apparently flung from his seat near the door without anyone noticing, and his body was found in the river the next day.

On a lighter note, the period between the wars was when Lesbury Feast was held at the end of June each year. Village sports took place on the Saturday afternoon at Townfoot Farm and gipsies camped in the Wynding. On the Monday there were sideshows on the village green, now sadly reduced to a small triangle, and there were donkey and mule rides through the village. It was all rounded off with a dance in the old village hall.

Today Lesbury has a vibrant community. The old school has been converted into the village hall which is the hub of many activities from bingo to WI, and from pre-school playgroup to the Music and Drama Society. Behind the hall are the popular tennis courts and bowling green and across the road the thriving village shop-cum-post office. Hipsburn boasts an important railway station for the surrounding area and nearby Ratcheugh is the setting for many a point-to-point meeting.

With its well tended gardens and stone cottages Lesbury is an attractive village, home to swans, herons, kingfishers, red squirrels and salmon, as well as a human population of all ages with a strong community spirit.

Linton 🦢

Most people think of a pit village as a dirty, depressed, horrible place to live, but not so. Linton was in the past a small 'model' mining village, near the market town of Morpeth, surrounded by fields, woods and streams. Yes, the pit was there and miners were to be seen coming home black at the end of each shift. Yes, their boots had to be dried, scraped and polished each day and their clothes had to be 'dadded' against a wall, then brushed to remove the coal dust, but as children, we thought nothing of that. We could creep into the pit yard and catch 'paddocks' (frogs) in the pit pond and get chased and scolded. That was all part of the fun of life.

Linton had all the necessities of life and quite a few of the luxuries. The church, made of corrugated iron, stood at the end of the village, near the bus stand where a bus came and went hourly to Ashington. It was surrounded by what we called the 'foxcover' – a small copse of gorse and hawthorn, a fine place to build camps and play wild games. The church was also the school with two classes in it, but in the early 1930s a new school was built – a fine affair with four classrooms, a hall and domestic science/woodwork room, and Mr Harrison began his long reign as headmaster.

Near the school stood the two shops known as 'the shop' and 'the store'. 'The shop' was also the post office and was run by Mrs Arnott, a tall, imposing lady who kept us all in order. Woe betide any child who was cheeky or forgot to say 'please' and 'thank you'. Sometimes you were sent to buy a carbide for your dad's pit lamp, or to do a message for a neighbour and were given a penny for going. What a dilemma! Should you buy sweets, sherbet or maybe a packet of candy cigarettes?

Apart from the colliery manager who had a big detached 'post' house, everyone lived in one of the five rows which made up the village. The houses varied in size but all had a front garden and a backyard in which were built the toilet and the coalhouse. Each coalhouse had a little door in it onto the street. These were high up in the wall and were there so that the miners' free coal which was dumped on the pavement could be tossed in. Eddy or Frankie Smith made their living by charging a shilling to throw your load of coal in for you. They must have had strong muscles – and sore backs.

The men liked to grow vegetables, onions, leeks, potatoes etc which the women made into broth and stews. The houses were clean, the gardens were neat and the village as a whole was tidy.

The miners enjoyed the fresh air after their long hours underground and ran successful football, cricket and tennis teams. Then there was the 'tute' – the miners' institute where they could play billiards, darts and so on. There was a ladies' room where they held whist drives and put the world to rights as they played. Later a bowling green was constructed and both men and women played and ran village teams. There was even a small cinema there with new programmes three times a week.

Now, inevitably, it is all changed. The pit has gone, the old church has been replaced by a brick one, the foxcover has largely disappeared and the houses are privately owned. But it is still a pleasant place and is loved by the people who live here now.

Longframlington ✺

Much of 'old' Longframlington dates from the late 17th and the early 18th centuries. A directory of 1828 describes it as a 'considerable' village which had been recently much improved 'by the addition of several neat houses and shops'. It had a population of about 500. Today it is an even more considerable place with a population of 1,109 at the 1991 census. The two annual fairs, for the sale of livestock, have long been discontinued and the site used for the extensive gardens of Wardle Terrace. These provide an agreeably open aspect at the southern end of the long, narrow main street which must surely give the village the first syllable of its name.

Whether from idleness or as a sign of affection, locals now refer to it as Longfram, or just as Fram. It was formerly known as Framlington and its principal family, the de Framlingtons, were recorded as the 12th century benefactors of the Augustinian priory of Brinkburn which lies within the parish.

What remains of the priory is hidden in wooded seclusion on the north bank of the Coquet and its site is as attractive today as it must have been to the monks who first found it. It now houses some pieces of modern sculpture. Each year a service is held on Ascension Day in the church, which is well preserved among the traces of the monastic buildings.

The church of St Mary the Blessed Virgin in the centre of the village still retains some features of its foundation in 1196. Nonconformist worship also has a long history here. A congregation existed in 1640, meeting in a private house, and a Presbyterian chapel built in 1739 was rebuilt in 1854. Members of the Anglican and the United Reformed churches are currently working hard to improve their churches again.

The village, perched on a ridge 500 feet above sea level, is approached from the south by a long steep hill, a toilsome route for travellers on foot or in a stagecoach. To the north lies a tract of land once frequented by highwaymen and described in 1828 as the 'wildest and most dreary moorland in the county'. From either direction Longframlington must have been a welcome sight, with its three coaching inns well placed near the roadside. Today it is still famed for its places to eat and drink: The Granby, The New Inn and Embleton Hall.

Near the old school, now housing for rental, is the lion trough. This is used now for flowering plants but is a reminder of the difficulty of water supply in the past. In 1821 public subscription made it possible to pipe the water to six or seven collection points each marked with a lion's head. It was not piped to houses until long after, though the date has not been ascertained.

Though never at the centre of trouble, the village has been affected by war. The Romans had a marching camp at the south end, the Napoleonic Wars brought a four-gun battery behind The New Inn and in the Second World War soldiers from the tank regiment were billeted here. The playing field is still sometimes called the Tank field because of their activities.

There are interesting records of the beginning of compulsory education in the log books of the old school. Parents then, it seems, did not always prize education as do their modern successors, who have campaigned for the retention of the school site and hope to see a village school built there. On 16th December 1883, three Anderson brothers are reported as being present only one day a week 'owing to working in the pit'. A local private school was patronised, according to another entry, not in a search for superior teaching, but because there they could 'attend as often as they pleased'. One transfer from this private school, Rachel Turnbull, was put into Standard V, presumably because of her age, but was found to be 'unable to do even Standard I sums'.

Besides coal mining, farming and trades provided much employment until modern technology transformed agriculture and shopping habits. Longframlington, however, still enjoys the advantages of having three shops, and there is one traditional professional craftsman, the maker of Northumbrian small-pipes.

Road building has always mattered here. The Romans brought the eastern branch of Watling Street west of where the village was to develop, on its way to Berwick. The main coaching road to Scotland ran through the centre, and now a bypass is being planned to dissuade heavy traffic from thundering through. Longframlington will continue to be worth a visit for those who seek a warm welcome and links with the past.

Longhirst

Longhirst stands on the Bothal burn on the roads from Morpeth to Newbiggin, Cresswell and Warkworth. The whole township contains about 1,500 acres. Ancient documents, dating back to 1629, show that Longhirst was commonly written 'Langhurst'. The railway station, which at one time played an important part in village life, lies one mile east of the village at Longhirst colliery.

At the beginning of the 19th century, Longhirst village was the property of the Duke of Portland and William and George Lawson, Esquires. Longhirst Hall, originally named Longhurst House, was built for the Lawson family. John Dobson was the architect and the foundation stone was laid in June 1824. It was William Lawson who took up residence at the hall on its completion.

William Lawson was followed by the Rev Edward Lawson MA who proved to be a benefactor to the village, building a National school situated halfway between the village and the colliery. Church services were held in the school until in 1876 the church was built at the cost of £3,950. He left his mark on village life in other ways too. An article dated 1873 stated, 'The village did at one time sport a public house which was closed by Rev Lawson, a staunch teetotaler, but villagers noted wine carts still went to the Rev Lawson's home at the hall.'

The parish of Longhirst was formed in 1875. Before that date it was part of Bothal parish. The church, dedicated to St John the Evangelist, was built at the south end of the village. Sir Arthur Blomfield was the architect. Inside the church, there is an oak chancel screen carved by the parishioners and Rev Proctor, vicar from 1885 to 1916, and a brass lectern presented by Sir James Joicey MP in 1888.

In 1858 the village trades included farmers, a shoemaker, a wheelwright, a draper, a tailor, a blacksmith and a shopkeeper. The population was 96. By 1902 the number of inhabitants had grown to 408. This rise was due to the opening of Longhirst colliery in 1868. Although the mine closed in 1896, the population remained more or less static, a possible explanation being the opening of mines at Pegswood and Linton, where redundant miners could seek employment. The village trades had by that time changed. There was a joiner who also ran the post office, a Co-operative store at Longhirst colliery, which had opened in 1875, a blacksmith and a cowkeeper but all the other trades previously noted had gone.

During the early 1880s Longhirst Hall and estate, the village, colliery and surrounding farms were sold to the Joicey family and Sir James Joicey took up residence at the hall. Village people found employment in the hall and on the estate. In 1921 Lieut-Col the Hon H. E. Joicey offered for sale the hall, the village, the reading room (church hall), the joiner's, the smithy, the colliery and houses and surrounding farms. The Joicey family stayed on at the hall. Statistics show the population to be

397 in 1934 and the village still had a blacksmith together with a market gardener, a smallholder and the other trades of 1902.

In 1936 the Hon Major James Arthur Joicey became Lord Joicey and moved to Ford Castle. The hall was taken over during the war by the Home Office and soldiers were billeted there in Nissen huts. In the late 1940s homeless squatters occupied these huts until they were rehoused. In 1952 the hall became a Home Office approved remand home for boys. In the early 1990s it underwent extensive renovation to become the county's first university campus combined with a management training and conference centre – the Longhirst Campus of the University of Northumbria.

The railway station closed in October 1951 and the years since then have seen a gradual erosion of other village services. Structurally, Longhirst village has changed little over the years but whereas a century ago, people traded in and around the village, now most people commute. However, there is still a very strong community spirit among the present population of 305.

Longhorsley 🎋

Longhorsley, population 500, straddles one of the main roads to Scotland and the north, the A697. Once purely a rural village, with three working farms and several agricultural smallholdings within its boundary, it has now mutated into a dormitory community, serving the needs of the business and commerce of South Northumberland and Tyneside.

The houses, some built several hundred years ago, have all been modernised and a modern estate has been built to the south of the village. An ancient pele tower lies to the west end of the village, a reminder of the violent past of this Border country. The pele tower, lately the residence of the parish priest, is excellently preserved, being now the residence of a village inhabitant.

The village churchyard is about half a mile to the south east of the village, where the old church, rebuilt in 1773, has been left to decay. Services are now held in the old village school, which has been converted to the church and dedicated to St Helen.

The present school, built in 1965, serves the needs of the village children until they reach the age of nine. They then have to travel the seven miles to Morpeth by bus, to continue their education.

Longhorsley could in the past claim to have been well sustained by the many shops, trades and professions, who provided the services that the local community required. Most of these have long ceased to exist. A frequent seven day bus service is now an irregular six day one. Shops, inns and tradesmen have all disappeared in the ever changing modern world of business. Only a general dealer's, a post office and a single public house remain. A welcome aid to village life was provided in 1988, when after many years of effort a village hall was opened; a venue for almost all village meetings and activities.

One mile north is Linden Hall, at one time the manorial seat. The splendid John Dobson-designed building is now a prestigious hotel. Many personalities of the arts, sporting and political worlds can often be seen travelling to take advantage of the peace and quiet of the hotel and its 300 acres of park and woodland.

Walkers have the opportunity to observe many varieties of wildlife in and around the village, even llama, wallaby and Gloria the camel at the home of the local vet! Short-eared owl, heron and, if you are lucky, hen harrier, are just a few of the species that the observant may notice locally. The pleasure of a walk is further enhanced as you discover the magnificent views of the Northumberland coast to the east or the Cheviot Hills to the north.

In July 1993 a plaque was placed on the wall of the post office to commemorate the death 80 years earlier of Emily Davison. For it was from that house, then her home, that Emily left on the journey that was to end with her fatal injuries under the feet of the King's horse at Epsom. Emily Wilding Davison is remembered for her suffragette activities by the Longhorsley WI each year, on the anniversary of her death, when local members place flowers in the colours of the suffragette movement on her grave in nearby Morpeth.

Women's lives were also enhanced in a different way by another Longhorsley inhabitant, Thomas Bell. It was in the village shop that Thomas Bell developed the first self-raising flour, which he called Bell's Royal. That flour, of course, is now known as Be-Ro.

Each year, under the auspices of the parish council, inhabitants of Longhorsley get the opportunity to walk the common boundaries. This pleasant ceremony, now a peaceful stroll over the moor, with refreshments provided on completion, was not always so.

In 1927 after a long dispute relating to a common boundary between a local family and villagers, a violent battle took place between the two opposing sides. This altercation resulted in much spilt blood and many battered heads, such was the fury. That occasion is the only time that Longhorsley made national news, for the national papers carried front page banner headlines declaring 'The Battle of Longhorsley Moor'. Even *The Times* thought it of sufficient interest to warrant front page attention. It is fortunate that disputes in Longhorsley are now resolved in a less violent manner.

Lowgate 🦋

Two miles west of the market place in the historic abbey town of Hexham lies the hamlet of Lowgate. Originally the site of the 'low toll gate' leading into Hexham from the shires, it has almost doubled in size during the last decade.

The pretty church of St Mary was built in 1895 for the princely sum of £200 with embellishments and furnishings gifted from its parishioners. Built to serve the scattered rural congregation of the abbey in Hexham, it continues to do so today. The original school was quarter of a mile from the cluster of houses and its pupils came on foot from a wide rural area. Destroyed by fire, it was replaced by a temporary iron building for 80 pupils in 1908. Today this building is in the capable hands of Lowgate Women's Institute. A new school in Lowgate opened in 1932 and this attractive white building provides primary education and a focal point in the hamlet.

Although there is no longer employment from the local landowners, commuters live in new houses which have been built alongside the original estate workers' cottages. The Methodist chapel built in 1858 stands solidly alongside and worshippers congregate every Sunday for the service. An attractive landscaped caravan site lies hidden well back from the road, giving city dwellers an opportunity to enjoy the country. The original wayside inn has reverted back to domestic use. However, a purpose-built nursing home for the elderly provides a peaceful haven for its residents amidst the beautiful countryside.

Lowick 🌿

Lowick has been careless in the retention of any of its old landmarks; scarcely anything remains. The penfold was the last structure to be removed after the Second World War.

At that time blackthorn trees, which marked the alleged burial place of victims of the Black Death, were cut down. The Plague Pit was a square hedged area on the north corner of South Road and the High Steads road. There was a sunken hollow covered by old brambles and surrounded by ancient blackthorns; these were destroyed and the hollow levelled.

There is a cottage in Main Street which was built on the site of the Covenanters' secret meeting place. These were Scottish Presbyterians who supported the agreements intended to defend or extend their faith. The Scottish Presbyterian congregation has been in existence here from 1662, and is one of the oldest nonconformist congregations in England.

In the mid 19th century there were five places of worship in the village – now there are only two: St John the Baptist's church, where the Roman Catholics also worship, and the Scottish Presbyterian church. There has been a church here since the 12th century, built by the monks on the route between Lindisfarne and Durham, but rebuilt in 1794. The route crossed the Roman road known as the

Penfold on Lowick Common in the 1920s

Devil's Causeway, and it was around these crossroads that the village began to develop.

The place we now call the Bastle Corner was the site of the old bastle or pele tower where local people took refuge during Border raids.

On the opposite side of the road to the Bastle Corner stands the war memorial. After the First World War money was collected for a memorial but General Sitwell of Barmoor Castle offered to give two large rocks to be placed one on top of the other, with the names of the fallen carved on the rock; harsh Northumbrian rocks to express the harshness of the war. However, the local people did not agree to this. They wanted an obelisk of marble or granite, so the rocks were carted away to the entrance to Barmoor Castle, and the present memorial was purchased.

Money continued to be raised until the present village hall was completed in 1959, by refurbishing the old Church of England school and school house built in 1842 and closed in 1923. 'The Public Subscription School' was built in 1876 and so for 47 years there were two schools in the village and many battles ensued between the rival pupils.

In the early part of the century, farm labourers were hired each year on 1st March; the workers stood while the farmers chose the men they required. At the time of the hirings there were shows, roundabouts, swing boats and coconut shies on the common. The day of the 'Flittings' was the 13th May when workers moved to their new homes and places of work. Farm carts moved all their belongings including the pig. A resident recalls that on one pouring wet Flitting Day three carts came through the village piled high with furniture, and on top of the last cart was lashed a large rocking chair, and in it sat an elderly lady carrying a baby, and behind her was a large pig in a crate. The rain streamed from her hat but she sat there dignified with her head held high as though she was the Queen of Sheba.

Other visitors to the village were the gipsies, in horse-drawn caravans which drew up on the common.

During the late 19th and early 20th century there were eleven shops in the village including a saddler and a blacksmith and a hat shop. There was also a doctor who lived and had his surgery in the village. He removed teeth without anaesthetic; the patient was seated in an armchair – the doctor put his knee on the chest and his hand on the forehead and pulled out the tooth.

Below the Public Subscription school there were two butcher's shops, one on each side of the road. The animals were slaughtered behind the shops. People were also employed in lime working and there is still a lime-kiln which can be seen to the north east of the Eel Well. Coal working was carried on and there are many shallow mine shafts about the area. The stream at The Black Bull was dammed to form a pool where carts could be washed.

At the beginning of this century the village was always busy on Saturdays when people from outlying villages came in to shop. On fine Sunday evenings during the summer after the evening services, most able bodied people took a stroll up to Barmoor and back to meet and to talk. There was very little road traffic and the road from the lower end of the village to Barmoor became quite crowded.

From the vicarage to the wood at the lower end of the village is one mile. Not surprisingly the village is known as 'Lang Lowick'.

Middleton 🐚

Middleton lies in the Wansbeck valley, in the heart of rural Northumberland. Down the hill and under the bridge is where the railway station used to be, built in the mid 19th century. Farmers could take their stock to market and get back home the same day. Cattle and freight, and milk for delivery in the towns, were loaded from the siding at this little station. Long passenger trains went through to annual events, like Rothbury races and Bellingham Show, and on one occasion a whole train was commissioned for a party, with food and drink served on board. The last train through Middleton was packed with people, and many were on the platform to see it. A huge wreath hung on the front of the steam engine with the words 'Will ye no' come back again?', a Northumbrian piper played, and the 'Wannie' line was closed forever.

Middleton burn flows through the fields to join the river Wansbeck. A pretty, arched dry-stone bridge spans the stream, and once hay carts and waggons trundled over it to farm buildings and cottages on the hill above the village. One cottage stands on its own. This is Trevelyan House, the oldest in the village. Years ago it was the butcher's shop, and old folks remember that animals were slaughtered there, and the hillside was red on killing day. There is a wood at the top of the hill that is full of snowdrops in springtime, and the cottages there look over the village to the Ox Inn – a cosy, old fashioned pub, where friendship abounds.

There is the manse and church, now privately owned, and the village farm was here, too. A low granary above the byres would resound to the music of fiddle and melodeon, for dances and wedding parties were held here. The oil lamps that hung from the beams were shaded with milk churn lids. A fire precaution! These buildings were developed into three houses.

The stream flows under a road bridge just a little way on, where there used to be a ford. Two houses were built conveniently near to the water, which had to be carried for home use. That was 170 years ago, and a member of the same family is there to the present day. His forebears were tailors, who travelled around the countryside keeping the farm folk suitably clothed. The first post office and telephone in the village were in one of these houses. The mail in bags, sealed with wax, was brought by horse-drawn mail coach. In severe winters, the letters were delivered by a 'postie' on horseback, to out-lying farms and cottages, up to quite recent times. The post office too has gone.

Up the road towards the end of the village is the village hall, built with money raised by local people in 1928, although the site for it was donated. During the war years, troops stationed here commandeered it. Nissen huts were erected, and the village overflowed with service people and vehicles. The farms were striving to feed the country, and Women's Land Army girls replaced conscripted farm workers. The village hall, with its old black coke-burning stove and oil lamps that had to be pumped up at intervals, was the heart of the village. The NAAFI canteen was here, and there was lively entertainment most evenings. The building beyond the village hall is now two cottages, but it used to be an old alehouse of very dubious repute. Electricity brought Middleton up to the 20th century in the early 1950s. We got three street lamps, and, surprisingly, not everyone was pleased.

On big national occasions, like the Queen's Coronation in 1953, the neighbouring villages of Hartburn and Angerton joined with us to celebrate, sharing the cost and the fun. The WI gave a display of country dancing, the children had a fancy dress competition, and a big bonfire was built over on Andrew's Hill. A firework display was to be the grand finale. But a lighted match was accidentally dropped amongst the fireworks, which exploded into a magnificent spectacle of colour – and the poor man who caused it crept off to his bike and peddled away into the night!

Children go to school by bus now, but at one time they walked two miles, taking sandwiches for lunch and a penny to buy a cup of cocoa. Many young people leave the village for further education, and don't come back, as the work they train for is not here. On the other hand, families move into the village to enjoy peace and quiet, and settle in well. There is a carpet bowls club and art classes, and what self-respecting village would be without its leek club? There is also a Northumbrian Evening, and a Christmas whist drive has been held each year since the village hall was built. The very first minutes tell us that the prizes were a pork pig and two turkeys, which together cost £7.

Milbourne 🌿

The village of Milbourne lies four miles north west of Ponteland and was divided into two townships by the deep, narrow glen through which runs the burn that gives the village its name. It consists of a hall, a church, a number of farms and cottages, a manor house or grange and a Methodist chapel.

Thomas Bates distinguished himself in battle against the Scots in 1552. He then purchased the estate of Milbourne from Robert de Meneville. His descendant, Ralph Bates commissioned the building of the hall in 1807, which was built of stone from the quarry at Belsay, so forming the beginning of the Quarry Gardens. The architect was Patterson of Edinburgh.

The beautiful church of the Holy Saviour was built and endowed by Miss Jane Anne Bates in 1868 and is a chapel of ease of Ponteland. It has a fine spire and handsome chiming clock. Services were held in the morning on the first Sunday and at 3 pm on the other Sundays. Now the service is at 11.15 am each Sunday, and is well attended.

The manor house or grange is on the north side of the burn. The Horsley family lived here in the 17th century and were nonconformists. George Horsley objected to the ritual of the burial service and chose to be buried in unconsecrated ground. His grave is enclosed by a circular wall near the grange.

The first Methodist services were held in a little disused cottage on the banks of the Mill burn and a children's Sunday school was formed. Great help was given by Mrs Elliott-Bates from the hall, resulting in the children going to part of the church service after their Sunday school, so beginning the ecumenical spirit in Milbourne which still remains, as members of the church and chapel have formed a choir in recent years. In 1903 a plot of land was acquired and a new chapel was built near the Bridge End. Services are held every Sunday evening and are well attended by local and more distant worshippers.

Agriculture was the main occupation and so the blacksmith played an important part in the life of the village. One blacksmith, Mr Jackson, a well respected gentleman, served both his village and district as a councillor, and his name lives on in Jackson Avenue in Ponteland. Mr and Mrs Jackson and most of their family emigrated to Canada in 1926, life being very hard for them for several years. Members of the family still visit Milbourne from time to time. The blacksmith's shop became a ruin and was pulled down when tractors took the place of the horse.

The school, built and endowed in 1852 by Miss Bell, was not in the village but at Higham Dykes on the Belsay road, so all the children had to walk or cycle or some were brought to school in pony and trap. Everyone carried sandwiches but in the 1920s it was arranged that a pail of soup or broth be brought twice a week from the Waggon Inn for the children. This was a red letter day! In the late 1930s the school was closed and sold. Now a bus comes into the village, collects the children and takes them to Ponteland to school. There are no shops or inns in the village and no public transport.

Many years ago dances used to take place in the granary at Town Farm, but after the bothy was built as a place of entertainment for the estate workers, dances were held there and were very happy occasions with faith suppers. A harvest supper was held there after the church service each year too. Milbourne formed a Women's Institute in the early 1920s which gave new life to the village, but it was disbanded when the Second World War commenced as soldiers, who manned the searchlight station in the church field, used the bothy.

Electricity and piped water did not reach the village until the 1950s. Houses were lit by candles and paraffin lamps, and farms had a manual pump for their water supply. In a drought year it was hard work pumping water for the cattle. There was a communal pump beside the smithy, which is still there.

At harvest time the corn threshing machine took about a fortnight to go around the farms, and the farmers and their sons helped each other. Now most of the farmers have their own combine, employing only two men, one on the combine and the other leading the corn away. This decline in agricultural employment has meant some cottages are now privately owned, causing a small influx of newcomers.

Milbourne is an attractive little village and a pleasant place to live. It is very popular with walkers, who enjoy the quiet 40 minute stroll around the 'Square'.

Milfield 🐑

Coming down the slope of Coldside, on the old drove road from the Cheviot Hills, the panorama of Milfield Plain lies below – an area submerged after the Ice Age and now rich agricultural land. To the east of the houses at Threefords, towards the river Till, the Saxon king Edwin built the palace of Meldrum, Melmin and later Milfield. It is now only discernible from the air as are many other ancient British remains nearby.

A month before the battle of Flodden Sir William Bulmer, though outnumbered, ambushed the Earl of Home's force and drove the Scots across the Border. They afterwards described the Milfield Plain as the 'ill road'.

Beside the present A697 stands the Red Lion Inn, built around 1740 with Venetian windows and now a listed building. There the drovers with their flocks found shelter and hospitality. It was in 1780 that George Grey, who became a well known agriculturalist and with the Culley brothers of Fenton introduced the Border Leicester breed of sheep, first started clearing the land of gorse and broom.

Milfield village developed around the demesne, the Home Farm and Milfield Ninth, now Whitton Hill Farm. The Greys lived on Milfield Hill in a house now demolished. Only the ruins of the stone kennels for the hounds and old barns and stables are to be seen. Here was born in 1828 to John and Hannah Grey a daughter, Josephine, who in married life as Josephine Butler became a vigorous campaigner on behalf of women. Her life is commemorated among the Lesser Festivals in the Alternative Service Prayer Book.

By the beginning of the 19th century Milfield was a self-sufficient village with all the requirements for country living: a general shop and post office, baker, two saddlers, blacksmith, joiner-cum-undertaker, cycle and shoe repair hut and even a Registrar for Births and Deaths. A stonebreaker's yard had provided the foundations for the road, which was then covered with soil and smoothed with water. Travellers on the London to Edinburgh mail coaches found welcome rest at the inn. The stables were later converted into dwellings, then demolished to provide a car park for the travellers of today.

January 1856 saw the opening of the Primitive Methodist chapel. Farmers and local businessmen gave their workers time off to cart the stone from Doddington quarry. Thomas Clark was thanked for overseeing the construction of this fine building. His nephew built the adjoining manse as a memorial to him. He also left a trust fund for the higher education of pupils and in 1891 built the reading room with a billiard table for use by the young men of the village.

From the new school of 1962 the pupils walk down to the old school of 1842 for their dinner. There also the youth club, Brownies, the Rainbows and the WI meet in comfort. It did not serve the early pupils so well. Some walked long distances to a poorly heated room with no toilets or kitchen. Meant for 120 children, the attendance fluctuated between 60 and 73 due to sickness, farm work and the occasional flooding of the river Till.

With the Second World War came evacuees to the school and an airfield on the plain. Two rows of headstones mark the graves of young RAF trainees at Kirknewton parish church. The airfield was later used by the US Air Force, and in 1944 a Flight Leader School was formed in preparation for Operation Overlord. Army officers were billeted at the Red Lion and the Methodist chapel used by the Ministry of Food for storage; £500 was allowed for redecoration after the war.

The returning ex-servicemen then needed homes. The huts on the airfield were where many families enjoyed their first years together. Glendale RDC built houses for them and other villagers from condemned houses, plus pensioners' bungalows on Wheatriggs, a field of that name. Their front gardens are a delight in summer and the long rear gardens produce excellent fruit and vegetables. Money was raised for swings and slides on the playing field. Milfield people provided their own entertainment, in particular the Youth Week with its fancy dress parades, dances and many other activities. This became so popular in the surrounding area that by 1980, when police had to be present, it had to be abandoned.

The yearly leek show is held in the pub hall and the indoor bowls club has a successful team, whilst the men enjoy quoits matches. In 1956, as the population of the village grew, the WI was formed. Members still enjoy talks and demonstrations, organising various functions and providing a meal and entertainment for the senior citizens at Christmas. The Tuesday Club started by Kirknewton church meets for companionship and entertainment for the over sixties.

The appearance of the village has changed only slightly in recent years. Cherry trees were planted on the green and a seat purchased to commemorate the Queen and Prince Philip's Silver Wedding, the parish council later planting five more trees. A rose garden was planted by the old village pump in memory of Ann Mildred, a councillor and WI secretary for many years, who loved and worked for Milfield.

The villagers are fortunate in still having a shop and post office, and a saddler continues his trade. When the village blacksmith retired in 1962 Andrew Wilson & Son moved from Kilham to continue the trade of farrier, and now have a thriving agricultural engineering business. In 1963 they opened a café in part of the smithy and today, as Milfield Country Café, it is a well known stopping place for coaches and commercial vehicles, as well as many tourists. A refrigeration catering firm now operates on the site of the blacksmith's garden and a drilling investigation firm is based in a building once used as a byre. Employment is also to be found at the chicken factory sited far enough away for the aroma not to spoil the country air.

The hills of spoil resulting from sand and gravel extraction are slowly vanishing from the skyline after 20 years, the land at last being returned to its former state. From the gliders circling above the gliding club site nearby, the old hangars now used for storage remind the pilots of wartime operations long ago.

Nedderton 🌿

Nedderton is a small village of approximately 80 houses in the district of Bedlingtonshire. It is a mile and a half west of Bedlington on the B1331 road, and three and a half miles from Morpeth.

The first historical reference to it was in the time of Bishop Hatfield in 1345. In 1404 Mary, widow of Sir William Swinburne, granted all her lands in Nedderton to Sir William de Angram. By this time Nedderton was in the bishopric of Durham. In 1426 the Earl of Westmorland died here of a sudden seizure and the village became known as 'Strangle-Place'. During Henry VIII's reign the land had passed to the Ogle family. By 1643 during the reign of Charles I, Lord William Howard had become the owner of the whole manor of Nedderton or Netherton, as it was sometimes called. This then passed to his descendants, the Earls of Carlisle.

The Carlisle family built a school in 1846. This is a very attractive stone building situated in the centre of the village. It is no longer a school but is in use as a training centre for young people.

Nedderton is in an arable farming area, corn and oil seed rape being the main crops, and there are three farms. Nowadays it is purely a residential village with residents leaving the area for their work in Newcastle, Morpeth, Cramlington etc. It was once in an important coal mining area, and this is mentioned as early as the 16th century. The population increased during the 19th century with the opening of Netherton colliery, about half a mile away. The sinking operations began in 1818 and it was in use for 156 years, closing in 1974. By 1873 Netherton had grown dramatically and had a population of 1,500 with its own Co-operative store, brass band and lively community. The coal was used locally and also exported from Blyth, using the river near the old Bedlington ironworks to which keel boats came to take it to the port.

Now there are only a handful of houses left, the pit buildings and spoil heap have gone and the whole area has been restored and landscaped. Trees and hedges have been planted to return it to a pleasant leafy area for people and wildlife to enjoy. The pit manager's old stone house, with its large garden and mature trees, has become an old people's home known as Howard House.

Nedderton has grown in the last few years with two new housing developments. Plans for more houses are in progress. Sadly the post office closed some years ago and the village does not have a church or community centre. The villagers were proud to win a trophy for the Best Kept Village in 1976, and were also runners-up in the 1988 competition. Wansbeck council keeps the village looking attractive with their beautifully planted flower beds and passers by can sit on the wooden seat presented by the WI in 1953 to commemorate the Queen's Coronation.

Netherton 🐚

Netherton is a peaceful country village with a population of about 60. The Star Hotel, now the Star Inn, was built about 1900–1910 as a railway hotel, awaiting the planned railway up the valley, across by Alnham and down to Whittingham station on the Alnwick–Wooler line, but this never materialised.

The former blacksmith's shop was bought by a local haulier and the house renovated in the 1960s. A garage was built in the 1970s for agricultural and mechanical repairs. The former school house, sold in the mid 1980s, used to be The Fighting Cocks Inn and has recently assumed that name again. Also, in olden days, there was another inn called The Phoenix. About 1990 Netherton Southside Farmhouse, a former coaching inn – with a cheese room, dated on the window sill – was sold together with three farm cottages and a farm steading, renovated and put on sale to owner-occupiers.

The stone Victorian school was built in 1890 on the site of the old Netherton Northside Farm, relocated across at Netherton Buildings. Behind the school part of the garden or stackyard wall can still be seen. Further across the mill field is a dug-out circle with a central mound of earth – thought to be a cock-fighting pit. From the marsh, clay was dug out and used to line and seal ponds in the locality. In the school field is Cherrywell, named after a wild cherry tree, and Barrister Well.

Netherton Memorial Institute, known locally as 'the hall', opened in 1921 on land donated by Henry and William Blakey. It contains the beautiful brass memorial plaque to the fallen of two world wars. The reading room was well used by the local lads but closed in the mid 1930s.

Newbiggin by the Sea 🪶

Newbiggin by the Sea, once a mining and fishing village, is now mainly a dormitory for workers in Newcastle and the surrounding areas of Ashington and Morpeth.

The pit which was opened in 1911 closed in 1967 leaving only the centuries old fishing industry. This has declined from 142 cobles in 1869 to nine, most of the boats fishing from Blyth. The remainder are drawn up by the lifeboat house at the east end of the sweeping bay.

Fisherwomen no longer bait the lines, a tedious job necessitating collecting mussels from the nearby rocks and baiting up to 700 hooks per line. Now very little line fishing is carried out. The cobles mainly fish for cod and haddock in the winter, and salmon from May to September, as well as putting in pots for crabs.

The bay has no natural harbour for protection. Newbiggin was once an important port for shipping grain, and many vessels rode in the bay. In the 14th century there was a pier and the Bishop of Durham granted 40 days indulgence to all persons in his diocese who contributed to its maintenance.

On the rocky headland of Newbiggin Point stands the ancient church of St Bartholomew. Built about 1200, it is conspicuous for miles and is a useful landmark for sailors. In 1771 the local fishermen refused to pay tithes to the clergy and the vicar retaliated by discontinuing services. The church fell into disrepair and was not renovated until a century later and regular services resumed.

To the north of the point is the moor and golf course, which has been owned by the freeholders or 'lords of the manor' since 1285. The freehold was granted to them by Edward II for building a ship for his war against Scotland. They still walk the boundaries once a year in May on Lady Day and distribute nuts to the children. New freeholders are still initiated by being 'dunted' or bumped on the dunting stone. In 1752 the freeholders agreed that no ducks should be kept in the town!

Newbiggin lifeboat has carried out many rescues. In many of them the fisherwomen have helped with the launching, and have twice been awarded the thanks of the RNLI on vellum, and these now hang in the lifeboat house. On the first occasion, in 1927, ten cobles were at sea when a severe gale blew up. Not enough crew being available, the women pulled the lifeboat down the beach in torrential rain and howling winds, and waded waist high into the raging sea to launch the boat. Nine of the cobles were saved, and the tenth managed to land at a nearby port.

In 1940, when a Belgian ship, the *Eminent*, was in difficulties, it was impossible for the lifeboat to round the point owing to heavy seas, so the women hauled the boat over the moor, rocks and sands for approximately a mile, until it could be launched safely. In 1984 this rescue was commemorated when members of the WI dressed in fisher costume hauled a small boat from the golf course down the main street to the WI hall.

Due to mining under the sea bed the bay has subsided and caused the main street to be flooded during the spring and autumn tides. Shopkeepers once bolstered up their doorways with sandbags, but since the building of the new promenade and wave wall flooding is a thing of the past.

Shelters which stood on the promenade have gone, together with the bandstand where people used to dance on summer evenings, the herring house and the fish auctions which used to be held on the sands. In 1868 the first cable to Scandinavia was laid from Newbiggin, but the cable house has gone. Now, heaped against the sea wall for nearly the length of the promenade are huge granite boulders, which although they give some protection from the pounding of the sea, add nothing to the beauty of the bay.

Large stone houses overlooking the sea used to house many summer visitors, and old photographs show ladders leading from the gardens to the beach. With the advent of the railway many day trippers came from Newcastle, but the railway has now gone.

The hand-cranked merry go rounds, and donkeys for riding have gone, as have the ferry boats which gave trips around the bay. Holidaymakers now stay at a caravan site overlooking the sea at the Church Point.

A mile to the north lies the village of Woodhorn, now only a handful of cottages, and the 8th century mother church of St Mary, said to be the oldest on the Northumbrian coast. It is now redundant and has been made into a much visited museum.

Coal is still gathered from the beach, but not in large quantities. None of the changes which have taken place detract from the atmosphere of Newbiggin, where horses are still tethered on the moor, and early mornings bring the sound of 'trotting' races down the main street. The church still holds its annual St Bartholomew's Fair, and the promenade is crammed with people on Lifeboat Day, to watch the water displays and buy from the stalls set up round the lifeboat house.

It has grown from a small fishing village and now has a population of approximately 7,000 and is in danger of being swallowed up by neighbouring Ashington. It no longer has its own council, but belongs to the greater Wansbeck council, which controls its affairs but has not succeeded in smothering its identity.

Newbrough 🌿

The village of Newbrough lies five miles north of Hexham on the north bank of the river South Tyne. It enjoys a pleasant, agricultural landscape and has been designated as a conservation area.

In 1217 Newbrough was granted a royal charter by Henry III and it became a borough town, hence the name, 'new market town'. In 1306 the people of Newbrough watched the arrival of Edward I with his retinue. He is said to have lodged at Thornton Tower and was in a poor state of health, leaving later in a litter. He died the following year.

The centre of the village, along the Roman Stanegate, is mostly constructed in stone. The village boasts some fine public buildings, all of which are listed buildings in their own right.

The oldest of these is the Red Lion Inn, a hostelry dating back to 1190, when King David of Scotland presented Thornton, the chief house in the parish at that time, to Richard Cumin. The Red Lion Inn takes its name from the Scottish royal lion. Today the custom of Carlin Sunday is still observed. On the fifth Sunday in Lent carlins (cooked dried peas) are served to customers, traditionally eaten garnished with salt and pepper and washed down with a tot of rum. On Easter Sunday a competition for an Easter bonnet, and for the best dyed egg is held, proceeds in aid of a local charity.

On the east side of the Red Lion, locally known as the 'corner end', sit two boulders which were found in the long field, Thornton Tower Lane, by a man called Corbett, who took a liking to these stones. Despite the fact that they were considerably heavier than his donkey and cart put together, he carted them to the corner of the Red Lion Inn. He was told by the authorities to take them away, which he did, but late that same night, muffling the wheels of his cart, he replaced them. There they remain and are a popular meeting and sitting place, now very shiny with use.

An imposing structure, Newbrough town hall was built in 1878 for the use of the inhabitants of Newbrough and Fourstones by the generosity of Miss Jane Todd, who lived at nearby Newbrough Park. In 1950 a serious fire destroyed part of the roof and the caretaker's flat. The damage was repaired and funds were raised the following year for improving and renovating the hall. It is the main social centre, widely used for wedding receptions, dances and by many local organisations.

In 1848 the building near the war memorial was built by public subscription by an organisation called the Mutual Improvement Society, later to be called the Mechanics' Institute. When in 1948 changing times made it apparent that the Institute had outlived its usefulness, the final few members presented the property, plus the sum of £100 for decorating and renovating the building, to Newbrough Women's Institute.

Approximately half a mile west, on what had been the site of a Roman fort, stands St Peter's church. The original chapel was built in 1242 but in 1865 this chapel was pulled down and replaced by the present structure. In 1930 whilst excavations were being carried out in the churchyard, the boundary wall of a Roman fort was discovered.

A relic of medieval life is St Mary's Well in a field close to St Peter's church. This field is called 'Nonnesfield'. In olden times it was reported to have effected many marvellous cures and it is still said that no aquatic reptiles can live in it. It has now almost vanished but underground, they say, there still runs a stream of healing water.

Further west on the Stanegate is the site of Nunsbush, one of the black thatch houses in the parish. It was inhabited until 1923 and then fell into decay. It was here that the nuns who attended St Mary's Well are said to have resided. Mary Teasdale lived here until her death in 1890, aged 101 years, and she enjoyed a clay pipe right until the day she died. There are other cases of longevity.

Newbrough also has a history of some violent deeds. A story often told is that of Old Meg. Less than a mile to the north of the village a burn runs from the fell above, through Meggies Dene. In the springtime a pink thorn blossoms there, and according to the 16th century legend it covers the grave of Old Meg, a witch, who was burned at the stake and buried in the Dene with a stake through her blackened heart, having been refused a Christian burial. As one pink thorn dies, another springs up in perpetual memory of Newbrough's witch.

On the eastern boundary is the sports field, home of the football and cricket clubs, both with long traditions and still flourishing. Nearby is the Wesleyan Methodist chapel, a fine stone structure built in 1876 and opposite the Church of England aided first school. The majority of the rest of the village consists of Sidgate housing estate, built by the council to relieve overcrowding.

Since the closure of the lead mines and Settlingstones witherite mine, most of the villagers commute to work within the Tyne valley, there being very little in the way of other employment.

New Hartley 🦡

New Hartley lies to the north of Seaton Delaval, off the A192. A disaster which occurred at the Hester pit on 16th January 1862 left its mark on this mining village. On that day the beam of the pumping engine, placed over the pithead and weighing 42 tons, suddenly snapped in two, half of it crashing down the shaft to entomb 204 men and boys in the pit below.

It was ten days before the funeral could be held, due to the extreme difficulty and danger in bringing out the bodies from the pit. The Primitive Methodist chapel in Hartley was used as a mortuary where bodies of the unknown were left for identification by relatives.

The funeral took place on 26th January 1862 and the correspondent of the *Illustrated London News* estimated a crowd of 60,000 invaded Hartley on that day. Queen Victoria sent a letter which was read out at a service in Hartley before the funeral. Not all the men and boys lost were buried at Earsdon, a few separate burials took place at Cramlington, Cowpen and Seghill. Although Earsdon church was four miles away, the funeral procession was so long that the first hearse reached the church before the last hearse departed from the colliery at Hartley. There wasn't enough room in the actual churchyard so a hole had been made in the wall into the field beyond. In one grave alone, there were seven people from the same family. There was also a mass grave which contained no less than 33 bodies, this being chiefly for the unknown dead. The gravediggers worked non-stop from dawn on the Saturday until after dark on the Sunday evening of the funeral. Such was this unforgettable day. One can feel great pity for the mourners as they made their weary way back to Hartley, and what was left of home.

The Hartley miners did not die in vain because seven months after the disaster occurred, on 7th August 1862, a special Act of Parliament was passed which made it compulsory for every mine to have two shafts. Later, a miners' permanent relief fund was set up, the necessity for which was forcibly brought home by the hundreds of dependants who would otherwise have been destitute.

The centenary of the disaster was marked in January 1962 by a special service at Earsdon parish church and by the floodlighting of the memorial. Inscribed on the memorial on its four sides are the names of the 204 men and boys who were lost in the Hartley disaster. A plaque was erected in the Garden of Remembrance at New Hartley near the shaft. The shaft, with the half of the broken beam still buried in it, is marked by a stone wall, in which the date stone of the old pumping engine house has been inserted.

Newton 🦋

Just a short walk uphill from the busy Carlisle/Newcastle motorway lies the peaceful, tiny hamlet of Newton. There is only a single road with buildings on either side, surrounded by scattered farms on the perimeter. It stands 400 feet above sea level, built on sandstone, facing south overlooking the lands of the Bywell estate and the ancient baronies of Baliol and Bolbec, of which it was once a part. It is surrounded by fertile pastures and extensive woodland and from Tofts Hill, above the village, Alston in Cumberland can be seen on a clear day.

The meaning of Newton is 'new town' and the belief is that, like Bywell, a larger village existed in the 15th–16th centuries but with repeated raids by thieves and Borderers, Newton became deserted and the buildings were left to deteriorate.

The ancient township of Newton in the 13th century was made up of a collection of small tenements which were owned by the Baliols of Bywell, the rest having a variety of owners. In 1426 there were six 'messuages' (a dwelling and some land) which were worth nothing, being 'debilous and ruinous, 120 acres of moor and 100 acres of wood which was worthless'. Rents at that time were four shillings a year for a cottage and a garden.

The lands became the property of the Crown in the 17th century. They were then sold to a variety of owners. The Fenwicks of Bywell were one of the buyers, who in turn sold to Joseph Bainbridge of Newcastle in 1816, making him the sole owner of the estate with the exception of Newton House, which was owned by the Joiceys of Newton Hall. The estate was sold to William Hedley of Wylam in 1842 and maintained by him till 1952 when it was purchased, together with seven farms, by the trustees of Viscount Allendale's estates for the sum of £80,000.

The farms surrounding the village and almost half of the houses today, the earliest built in the 18th century, are still part of this estate. Some of the local families, the Telfers at Newton High House and the Woodman family at Town Farm in the centre, have been tenants for generations.

Until 30 years ago the village remained unchanged, consisting of an inn, The Duke of Wellington, two farms, a chapel at its west end, the WI hall at its east end, and an agricultural workshop. A cutting from the *Evening Chronicle* in 1930 states, 'A remarkable instance of a 300 years old business surviving in tense modern competition is provided at Newton, near Stocksfield, where the manufacture of farm implements is carried on in a small workshop by two brothers, John and James Symm, who inherited the business. The products of their workshop are famous throughout the north country. The two brothers are able to trace the origin of the business as far back as 1770, though it is known that it had then existed for over a century. Mr John Symm estimates that from tales told by his grandfather, it had been in existence for 300 years and was established in the time of Oliver Cromwell.'

This historic firm remained in the hands of one family through the generations, designing and constructing from their own ideas, a mower/reaper being their most successful product and for which they gained their reputation. In pre-war days their implements were exported to Australia and South America but the war stopped the development of the business overseas.

In 1963, Tom and Charlie Symm retired and wound up the business. Other firms continued repairing farm machinery in the workshop, until its final closure in the 1980's, when the site was sold for residential development. There are still Symms living in the village today.

The chapel at the west end was supported until the 1960s, when it was sold and made into a dwelling house, the first conversion from its original use. Further developments followed, when South Farm was split up and the house and adjoining buildings were converted into attractive properties. The old estate houses had indoor toilets and bathrooms installed about this time, to bring them up to present day standards.

The parish church of St James lies half a mile to the north east, extended in 1873 at a cost of £4,500 by the Joicey family of Newton Hall, to provide a church of great beauty. The old hall is now known as Mowden Hall and has become an independent school. The old vicarage was built in 1877 at a further cost of £5,000. A village school existed behind the church until the end of the war when numbers of children had greatly diminished.

The boundaries of Newton have not altered through the last century and recent designation as a conservation area should secure its future as it stands today, a small, delightful place in which to live.

Newton by the Sea

Newton by the Sea is on a beautiful sheltered bay on the north east coast, with a long stretch of beach tipped by the picturesque ruins of Dunstanburgh Castle. Tucked among the sand dunes are a few wooden chalets, but the tiny village is concentrated around three sides of a square just yards from the beach. As well as the inn, the square is made up of small grey stone bungalows, once, but no longer, fishermen's cottages. Only the odd coble floats on the bay now, and the walls are no longer draped with drying nets.

Over 50 years ago, the village school had the incredible attendance of eight pupils. The morning milk was delivered there by pony and cart by the local farmer, and after the pony had been duly patted in appreciation, the milk was warmed on the black smoke-billowing pot-bellied stove. The resulting tepid, sooty liquid was noisily drunk with great relish through bent straws, and bubbles blown in for extra enjoyment. Sandshoe-clad and bare-kneed children played in the school yard – old fashioned games requiring extensive improvisation and imagination to compensate for lack of participants and materials. In the distance could be heard the jubilant cackling of hens as these individually-named little brown ladies completed their daily task, to give great enjoyment at dinner time, when eager hands felt into soft, warm, hay-lined nests to capture the neat brown eggs which were then carefully carried home to be relished at teatime.

After school came the excitement of milking Daisy, the large, placid doe-eyed long-suffering pet cow, who suffered with great tolerance the indignities of small hands learning to milk. The reward for a pail full of creamy, warm, frothing milk, was a full mug and a telltale moustache as proof of a 'pint' enjoyed.

The cows have long gone to the dairy in the sky and the milk is delivered by unknown bodies driving ghostly vehicles in the night. There is no joy in collecting the pint from the doorstep. The school doors are closed and the yard is silent, the hen's happy clucking no longer heard, anonymous eggs being delivered in regulation boxes. The simple country joys of childhood have gone, but holidaymakers and tourists are the new generation finding delight in this beautiful, hidden little village.

Norham 🦢

Norham, a village of some 500 inhabitants, is situated in the Tweed valley eight miles inland from Berwick upon Tweed. All three approach roads are downhill, the one from Scotland leading onto the bridge built just over 100 years ago to replace a wooden one. The castle on its rock dominates the east end and looks down onto the main street and the triangular village green.

This deceptively peaceful village has a turbulent history of Border warfare, both the church and the castle being built in the 12th century by Bishop Pudsey of Durham. Norham was the northernmost outpost of the see of Durham and the defensive castle was built in Norman style with a large square keep which though ruined is still an impressive building. The inner ward was used as a refuge for villagers and the ruined walls are quite extensive, the moat only visible at the Marmion Arch. The ruins were made safe by the Ministry of Works during the 1920s, and at the same time the steep road was reconstructed and widened; the inner ward is grassed and beautifully kept by English Heritage. Formerly the custodian lived in the small cottage in the walls with his family, and during the Second World War the grounds were fenced in and kept grazed by sheep from the adjoining farm. Chilli Hill, opposite the castle, is a favourite place for 'rolling eggs' at Easter and sledging, with even the occasional skier in winter if there is snow.

The wide street with its grass verges softens the rather Scottish and austere looking houses on either side, while the green with its market cross lies at the road junctions. The cross, played on by generations of children, shown by its well worn steps, dates from the 14th or 15th century while the top pillars are 1879 and the salmon weathervane surmounting it dates from 1925. The cottage on the corner of the street behind was in bygone days the Salmon Inn.

Salmon fishing was one of the chief sources of employment, with net fisheries from Berwick to Coldstream along the river banks. The fishery, Pedwell, gave its name to the street leading to the river. Pedwell was the scene of the custom of 'blessing the nets' by the vicar of Norham at midnight on 14th February each year. The salmon net fishing has ceased excepting at the river mouth and the small fishery of Canny, the rest of the river being given over to rod fishing. There is also trout fishing by permit from the local pubs. Pre-war, fishing cobles competed in the annual boat races when crews from other fisheries came to join in the fun. Families would sit on the river banks along the route, picnicking and enjoying a day out; tug-of-war and quoits were part of the event.

The old school building in Pedwell Way, now a house, adjoins the former school house, situated at the east end of the churchyard as befits a church school. The school closed in 1911 and was then used as a church hall. There are a few who can remember going to the old school and how they marched up to the new one. Then there were 120 pupils up to the age of 14. Now there are 42 pupils up to the age of nine, at which age they are transported by bus to Berwick middle school, and at 13 to Berwick high school. Formerly children who passed the entrance exams went by train to the grammar school at Berwick.

The pre-war train was the *Royal Charlotte*. The station half a mile out of the village was the main transporter of parcels and papers to and from Berwick. Milk was taken to the station from Galagate Farm in large churns in a pony and trap. The last signal porter and his wife still live in the station house from where they run a coal business. In addition they have restored much of the station to become a comprehensive private museum with porter's room, office, waiting room and signal box complete with signal man, who stands at the ready in case a train should ever come that way again. A far cry from the hectic days following the 1948 flood when the main East Coast trains were diverted for a time through Norham (numerous bridges having been washed away).

The Norman church too suffered during the 27 foot spate of 1948, which disturbed the gravel bed and caused the east end to subside, needing a large amount of restoration. It had been subject to many restorations previously, as it was also damaged in the 16th century. The pillars on the north side are octagonal and those on the south side round, the whole structure now lovingly kept by members of the congregation. The church is situated at the west end of the village and stands between the river and the village surrounded by its large churchyard. Built on the site of a Saxon church, some stones of which are still kept in the church, which is dedicated to St Cuthbert, it is active in the community, all denominations joining in activities.

A good bus service has been maintained between Berwick, Norham, Cornhill and Kelso run by two different companies working together. Pre-war the service was well used by workers travelling to Berwick. Those days people did not travel far. The bus stops outside the stone-built village hall, which is over 100 years old and is the centre of village life, both geographically and socially.

North Seaton Colliery ✣

History records that there was a Roman settlement at the mouth of the river Wansbeck, but North Seaton Colliery was born the day the pit shaft was sunk in 1859.

The original homes for the miners were two rows of wooden houses cut into the hillside on the north bank of the river, with outside staircases leading up to the bedrooms. As the pit developed and the work-force grew, 14 rows of houses were built with stone from the nearby quarry and were eventually supplied by the pit with electricity and outside water taps, two or three taps per row. Toilet facilities were very basic consisting of detached 'dry netties' with toilet paper being squares of newspaper threaded on a string. These were hung on a convenient nail! It was considered a grand place to live and many local couples married to establish a closely-knit community.

The first of two schools was built in 1859 and the first of two chapels appeared in 1876. Originally food was brought into the Colliery by the one access road and sold from a horse and cart, as Royalty had decreed that no shops could be erected on the private land. Eventually the provision of a Co-operative store was granted and this catered for all the needs of the growing community. The grocery department became a popular place to exchange gossip and news, with two or three strategically placed chairs in front of the long wooden counters.

In 1924 a miners' Welfare Hall was built which became an important focal point of the village. It has been much used over the years for functions such as the children's galas, meetings, wedding receptions, and our own Colliery prize brass band played for family dances. Upstairs was a billiards room, a reception room and small ante-rooms while in the grounds were the tennis courts, bowling greens and flower gardens. Nearby were two football fields and a children's playground complete with swings etc. All this was paid for by a miners' levy deducted weekly from their wages.

In addition to these amenities, the levy helped support our own doctor and nurse who lived in the Colliery, and our own ambulance was garaged in the village, being driven and maintained by Mr Joe McLean, a local miner.

We were the proud owners of our own Co-operative Dairy with fresh milk delivered daily by horse and cart. Families who were shareholders received a yearly dividend. There was also a brick-built fish and chip shop and next door the wooden hut of the local barber.

Each housewife was proud to display her home-made 'proggy' and 'clicky' mats with their own original designs. A new mat was a must to lay in front of the fireside at Christmas. At New Year, with parties everywhere, it was open house to friends and first-footers who came carrying their traditional lump of coal and 'wee dram' in their pockets. No one was ever turned away, even the few who had over-indulged in the festivities.

Many miners owned their own boats and went fishing to provide an outdoor recreation with fresh air to compensate for working under-ground in very adverse and dangerous conditions. They built their own harbours to moor and maintain the boats.

The river was used for the annual regatta which attracted many well established crews of rowers from all over the North. This was a very special long weekend when everyone participated by hosting visiting crews and supplying refreshments for spectators, culminating in a Grand Dance in the evening held in the Welfare Hall.

There were about 25 pigeon lofts on the riverside and the men formed a racing club. The birds were sent in special baskets by train to various starting points in the South and eventually to France.

The sand dunes at the mouth of the river had many sheltered and safe places where families gathered for playing games and having fun. Camping out was a favourite pastime as food cooked outdoors was considered manna indeed. In the evening, wandering their weary way home, trailing towels, wet bathing costumes, tents etc, dog-tired but still laughing and singing; the end of a perfect day.

Circa 1950 saw the start of the modernisation programme of the village. Tarmac roads replaced the dirt roads, each house was provided with piped water and the 'netties' became flush toilets. Twenty four council houses were added to the 40 houses built a few years previously, so there were now 64 'modern hooses' in the community.

Unfortunately, the early 1960s heralded the end of this closely knit community with the closure of the mine and the dispersal of the working miners to the surrounding pits. Another blow was the declaration by the powers-that-be that the 100 year old stone houses were now becoming unsafe for habitation, and that the lease on the land was now up and not being renewed. Consequently a new estate of council houses was built two miles away and families moved there as new houses were available. Only the 64 brick houses remain now in the old village of North Seaton Colliery.

The demolition programme also included the Welfare Hall, Co-operative store, chapels, schools and all pit buildings above ground. As the community was uprooted a way of life disappeared. Eventually, other families from surrounding districts were integrated and the closely knit feeling seemed to be gradually eroding. A communal meeting place was badly needed and with help from the local council and many fund-raising events, money was raised to build a community centre. This was instrumental in helping to encourage and reintroduce neighbourliness.

Otterburn 🦌

A village in the Rede valley situated on the main road to Edinburgh and 15 miles from the Scottish border, Otterburn has a thriving community of around 400. It is almost entirely surrounded by the Ministry of Defence training area and is within the Northumberland National Park.

The area contains many working farms, but the MOD is the district's main employer. There is little unemployment in the area, with the village's three hotels, The Percy Arms, Otterburn Tower and Otterburn Hall, also employing local staff.

The village originally had four churches and three are still used for worship. The Anglican church of St John the Evangelist was designed by John Dobson and cost £3,000. It was dedicated in 1887 and the first vicar was the Rev Mr Brierley (1919–1949). Mr Brierley's memory lives on as the village council estate of 60 houses is named Brierley Gardens. The Presbyterian church, a much older building, now houses a riding school and the worshippers attend Birdhopecraig in the village of Rochester. The Methodist church was built in 1909 and is still in constant use. The Roman Catholics of the district once worshipped in a loft above a barn next to the old vicarage and had an outside stone staircase before St Peter's was built in 1953.

Otterburn was famous for its woollen mill, dating from the early 18th century. Once a hive of industry producing rugs and blankets for sale worldwide, the mill itself now stands empty and silent. The smart showroom, however, is still busy and attracts many visitors.

The exact origins of the village school are not known, but there was a classroom in the school house in 1828 named after Lady Murray. By 1930 there were three classrooms housing infants, juniors and seniors. The school is now a primary and the older children of the village travel to Bellingham, Ponteland and Haydon Bridge.

Otterburn Tower, once a fortress that held off a siege by the marauding Scots before the battle of Otterburn in 1388, was built by the Umfraville family. It is now a quiet and peaceful hotel, attracting visitors with the promise of 'spending a night in a castle'.

The Percy Arms, a former coaching inn, stands in the village centre. Before the 1930s it was attached to a row of stone cottages which were demolished to make way for the hotel as it is today.

Otterburn Hall, built in 1870 by Lord James Murray and later owned by Sir Charles Morrison-Bell, became a military hospital during the Second World War. It is now a hotel and adventure centre owned by the YMCA.

Otterburn has many activity groups, including popular indoor bowls sessions, a successful football team, a working men's club and a sports and leisure centre.

Ovingham 🐾

Ovingham lies in the Tyne valley, twelve miles west of Newcastle. The name is Saxon and probably means 'homestead of the sons of Offa'. It is first mentioned about the year 1200 although the village had been established three centuries earlier when the church tower was built. Although Ovingham had a weekly market in the 13th century and a yearly fair on St Andrew's Day it was never wealthy in medieval times. In 1312 the Bishop of Durham was unable to obtain any taxes from the parson 'because the church and villages in his parish are burnt by the Scots'.

The church of St Mary the Virgin has the tallest tower in Northumberland at 105 feet. The tower was built in the early 9th century, the rest of the church in the 13th. Across the road lies the old vicarage, the east end built in the 14th century to house the Augustinian canons from Hexham, along with the vicar. The remainder was erected in the 17th century, but greatly altered in the 19th. It is rumoured that a tunnel connects it with Prudhoe Castle across the river, but it has never been found. Today it is a private home, the present vicar living in a modern house on a small estate close to the church.

Thomas Bewick, the famous wood engraver, was born across the river at Cherryburn in 1753, but received his early education in Ovingham, and is buried along with his wife in the churchyard. In his day the village had its industries, among them dyeing. Bewick's grandfather was a dyer, as was George Stephenson's, his mother being a native of Ovingham. He is represented with his employer in Bewick's woodcut, *The Ovingham Dyers*. The Bleach Green is still to be seen today, along with the remains of the old mill.

It was only in 1883 that Ovingham was connected to Prudhoe by a bridge, though since the 15th century a ferry had existed. Another bridge is the 17th century packhorse one, which spans the Whittle burn. It was once very busy when the Newcastle–Carlisle turnpike road passed through the village, but now a concrete bridge crosses the burn.

There are two village halls, one the reading room which is 100 years old but has recently been modernised and extended. It is used regularly and its committee organises the Goose Fair every year. This was first held as a hiring fair in medieval times and was revived about 20 years ago. It is held on the third Saturday in June when Morris dancers and other folk groups lead a procession through the village.

The other hall was bought by the members of the Women's Institute in 1939. The hall was not used by the WI until after the war as it was commandeered for the billeting of soldiers. Today it is maintained by the hard work of WI members, and is used for a weekly doctor's surgery, for parish council meetings, at election times, and by a carpet bowls club.

The population of the village has more than doubled in the last 25 years, with the building of five estates of houses. However, it still maintains a village atmosphere; it has an excellent first and middle school and people care about the elderly residents and help at a lunch club and day centre held every week. The church and Methodist chapel are well attended, as are the two public houses. Ovingham has two shops, a post office/newsagent and a general grocery shop. There used to be a butcher, tailor and hairdresser but these have all ceased to trade.

Ovington 🦗

The village of Ovington lies a mile west of Ovingham and is situated about a mile north of the river Tyne.

It was founded as an offshoot of Ovingham, but in 1296 it was noted to be the wealthier of the two villages. Ovington Hall is first mentioned in 1525; the only relic of this is a pointed window in an outbuilding facing the road.

The population has increased in recent years, with the building of a council estate and more recently private houses, but it still retains a good community spirit. There is one small shop and post office, a well established plant nursery, a social club and two public houses with restaurants attached. There was a lovely chapel that is now converted into a private house.

Ovington is well known for its prize winning silver band, although it no longer has its own hall in the village.

Pegswood 🦗

In the 18th century, Pegswood was known as Pegsworthe and consisted of ten cottages and one inn. Most of the original cottages are still standing today. These were homes for estate workers. The inn is now a house with riding stables attached. It is still owned by the estate and rented out, as are all the remaining cottages.

In 1867 Pegswood colliery was sunk and with it came the beginning of Pegswood village. The first eight colliery rows were built in 1867 and the remaining six in the early part of the 20th century. The streets were named after the Duke of Portland and his family titles, beginning with Portland and ending with Langwell Terrace. The houses built for the colliery workers were well built but with no amenities, no running water or electricity. Toilets were across a dirt road, and of course were earth closets. These were emptied at night by men with a horse and cart. Electricity came in the 1940s and also flush toilets. The National Coal Board modernised the houses in the 1960s with bathrooms and kitchenettes.

Council houses were built on land acquired from the Portland estate – very modern compared to the colliery rows. Pegswood now has seven housing estates. The colliery has only three and a half long rows and two small rows left standing. The others were demolished and people were rehoused on the new council estate.

The first school had three classrooms. In 1901 a junior and senior school was built on the Longhirst road. In the late 1930s a further six classrooms were built and the infants lifted up their chairs and marched to the new school. The old school housed soldiers during the war. After the war, the Church of England rented it out for a church hall and later, it was used as a church. Now it is to be returned to the education authorities.

Pegswood had two chapels, Wesleyan and Methodist. The Wesleyan chapel is now owned by the Catholic church and holds services every Sunday. The Methodists and the Church of England have united in worship in one church, called St Margaret's.

The highlight of the Sunday school year in the past was the Whitley Bay trip. This was a family day out for the village, when a special train was laid on. If you were a good attender at Sunday school you went free. The village came to life altogether on that Saturday morning, everyone making their way to the station, laughing and so excited. Mothers and fathers carrying bags with the bait, towels and swimming gear, children carrying buckets and spades. What a day!

The second highlight of the year was the children's gala held in the Welfare Park and paid for by the miners. The committee, helped by the school teachers, organised a great day.

The miners' Welfare Hall was built in 1927. Each man gave twopence out of his wages towards the upkeep. The hall was used for dances and wedding receptions. A cinema was opened in 1928, silent movies of course. Later, they used to show films five nights a week and a matinee for children on Saturday mornings.

Retired members of the colliery had an annual outing with everything paid for by the 'Welfare'. In the 1960s, an extension was built with a modern dance floor and bar. Sadly, it is now an uphill battle to keep the building open. With the closure of the pit in 1971, all revenue from the miners ceased and it became self-supporting. Bingo was started to help raise money and is still played today four times a week.

The Welfare Park had a children's playground and a football field. The flower park had tennis courts, putting greens and a six lane bowling green. Pegswood had very good men's and ladies' bowls teams, and often won the league cups. Today, the football field is still used but the tennis courts and putting greens are flower beds. A few years ago the bowling green was relaid.

In the late 1940s a boys' club was formed, and the Duke of Gloucester came and officially opened the new building. A greengrocer's shop now stands on the site. Pegswood had Cubs, Scouts, Brownies and Girl Guide packs and all are still going strong today except for the Girl Guides. The over sixties club was founded in the 1950s and has a good attendance. They meet once a fortnight in the Welfare Hall. They also have a good choir and often give concerts to other clubs in the area. Pegswood has two club buildings. The social club was originally a house and when it first opened, beer was only twopence a pint. The British Legion club was built much later, next door.

Ponteland 🪶

Modern Ponteland is a large village with origins going back to Saxon times. The present population is about 12,000 including those living on the Darras Hall Estate which adjoins the original village.

Very slender evidence exists for the earliest inhabitants of the area, but there is a good example of a beaker which was left by the people who probably lived here about 3,500 years ago. Roman artefacts found in a nearby peat bog at Prestwick Carr may have belonged to a hunting party. Hadrian's Wall is only two miles to the south, with wall forts within five miles, so there would have been Roman troops in the district for nearly 400 years.

The parish church, dedicated to St Mary the Virgin, is undoubtedly the oldest building in the village with stonework almost certainly of Saxon origin. There is much original Norman work, including the tower with the west door and western end of the nave. The chancel, transept and aisles are 13th/14th century, and there were 19th century additions and alterations, mostly done in 1881 when the building was in a very dilapidated condition. Since then the church has remained virtually unaltered. Dowsing by Dennis Briggs and Prof Bailey has revealed the presence of two earlier buildings, with apsed ends, underlying the existing structure for the most part. Outside the north aisle, however, their existence has been confirmed by limited digging.

After the Norman conquest, the knights who had supported King William were granted lands for their services. The de Bertram family settled Mitford, and built a large castle there; whilst one of them became lord of the manor of Ponteland, also building a castle, although a much smaller one. The core of this building, the barrel-vaulted ground floor, remains as an interesting part of the Blackbird Inn. Tales of secret passages from the castle are true and some older residents know where they ran. The castle suffered many vicissitudes, including being burnt in 1388 by the Scots under Douglas, following a raid on Newcastle. They were pursued by Harry 'Hotspur' Percy and at the resulting battle of Otterburn, Douglas was killed and Percy was taken prisoner. Much earlier an attempt to bring peace to the constantly warring nations had been made in 1242 by the signing of a peace treaty between Alexander of Scotland and Henry III of England, in Ponteland, reputedly in the church, but Border raiding continued until 1745, when the last great Scottish rebellion was decisively crushed at Culloden.

Following the destruction of 1388 the castle seems to have remained a ruin for some 200 years, when the then lord of the manor, Mark Errington, turned the ruins into a manor house. The family remained there for 200 years, when the building again fell into disrepair, until bought by a brewery company and turned into an inn in the 19th century.

No building was entirely safe in such troubled times. Only one of stone gave any degree of protection against raiders, and this would be why the vicar's pele tower was built at some time in the 14th or 15th century. Several of these peles exist in the county, some being incorporated into later vicarages. As the tithes were an important part of a vicar's stipend, it is possible that a tithe barn was constructed near to the church. Such a barn was known to exist, and last appeared on a tithe map of 1841, but no other records are known to us. There are no other old buildings of medieval origin in the village, and it was to be the 18th century before any other structure appeared, a common feature in Northumbrian villages.

Possibly the next building would be the rectory, a pleasant brick house in large grounds in the centre of the village and just across the road from the church. It was built to house the visiting rectors of Merton College when they came to collect tithes and generally to attend to their property. From the same period dates the former coaching inn, The Seven Stars and its brewery. This latter closed in 1906 and only vestiges of the brewery buildings remain, although the inn still exists, but it is a long time since coaches en route from Newcastle to Edinburgh were seen changing their teams of four horses outside. The Diamond Inn was built around 1830, the smithy next door in 1822 and, further along the road to Newcastle, in 1826 nine houses were built for freeholders who would vote for the landowner, Charles Lorraine Bell, in the parliamentary election of that year. In those days the people allowed to vote were few, and as the ballot was not secret and was published after the election, a candidate knew whether his nominees had in fact voted the right way. If they did not then he had a remedy!

An unusual event had taken place in 1722, when a small school was built in the village, under the terms of a trust given by Richard Coates of Horton Grange on his death. This trust still exists, with a new Coates middle school built in 1960.

No other developments of note occurred until the turn of the century, thus the 1901 census shows Ponteland as having a population of only 401. Although only eight miles from Newcastle, access to the city was difficult for ordinary people before the coming of the railway in 1905. With very limited possibilities for using horse-drawn vehicles, people could do little commuting for work or go for excursions or holidays, which were rare events in any case at that time. The railway opened up endless opportunities for travel for all purposes, and even more so for the future development of housing and industry. Landowners were soon alive to these possibilities and land was offered for sale for building all along the route of the line from South Gosforth, now used by the Tyneside Metro trains. The new electric loop line to the coast had been opened in 1903, but the branch to Ponteland was never electrified, and was worked by steam trains until its closure to passengers in 1929, and by diesels until goods traffic ceased in 1960. The result of the railway activity was an escalation in the population as people moved out from the city.

Public facilities are very good, all four churches in the village having halls, and there is a fine Memorial Hall which provides a venue for large events. Sport is well provided for with a sports centre and swimming pool complex owned by the council, as well as a golf course; good shops and a large supermarket provide for the inner man, and there exists a multiplicity of organisations active in all kinds of fields. Eating and drinking facilities are offered by the three public houses, the sports centre and many restaurants and hotels, including the airport which is situated only one mile away. Commuting to the city and further afield is rapid, as we are linked by a fast main road, and Newcastle International Airport is now one of the foremost in the country.

Prudhoe

Prudhoe stands on the great bastion of hills which form the south bank of the river Tyne, lying halfway between Newcastle upon Tyne and Hexham in an area which has regained all its former natural beauty.

Bronze Age man lived and died here; a stone axe hammer and two burial cists were discovered. Hadrian built his wall just a mile north. In the 10th century, we find Prudhoe within the parish of Ovingham, which lies on the north side of the river Tyne. The church dates from before the Norman Conquest.

The Normans quickly set about subjugating the locals and a timber castle was built on the haughs of the Tyne by one 'Robert with the Beard' Umfraville. He was first given the barony of Redesdale, which commands the pass into Scotland, and later the barony of Prudhoe, which, lying across the Tyne, commands the route between Newcastle and Carlisle. King William of Scotland laid siege to Prudhoe in 1173 and 1174 and by the end of the 12th century, Baron Odinelle had rebuilt the castle in stone. The barony consisted of 1,108 acres of arable land, 40 farms, a fishery pool, two water mills, a pigeon house, 16 cottages, brewhouses, two woods, a park, pasture for 200 sheep, and 50 bond servants. Rent was paid in cumin, pepper, salmon, corn and hay.

Henry Percy, Earl of Northumberland, acquired Prudhoe when he married Maud, widow of Baron Gilbert, in 1398. He led a revolt against Henry IV, who came north with an army of 30,000 and took Prudhoe, Alnwick and Walkworth. During the Wars of the Roses, Prudhoe changed hands repeatedly. Henry VIII sent fire and sword through the Northern counties when rebellion broke out, Prudhoe was searched and Sir Thomas Percy was imprisoned in the Tower of London and beheaded. Many years later, after the startling revelation of the Gunpowder Plot, the castle was again searched. A later Thomas Percy was one of the chief conspirators.

In the 18th century, the Duke of Northumberland tidied up the now ruined castle and built a hunting lodge in the grounds. Today the fabric of the castle and the environs are beautifully cared for by English Heritage.

During the Civil War, Prudhoe was occupied by both Royalists and Roundheads. There is an area known as Drawback, and legend has it that from there, 25,000 Scots Covenanters were ordered to draw back over the Border.

After the Reformation, the people of Prudhoe needed the ford and ferry over the turbulent Tyne to get to church in Ovingham. They waited until 1883 for the present narrow bridge to be built, but St Mary Magdalene's parish church was built in 1880. John Wesley visited Prudhoe on four occasions and a Wesleyan Methodist chapel was later erected.

The Gateshead Turnpike Trust pushed a new road through to Hexham in the 17th century, and the Dr Syntax Inn became a staging post for considerable coaching traffic. Fairs and hoppings were held there but when the railway was laid from Newcastle to Carlisle in 1838 the inn fell into decline, was demolished, and a new one built in the 1900s.

Coal mining was first mentioned in 1434 but when Matthew Liddell opened two mines in 1860, the population increased from 386 in 1851 to 1,995 in 1871. The coal found was good coking coal and clay was dug from the coal seams, so coke ovens, brick kilns and pipe works were

Prudhoe Castle

built. Waggon-ways were built to convey the coal, horses were replaced by stationary steam engines which in turn were replaced by locomotives. Later, ICI built a plant at Low Prudhoe, the Co-operative movement built large premises on the Main Street, and new housing estates were erected.

None of the heavy industries have survived. Local councils have joined forces to create a country riverside park which runs from Prudhoe to Newburn, with car parks, for fishing, canoeing, walking, running, cycling and picnics.

Annually, there is a Town Fair Day, a Gardeners Association Flower Show, a Remembrance Sunday parade and a Christmas meal with entertainment for every pensioner. The schools are rated very highly and many pupils go on to further education. There are good shopping facilities and a new leisure pool with a bowling green and park and the long awaited bypass were opened recently. The Prudhoe Gleemen have been singing for 90 years. The dialect, with its rolling gutteral 'r', broad vowel sound and upturned endings is still spoken and family names are still here from the 15th century.

The people are slow to accept newcomers, but when they do, they are friendly and kind. They are a hardworking community with a distinct pride and ruggedness of their own and are tough in outlook and behaviour, with a strong sense of family life.

Radcliffe 🦡

The name of the village of Radcliffe was derived from 'red cliff'. Spacious buildings in the centre of the village were erected by Messrs Ladbroke & Brown, for the education and religious instruction of the workmen and children. Services were held until 1893, when a new chapel was built, the Co-op lecture hall and workmen's social club having been built in the previous year.

The people of the village lived in back-to-back houses, built in long rows, with no running water, just an outside tap to every ten families, which meant that the tap was a good place for a gossip when you went to fetch water. Often the gossip was finished off over a cup of tea with some neighbour. Firesides were big and were blackleaded once a week. There was a big round oven at one side and a set-pot (for hot water) at the other, with the kettle always boiling on the hob.

When the miner came home from his shift, he would bathe in front of the fire. Some miners would leave a trace of coal dust on their backs because they believed washing weakened the back. Men had their allotments, growing vegetables, prize leeks, onions and tetties (potatoes). They were often pigeon fanciers and breeders, while some kept pigs and chickens. A grand day was when the pig was killed at the bottom of the garden. Black and white pudding and spare ribs were distributed to the neighbours who had helped to feed the pig.

Radcliffe had its own brass band, which practised in the Mechanics' Hall, sometimes called the 'tute'.

Mining was the main employment of the village, which suffered through many strikes, the first one in 1844 when the whole county was on strike. The men were supplanted by miners from Cornwall, known as blacklegs. People were evicted from their houses and camped out from Green Lane to Hope Farm. Miners' wives serenaded the blacklegs with rude and abusive songs which had some good effect, for the second strike which took place in 1847 (over weighing-in) lasted a much shorter time.

Coal from Radcliffe was sent to the harbour at Amble. The colliery was worked until 1892 when a fault was found and new shafts were sunk at Newborough. In 1928 the colliery closed and miners went to nearby collieries. Sadly, in 1930 the passenger train service finished and people relied on the buses.

There were two bus companies in Radcliffe, Longstaff Brothers and Craigs, both serving the community. Longstaff gave film shows – someone would ride around the village on a bicycle spreading the news that there would be a film show that night. If people could afford it they would walk to Amble and take the train to Newcastle, see a show and have change left out of half a crown (two shillings and sixpence).

Gloom fell when war was declared, and, one Sunday night in September of 1942, a land mine struck the village, shattering windows, destroying the chapel of the Good Shepherd, and killing three members of the Craigs family.

There was great celebration when peace came, but rumours of either improving the houses or moving people away from the village started at about that time. However, it was not until 1970 (12th October) that Radcliffe WI entertained the senior citizens, each person receiving a small gift, their last free supper before moving to Amble. In 1971 the villagers bade goodbye to the 'Holy City' of Radcliffe, moving to Amble (and water indoors at the turn of a tap).

Rennington 🌿

From earliest times this has been an agricultural area, for the name Rennington is derived from the Anglo-Saxon – the farm of Regna's people. Until recent years almost the entire population was employed on the farms. In 1618, in addition to Tristram Philipson's farm, there were two freehold and twelve tenement farms. Tenants were bound to plough a 'yoakinge' of the demesne at Alnwick Castle, to bring lime for repairs and straw for the castle stables. They also had to provide two pecks of oats to feed the bailiff's horses, and still, today, most of the village is part of the Duke of Northumberland's estate.

Although there are some new houses, including a small estate on the edge of the village, Rennington has changed little in general plan during the last 300 years. To the south east of the village there stood a wood of oak trees. This part was called Hockwood, a name which is now recognisable in the corrupted form of the Hocket.

The houses, some new, some modernised, are largely grouped around the village green, with the Victorian school, now used as a village hall, in a prominent position, and the earlier, original school converted to a private residence.

Despite, or because of, its peaceful occupation the village suffered much from attacks from Scottish raiders, though it is reported that inertia on the part of the inhabitants encouraged the spoilers to re-visit at frequent intervals.

The present church, dedicated to All Saints, was built in Victorian times, replacing an ancient Norman chapel which was demolished in 1831. The notes and sketches of Rev Hodgson, made in 1825, show that this early church consisted of a nave and chancel, and in 1828 the Archdeacon's visitation revealed that the whole fabric was in an unsatisfactory condition. He called for immediate repairs to the roof, and described the vestments as barely sufficient, the communion vessels as being of base metal, and the books no more than legible. The modern church, begun in 1835, originally had a nave and a tower, but a chancel and north aisle were added 30 years later. The font now in use is early 14th century and came from Embleton church, where the incumbent was the patron of the living at Rennington. The population in those days was around 300, now it is less than half that number.

The Horseshoes public house, built in the 1800s, incorporates the blacksmith's shop, converted to a restaurant. A small post office is the only shop in the village, inhabitants relying on private transport or the once weekly bus service to take them to the local market town of Alnwick.

Rennington was the home of Henry Ogle who, in conjunction with John Common of Denwick, has a strong claim to be the inventor of a reaping machine. Unfortunately the machine was improved and extensively adopted in America, so Ogle gained nothing from his ingenuity and died a pauper in Alnwick workhouse, having been school-master and parish clerk of Rennington for 24 years.

Riding Mill 🦋

The village (Riding meaning a clearing in woodland), population just under 1,000, stands where the March burn enters the river Tyne – six miles from Hexham and 15 miles west of Newcastle. Standing as it does at the convergence of a ford over the Tyne and the old Roman Dere Street, it has been inhabited since time immemorial. The ford and boat crossing was once overlooked by a motte and bailey castle of William Rufus' time – the mound remaining can be seen from the A695, just west of Riding Farm. These crossings were a natural route for the Scots (and English) in their sporadic raiding days and two of the houses, in the part of the village known as Broomhaugh, are based on the old bastles essential for protection of families and stock.

The village was originally based on farms in Broomhaugh, Riding, the Lee and one opposite the mill. This mill, 'Rising Water Corn Mill' (now a private residence), was in use in the 12th century, when it was gifted to the white friars at Blanchland. It was devastated at least four times, with the surrounding habitations, by the Scots, but was finally rebuilt and in regular use by 1565. Opposite the mill is The Wellington public house, which was built in 1600 as a home for Thomas Errington, the Postmaster of Newcastle. It was the scene of remarkable 'happenings' in 1669, culminating in the famous witches' trial at Morpeth, at which they were fortunately acquitted. The alleged witches were reputed to meet at the packhorse bridge, which was built (and still stands) to enable farmers to bring their grain to the mill when the March burn was in flood. After their outdoor meetings the witches were said to retire to The Wellington!

The old village life was changed when the railway was finally built. The station opened in 1835, the main traffic at the time being coal, coke

The mill at Riding Mill

and livestock. However, it also provided easy transport for the industrial magnates of Tyneside, who built most of the large residences of the 19th century. Now unmanned, it is one of the oldest stations and the station house retains its original external appearance, although, today, it is a private residence.

Good communications are still a feature of Riding Mill – the journey to Newcastle takes approximately 25 minutes by train and buses run every half hour into Hexham and Newcastle. Although Riding Mill is now mainly a dormitory village for Newcastle, it still retains its village community spirit. There is a post office and a village shop (where the shopkeeper is the eyes and ears of the village for all needing help of any kind). A cricket field, three tennis courts, attractive village hall, youth centre and first school provide opportunities for all kinds of sport, social clubs and societies. The church and Methodist chapel are both very active in the community and newcomers to the village are always made welcome.

The houses are of varying age and design, both of stone and brick and many are set in cul-de-sacs overlooked by a wonderful variety of trees, some of which are indigenous species. A small area of ancient woodland, by the old mill weir, is publicly owned. The March burn, which meanders through the village to join the Tyne, is a delightful feature and encourages a variety of wildlife, including herons, otters, red squirrels and many species of birds.

Rochester 🦌

Ro(w)chester, not to be confused with Rochester in Kent where the mail goes if it is not correctly addressed, is in Upper Redesdale, about ten miles south of the border with Scotland. It is a linear village straddling the A68, houses on one side, gardens, coalhouses and erstwhile netties on the other. The village has a hall, filling station/post office, café/grocery store, a United Reformed church, a parish church at Horsley half a mile down the road, a football team, and it hosts the annual Upper Redesdale Show on the last Saturday in September.

Rochester really consists of three separate little communities together with the farms in the immediate area. Until the mid 19th century the original village and the green were higher up the hill, inside the ruins of a Roman fort. However, around 1849, after a new road linking Newcastle and Jedburgh (the A696/A68) had been constructed through the valley, the then Lord Redesdale built a row of cottages and a school for his tenants along this road which has since become a busy trunk route. The name Rochester was adopted by this larger community; the old village on the hill fell into decline and became known as High Rochester. Finally in the 1950s a few prefabricated houses were built 'up the back road' between the other two settlements. These were replaced in 1989 by more attractive stone-built semi-detached bungalows and houses.

Most travellers on the main road today barely have time to register the name of Rochester before they're through. But there's a stark beauty about the surrounding hills and a wealth of fascinating history. For centuries this was frontier country. Two thousand years ago, the armies of Imperial Rome came to this wilderness and built a fort to guard troops, messengers and traders who travelled along Dere Street, the main road between York and Inverness. The Romans called this outpost Bremenium, the place of the roaring stream; for 200 years it was the most northerly occupied fort in the whole of the Roman Empire. When the empire collapsed and the garrison withdrew, the local population moved in. The fort walls provided security and the internal buildings a good supply of stone for cottages. In later centuries stone from the fort walls and gateways was used to build field walls, the porch in Lord Redesdale's school and new cottages, one of which has a recycled Roman altar built into the main wall!

In the turbulent years before the union of the Crowns in 1603, this area was in a state of constant unrest. The opposing armies of England and Scotland swarmed over the countryside and rival families on both sides of the Border took advantage of the situation to settle old scores and indulge in 'a little shifting' for their living. Shifting or reiving (stealing) involved cattle rustling on a massive scale and the theft of any property that wasn't firmly attached to the ground. In 1581 the villagers of Rochester lodged a complaint with Elizabeth I's commissioners against the Elliots of Liddesdale, whom it was claimed had attacked on several occasions, 'taking kye and oxen, goates, sheep and household stuff, so that the town has laid waste for five years.' To defend their possessions against the reivers, the Borderers were advised to build bastles (defensible farmhouses) which had thick stone walls and strong doors protected by an iron yett (gate). High Rochester has two bastles, both occupied.

The hills around Rochester still echo to the sound of military men. Behind the village is the Redesdale army camp. In 1911, Winston Churchill, Secretary for War, visited the area as a guest of Lord Redesdale to hunt, shoot and fish. But the weather was so awful and the sport so poor that Churchill is reputed to have said that the only use for this area was as an artillery range. So the War Office bought 19,000 acres of land for the newly-formed Territorial Army. Today British and NATO forces train over the same ground as their counterparts from Belgium, Eastern France, Spain, Portugal and Yugoslavia did 2,000 years ago, and armoured vehicles rumble up Dere Street where once there were chariots and cavalry.

Apart from Churchill, the only other visitor of note to Rochester was Elizabeth I's historian William Camden, who came to see the Roman remains during his tour of England in the late 16th century. In the early 1850s, under the direction of Dr John Collingwood Bruce, the Newcastle Society of Antiquaries excavated much of the fort, which was owned by the Duke of Northumberland. At the same time the Duke's land agent William Coulson, who was also the local Excise man, excavated the Roman tombs nearby. Further work was carried out in the 1930s and 1980s and currently a five year training programme has been initiated for students from Newcastle University.

In Coulson's day, long before the advent of the car and public transport which enabled people to leave their villages, Rochester supported five shopkeepers, three shoemakers, a butcher and a police constable. In 1923 when Winifred Foreman came from Ashington as a pupil teacher, there were 39 children in Rochester school. Forty years later when the school was closed, she and her pupils moved to Otterburn school five miles down the valley. Rochester children are still taught at Otterburn, middle school pupils have to travel twelve miles to Bellingham, high school pupils board weekly at Haydon Bridge, 35 miles away.

In more recent years as road links have improved and people have become accustomed to using their own transport, there is less need for reliance on village services, although travelling shops still come regularly. Community activities continue to thrive. At the centre of village life is the village hall, the venue for Halloween and Christmas parties for the children, coming-of-age parties, dances, whist drives and the WI. In addition there are regular outings to theatres and to the seaside and Bonfire Night is always a popular occasion.

Roddam 🦡

The hamlets comprising Ilderton parish, of which Roddam is the southernmost one, are strung out like beads along the eastern edge of the Northumberland National Park and the Cheviot Hills, around the great massif of Hedgehope Hill. The road that strings them together is the old or original road and even today one can easily trace its path, for this was the life-blood of the community for centuries, along which the drovers and carters, travelling north or south, would slowly wend their way, greeting householders and other travellers as they passed by. Contrast this with the relatively new road, the A697, with its hustling cars and lorries greeting no one in their sole aim of reaching their journey's end as quickly as possible.

Mechanisation and the growing of more corn have diminished the need for workers and hence reduced the need for schools and local services. Gone are local schools such as Roddam, post offices such as Wooperton and stores, but thankfully still in use is the parish church of Ilderton and its meeting hall. Here meet the worshippers after morning service and the small youth club. Roddam has its lively WI which has now found refuge in a one-time tack room above the stable at the hall. Every family has need of a car and it is to towns that people must go to obtain their provisions and amusements. Thankfully television and electricity are boons that alleviate the tedium of the long, dark nights of long ago.

But this quiet way of life is now being sought by town and city dwellers, with empty farm cottages in great demand, and looming on the perimeter is the ever-growing caravan site at Wooler. The hamlet of Roseden at one time consisted of 14 houses with a population of 60 people and was held by the Ilderton family. A stone above the doorway of Roseden House bears the arms of Ilderton/Cross, the original house being built by George Ilderton who married Margaret Cross in 1665. Today Roseden boasts a popular tea room managed by Mrs Walton, the farmer's wife, whose husband is a noted breeder of Suffolk sheep.

The Roddam family, one of the oldest in Northumberland dating from 1279, has left the area. Lord Vinson, the present landowner who lives in Roddam Hall, has an indenture bearing instructions from the government of the day addressed to Admiral Roddam stating what had to be done if Napoleon invaded from the coast. To make the hall more amenable to modern living Lord Vinson has had the top storey removed from the building.

Those who remain of the famous Collingwood family no longer run the large estate centred on Lilburn Towers. Their place has been taken by the Davidson family. Duncan Davidson is the power behind the Persimmon building firm and he is, with the acquisition of estates like North and South Middleton, Ilderton, Commonburn and South Hazelrigg, one of the largest landowners in the north and farms the estates from a central office at North Middleton House. The owner of the Middleton Hall estate, Austen Kirkup, was killed in a road accident but the name remains with the ownership passing to his nephew John Kirkup. His uncle was a great authority on trees and the tree clad slopes of Happy Valley are a living testimony to his expertise. Each year hundreds of hikers enjoy this, the prettiest of the Cheviot valleys.

The Wooperton estate, where at one time there was a chapel of ease, is now owned by Miss Stanton. In the 1950s 500 couple of rabbits were sent weekly to Newcastle market. Sufficient income was derived from their sale to pay the tenant's rent.

One can still see the remains of supports of three railway bridges washed away in the disastrous flood of 1948, and the buildings at Ilderton station are being converted into a restaurant.

The great outdoor event of the year is the Glendale Show held on land near Surrey House. It now attracts up to 10,000 people, so much so that the speed of the cars along the A697 for one day approximates to that of centuries past.

Rothbury

The village of Rothbury lies in the valley of the river Coquet, about halfway between its source in the Cheviot Hills and the sea. It consists essentially of three streets: Front Street, High Street and Bridge Street. The first two run parallel with the river on its northern bank and the latter leads at right angles from Town Foot to the river.

Front Street is lined with houses on the southern side, looking across the river to the Simonside hills beyond, while the shops are on the northern side of the High Street. Between the two lies the gently sloping strip of the green, shaded by chestnut, oak, sycamore and beech trees. The parish church lies in the angle between these two streets and Bridge Street, at the south eastern corner of what was the market place, where the market cross once stood but which is now another green triangle edged with pink and white cherry trees. In whatever direction you look, the grey roofs of the village are outlined against a background of hills.

The village is very old, as shown by the Saxon derivation of its name, and the church is an ancient foundation, though almost entirely rebuilt in 1850. Its Saxon origin is attested by the remains of an 8th century Northumbrian stone cross, part of which now forms the base of the font. Life in the valley was hard, and Coquetdale was inevitably subject to Border raids. It has its defensive castles and pele towers, and the 14th century pele at Whitton, across the river, was for many years the home of the rectors of Rothbury. As late as the 18th century, the village was described as little more than a church, an inn and a cluster of mean cottages thatched with heather.

Nevertheless, as times became more peaceful and farming improved, it was the natural market place for upper Coquetdale, to which cattle and sheep were driven for sale, and where their drovers were provided with a great many public houses and the services of various tradesmen. The cattle mart remains of some importance, and Rothbury is also a centre for banking, with good shops for country clothes, shoes, ironmongery and food. Here also are the middle school for children aged nine to 13 and the cottage hospital which serves all Coquetdale and beyond.

Rothbury began to grow rapidly after 1865 when Sir William Armstrong, the wealthy owner of engineering works in Newcastle, bought 900 acres of the Debden valley to the north to build himself a house and estate which he called Cragside. From 1870 to 1885 he employed Norman Shaw to extend the house and make it suitable to entertain royalty and many other wealthy guests. He planted thousands of trees and shrubs and employed members of most of the village families in the house or estate. An ingenious practical engineer himself, he organised various pieces of hydraulic apparatus for the house, and with his friend Joseph Swan installed the earliest domestic electric lights, generated by water power from the three lakes in the grounds. When the railway reached the village in 1870, largely at his instigation, Rothbury felt it was finally on the map. These were its great days, now remembered by local families.

The Armstrong family lived at Cragside for four generations, but in 1977 the estate was acquired by the National Trust. It was then in a fairly dilapidated condition, but the Trust restored the house ready for opening to the public in 1979. They are still at work managing the woodland and restoring the Victorian pleasure gardens and extensive glasshouses. Nowadays more than 85,000 people visit the house annually, especially when the rhododendrons are in flower.

Since the mid 19th century Rothbury has been a holiday resort for walkers and fishermen; there was even a race course, which is now converted into a nine hole golf course, and although the railway was closed in 1952 the village is still full of visitors in the summer. They are well provided with country hotels, cafés, guest houses, bed and breakfast accommodation and three caravan sites. In July there is a festival of folk music which is very popular, especially with local musicians – fiddlers and players on the Northumbrian pipes, who are known even beyond Northumberland. Interests and hobbies are well provided for in many other directions; apart from the adult education classes in subjects as diverse as languages, stick dressing and lace-making, there are dozens of clubs, such as the Photographic Society, the bowling club, the youth club, the over sixties club and the Local History Society. The Jubilee Hall is in use every night of the week and every Saturday for coffee mornings and jumble sales in aid of various charities.

Of course, the village has grown with new houses occupied by 'incomers', many retired people or commuters from Morpeth or even Newcastle, so that the population now numbers about 2,000. But it is still surrounded by unspoilt country and hill farms; many of the old families are still here and you can still hear the shopkeepers address their customers by their Christian names. There is a strong underlying current of continuity and all who are fortunate enough to live here respect and share the local feeling of pride and loyalty to the village.

Seahouses 🍃

In 1820 North Sunderland was recorded as a considerable maritime village, with 560 inhabitants. There were dark days in the history of North Sunderland when, in 1832, there was an outbreak of cholera. In contrast, however, the district basked in the glare of publicity following the heroic lifesaving deeds of Grace Darling, in 1838.

In more recent times the name Seahouses has taken over in preference to North Sunderland, deriving its name from the days when the 'sea houses' of North Sunderland were little more than a cluster of fishermen's homes nearer the shore. There has been a harbour here since 1318, if not earlier. Possibly little more than a sheltered creek originally, it has always been known as North Sunderland Harbour.

Boats sail from here to the Farne Islands, visiting the Inner Farne where St Cuthbert lived until the time of his death in AD 687. There is a small building on the island called St Cuthbert's chapel, supposedly built on the site of his hermitage. You can also land on Staple Island, and on the Longstone, where Grace Darling lived. The Farne Islands

Seahouses

are one of the most famous breeding sites for sea birds in the British Isles, and along with miles of sandy beaches and historic castles nearby, attract many people to this area.

Seahouses once had its own tiny railway, with a station adjacent to the harbour. Two small steam engines used to carry passengers and fish from Seahouses to connect with the main line trains at Chathill. It was said that a passenger had time to get out and pick daisies and catch up his carriage again with ease. This service was discontinued soon after the war, and a large caravan site now stands on the site of the old station.

In summertime the harbour would be a hive of activity as the herring fleet worked its way around the coast, and fishing was the livelihood of many families in the village. Pleasure craft and 'trip' boats now outnumber the fishing boats, and the old fishing village has become more of a holiday resort.

Seaton Delaval 🐟

The village of Seaton Delaval, originally a hamlet, had its origins after the Norman Conquest when William the Conqueror allotted these lands to the De La Val family. For many years agriculture was the only industry in the area, along with a little mining for coal, dug by hand by local monks. The outline of these old mine shafts can still be seen from the air.

A population explosion occurred in the 1830s when deep mine shafts were sunk and miners arrived from many areas including Ireland, Cornwall and Norfolk. Long rows of pit cottages were built to house the miners and their families and this was soon followed by the building of churches, schools, public houses, a miners' institute and general village amenities. The main 'shopping centre' of the village, as in many other mining villages, was the local Co-operative Society which catered specifically for a working class population. With the advent of the railways a railway station was built which linked Seaton Delaval with nearby villages and the towns of Newcastle and Blyth.

In the 1950s mines in the Seaton Delaval area became exhausted and were closed, throwing many men out of work. Fortunately at about the same time new factories were built in the nearby village of Cramlington and this absorbed much of the unemployment. It was amazing how men who had spent all their working lives below ground in the mines quickly became familiar and competent in factory routine and procedure.

Coincident with the closing of the mines the old pit cottages which were rapidly falling into decay were demolished and this meant a huge rehousing programme. Over a period of time a large new housing estate was built linking Seaton Delaval with the adjacent village of Holywell. Although much of this estate consists of council housing there is an intermingling of private houses which has resulted in an influx of newcomers to the village.

The village today has no focal point in so far as employment is concerned. The biggest employer is probably a local cosmetic factory which employs mainly female labour. Most people have to travel to their employment ie to factory work in nearby villages, to Tyneside and to the busy town of Newcastle. The big employers of the past, mining and shipbuilding, have gone and farming, which employed so many, is now largely mechanised.

The general amenities of the village are adequate for the needs of the population ie a United Reformed church; branch library; three schools catering for various age groups up to the age of 18 years; a community centre which caters mainly for an amateur dramatic society, Women's Institutes and dancing; evening classes held in the high school; and a park containing bowling green, tennis court and children's playground.

Perhaps the main feature and centrepiece of the village is Delaval Hall, home of the Delavals since the time of William the Conqueror. The latest hall, which is approached from the village by a mile-long avenue of trees, was built in the 18th century by Vanburgh. It is lived in by Lord Hastings and family, descendants in the female line from the Delavals. Nearby is the parish church of Our Lady built in 1102 and once the private family church of the Delavals.

Seaton Sluice

Situated on the north east coast, the village is in the barony of Delaval, Sir Ralph Delaval being created a baronet by George III. The village of Seaton Sluice has a very picturesque harbour, once known as Hartley Haven, rivalling Blyth in importance with regards to seagoing commerce. Around this harbour most of the dwellings were situated at that time, on the south side of the Seaton burn.

The name Seaton Sluice came into being after the building of sluice gates in 1690, the purpose of these being at high tide to trap the waters upstream, then at low tide they were lowered to sluice out the sands and prevent silting up of the harbour.

With the increase in trade, Lord Delaval prepared plans for a new harbour or dock and resolved to make a new entrance eastward through solid rock with dock gates at both ends. This provided not only an additional entrance to the harbour but also a deep-water dock where vessels could be loaded at any state of the tide. Lord Delaval's brother Thomas, who had received training in Hamburg, came over and supervised the cutting of the rock by hewing and splitting with burnt lime. The north entrance was used in stormy weather and the 'new cut' or south entrance in moderate weather. This 17th century engineering scheme cost £10,000 in those days and to this day is unique, with recognisable remains of the work still visible at low tide.

The village was also known as Hartley Pans, due to the salt making industry. Salt was produced at the mouth of the burn from as early as 1236, the sea water being evaporated in huge pans heated by coal fires. This industry continued for centuries and it was only due to the levying of heavy excise taxes on salt that the industry died out. By 1798 the shipping of white salt ended, though salt continued to be made for a few more years with the pans closing down in the early 1820s. (Salt used to be smuggled to North Shields and sold by the locals.)

For 200 years this small village was a hive of industry – salt, glass, copperas, beer, pit winding-engines and ships were all part of the lives of the residents.

The manufacture of glass was established by Thomas Delaval. He realised that all the raw materials necessary were readily available in this part of the coast, so with the aid of an Act of Parliament and his brother Sir Francis Blake Delaval, the glassworks were built; to this day pieces of Seaton Sluice glass can be found along the bank of the burn.

The bottles manufactured at the works were sent down to the harbour to be loaded onto vessels via a subway on trolleys running on one of the first iron 'rail-ways'. Loading the still warm bottles was very hard work and the loaders were given ale to quench their thirst from one of the six alehouses situated on the harbour banks. Each alehouse was named for a day of the week, and the women who carried the ale to the workers obtained their supplies from the alehouse named for that particular day.

Near the glassworks offices in Glasshouse Square stood the old granary and it was from the steps of this building that John Wesley preached to the good people of Seaton Sluice in 1744.

One of the more romantic pieces of folklore concerns the building of the castle. Sir Francis Delaval took a wager that within 24 hours he could build a castle suitable for a lady to dwell in. The result was that Sir Francis won his wager and Stirling Castle (locally known as Starlight Castle) became the wonder and admiration of all visitors. The ruins can still be seen in Holywell Dene.

Today the harbour is a haven for the many small fishing vessels of the local community, whilst still retaining much of its historical character. This quiet residential village boasts a beautiful wide sandy beach stretching three miles to Blyth on the north side, on the south side the two picturesque bays of Collywell and Hartley, and on the west and inland side of the village the Seaton burn, which winds its way past the old site of Seaton Lodge, the home of Sir John Delaval, who claimed that it was the finest thatched house in the kingdom. The burn continues past the remains of the ruins of Stirling Castle and the now extinct village of Gouldens Hole towards the neighbouring village of Holywell.

Sheepwash & Stakeford 🐑

Cleaswell was a hill farm contained within Choppington ecclesiastical parish, formed on 5th September 1893. The farm overlooked Sheepwash village and the river Wansbeck.

The Ogle family, who owned nearby Bothal Castle, established a farm on Cleaswell Hill in the late 14th century. The name Cleaswell is probably a corruption of the word 'twyzel' or 'tuysil', both derived from the Saxon word 'twisla' which means a tongue of land between rivers.

Early in the 20th century the farm was taken over by Ernest Wheatley and his brother Henry. Ernest lived at the farm with his family, and Henry lived in Sheepwash. The Cleaswell Hill farmhouse at this time was a substantial stone building with a hind's house attached to one end. In front was a large garden and pond – the cause of dampness experienced by the modern owners of the site, at least in the early days of the house.

The farm fields extended to the river Wansbeck. In a hand-drawn map of 1788 there were very few buildings marked. Cleaswell Hill, Whinny Hill Farm at Scotland Gate, a public house at Guide Post, and the East Bank House farm, where the Half Moon Inn is at Stakeford. There, fields rejoiced under the names of Ewe Close, Budy Gap, Clay Banks, Little Close and Earthquake field.

The back of the house overlooked the edge of the hill, so there was no back garden. Next to the farm and hind's cottage was a water tower which was a reservoir for water from the river, and supplied water to the railways. This was dismantled in the last 25 years.

At the end of the hind's cottage, a path turned at right angles down a very steep and rough path, down to Sheepwash in the valley below. This track, very rough, overgrown, and largely unused still exists. Harold, Robert and Norman, sons of the family, climbed the track every morning before school and every evening after school to collect the milk, and do their milk round at Sheepwash. They did this winter and summer, in the dark and carrying no lights. The milk was in three gill cans, although not always full, depending on the needs of the families they were being delivered to. This milk was fresh and untreated.

Sheepwash, to which the track from Cleaswell dropped, has its origins a long way back. It was a river crossing from earliest times and of some importance. By 1379 it had a church and a hospice. Hospices were commonly built for the benefit of travellers, often at the end of bridges or by washes, a shallow or fordable part of the river. James VI of Scotland crossed there on his journey to claim his throne in London in 1603. By 1764 the hospice had completely disappeared.

A bridge, first mentioned in 1735, was destroyed by a flood in 1894. There is now a modern, small bridge, overlooked by Cleaswell Farm. Beside it was a mill of ancient origin, which in 1635 was paying rent to the Church at Durham. This was demolished in 1973, although the mill house still stands. It was beside the mill that the pumping station for the water tower at Cleaswell stood. There were, right at the river's edge, two cottages for the men who worked the station, Bill Brown and Tommy Graham.

On the north side of the river stood a fine old house, the rectory which was used by the clergy from Bothal village, two miles distant over the fields. Local legend has it that a tunnel runs underground from the rectory to Bothal Castle. The former rectory, privately owned for some years, has fallen into disrepair. Opposite the rectory was the glebe farm belonging to Bothal. It was demolished for modern housing and only an old dovecote remains.

Pancake Row was a street of six houses beside The Anglers Arms. This was called after the Pancake Well which supplied Sheepwash and Guide Post with water. The houses were one up, one down in which whole families lived. The top house was also a tiny shop selling sweets and tobacco. Pancake Row has gone. Its site is a green maintained by the council and a wide road leading up to the estates.

Cleaswell Hill Farm was sold by the Wheatleys to the Whites, and then to Leech and Bell, two building firms, in 1950. The Wansbeck estates were built over the farm site and covered most of its fields, yet it is known as Stakeford, the village name, not that of the farm.

Cleaswell Lonnen was the track from the main road between the old villages of Guide Post and Stakeford up to Cleaswell Hill Farm. This is now a modern road through the estate called Wansbeck Avenue. The dreadful bend at Ashington Drive, Cleaswell Hill corner, echoes field boundaries of 1788. These, and the name Cleaswell Hill as a road name through the estate to Guide Post, and the track behind the farm, and the almost lost track to Sheepwash, are about all that remains of the past.

Shilbottle

Shilbottle is situated four miles south of the ducal town of Alnwick and three miles from the sea. Vikings and other settlers called it home, then came the Normans, whose mark can still be seen on the beautiful little church which was rebuilt in 1875. Care was taken to preserve the original Norman arch and two small windows. There is also a fine 14th century pele tower which was converted into a vicarage during the Reformation. It was renovated by the then vicar in 1864.

The main providers of work were agriculture, lime works, quarrying and drift mining for coal. A deep mine was sunk in 1921 to extract coal from the rich seams under the area. So good was the quality, it has even been delivered to Buckingham Palace. New houses and roads extended the village as the population increased.

A thriving community, it supported a football team and a cricket team which, along with the annual flower show, are still going strong today, with the addition of an indoor bowling club. The successful twinning with Hery in France, which began in the 1960s, has brought a new interest with alternate visits.

The old custom of holding a feast week where there were games and parades for the children, sports and comic football for the adults, has sadly gone, along with others that are only talked about by older members of the community. One custom that has survived is performed after a wedding. The bride is helped to jump over a stool (petting stool) when the couple emerge through the church gates – for good luck!

Up to the coming of the superstore most shopping was done in the village, which had a post office/shop, butcher, newsagent (which sported a petrol pump on the forecourt) and a Co-op store. Alas! none of these, apart from the post office have survived, but memories of divi-day at the Co-op still linger. However, in recent years, new businesses have flourished. The village now has a 'chippy', a general dealer's-cum-newsagent and a small garden centre on the old colliery site.

The elderly have been well catered for. Nowadays, the village has two additional sheltered schemes, plus a drop-in centre organised by the CRI and the Red Cross. The change in the education system has meant losing the old C of E school, leaving a county first school for children up to nine years. The school is also a base for a youth club, playschool and adult education.

The colliery was closed by the NCB in 1982 and other means of employment had to be found. As property was sold off by the NCB, new people have come in and others have bought land to build their houses. This means more people choose to commute to jobs outside the area, rather than leave the village. Some have come back to their roots to retire. Again, as in the past, the influx of new people has been absorbed into the village, bringing ideas and participation in the life of the community and the church.

Shilbottle can be said to be an ordinary village in its lifestyle, but not ordinarily situated, on rising ground up to the Beacon Hill (approximately 500 feet above sea level) on which bonfires could be lit to warn of Napoleonic invaders. It commands a view of the sea, Coquet Island with its lighthouse, Warkworth Castle, the river Coquet with its marina, and at the river mouth, the fishing port of Amble. Looking west, the view over the Cheviot Hills is something a visitor will never forget. Other castles and historic houses are near, the Farne Islands and Holy Island are but a few miles up the coast. This brings visitors to the village using the holiday accommodation now available.

Shotley 🎐

Steeped in history, the parish of Shotley Low Quarter is set in an area of outstanding natural beauty. English Heritage, conservationists, wildlife experts, scientists, photographers and antiquarians beat a path to its boundaries to learn, research and simply enjoy and admire. Yes, it is a joy to live here and the people of Shotley are proud to do so. This scattered, mainly farming community consists of two wards:

Shotley and Whittonstall. Shotley does not boast a village but lays claim to fame in being mentioned in David Bellamy's book *England's Last Wilderness*. Part of the Derwent reservoir is in Shotley, giving opportunities for sailing and trout fishing. The views of the Derwent valley are breathtaking. Perhaps the lack of a village strengthens the vigorous community spirit which prevails.

By the Derwent river are ancient stones which form the southern boundary. A previous parish council, led by its then chairman, Edwin Taylor, an internationally known dowser, fought Whitehall mandarins successfully to retain this historically important boundary in the teeth of Government changes. The whole community made its views known and prevented the threatened closure of Whittonstall school.

The general meeting place and metaphorical 'parish pump' is St John's church hall situated at Snods Edge, which means the edge of the snow. This hall, winner of several awards, is the envy of neighbouring parishes being beautifully and comprehensively furnished and equipped for everything from wedding receptions, dances, fairs, shows and exhibitions to meetings of the numerous clubs and societies, not forgetting the parish and parochial church councils, fulfilling the needs of all ages and interests. It is a tribute to the combined efforts of local organisations, giving practical and financial help for the common good. An annual trade fair at the hall attracts small businesses, craftspeople and visitors from far afield. During the summer months there is an annual art exhibition and Sunday teas are available offering reasonably priced, delicious food to appreciative visitors. Enterprising residents provide bed and breakfast accommodation in addition to the Manor House Inn and the Royal Derwent Hotel for the growing number of holidaymakers.

Jane Frizel lived at Crooked Oak Farm in the 17th century and was tried for witchcraft at Hexham assizes. Alas, she was hanged for the sin of bewitching local farmers. Talking of Crooked Oak, there is a wild and hauntingly beautiful place close by called the Sneep, which has strange rock formations in the river Derwent. Legend has it that one day King Arthur will be enthroned there again in the company of his Knights of the Round Table.

As one would expect, there were lead mines at nearby Leadmill bordering the river and a footbridge there crosses the river into County Durham. A charming story exists that the hamlet of Grey Mare Hill, which contains St Andrew's church, is named after the grey mare ridden by the luckless but dashing Earl of Derwentwater in the Jacobite rebellion of 1715.

Shotley Field contains, probably, the smallest cemetery in the country, comprising one grave and tombstone. When there were Border troubles, Shotley was a happy hunting ground for the Border raiders. Because of rich grazing land, cattle was worth stealing. The common of the barony of John de Bolbeck was added to Shotley in the 18th century and now the hamlet of Bullbeck adjoins Washpool Lane. Long ago there was a stage coach to Edinburgh and travellers could ford the river at Allen's Ford, Eddis Bridge and Ratchwood Ford. Water abounds; Shotley burn flows through the grounds of Shotley Hall, which was the home of the Walton-Wilson family, antecedents of the present Martell family.

The spiritual soul of Shotley is the 19th century St John's church complete with churchyard, lychgate and mounting blocks for riders and, of course, the church hall with its adjoining tennis court and sports field is a hive of activity. There are no shops now in Shotley but local people and visitors are well served by the Manor House service station and the Manor House Inn near Carterway Heads. The inn is set against panoramic views and offers the comforts of a traditional country public house with real ale plus cordon bleu cooking. Summer is long gone when we see the flash of bright pink coats, hear the hounds in full cry and we know the Braes of Derwent Hunt is following the chase.

Redundant farm buildings have been converted to houses and the new merges with the old. Newcomers are given a warm welcome to Shotley. In return they are wise enough to appreciate and respect traditional country values which still flourish.

Simonburn

The name suggests there would be a Simon burn – not so! The village is believed to take its name from one Simon de Burgh, altered over the years to Simonburn.

An original village was sited at Nunwick approximately half a mile away. This was demolished about 200 years ago by the owner, Mr Allgood, who decided to landscape the gardens at Nunwick and moved the village to its position today, close to the church. It is still largely owned by a Mr Allgood. Two hundred years has proved long enough for the village to blend gracefully into the landscape, sheltered by mature chestnut, oak and lime trees, which border the green, churchyard and fields.

The ancient 13th century church of St Mungo lies at the south west corner of the green. The parish of Simonburn was the largest in England, stretching from Carter Bar and the Scottish border to the Roman wall, containing some 50 villages. A survey dated 1522 stated: 'All the countye of Tynedale is in the Parish of Symondburne and there standeth the Parish Church thereof.' As the mother church of such an enormous parish, St Mungo's is impressive, of great historical interest and stocked with surprises.

The church is approached through a handsome lychgate built by tenants in memory of John Hunter Allgood in 1885. It is one of the finest in the county. The rectory close to the church was built in 1666 with a fine three-storey front added in about 1725. It is now a private residence. A small tithe barn at the end of the village is also privately owned.

The green is flanked by stone cottages, including what used to be the Red Lion Inn and its three cottages, built in 1702. Along from the churchyard is Rectory Terrace, once a large tithe barn bearing the date 1813. A blocked archway can be traced on the front of the building. Presumably the date refers to alterations. The village shop/post office and Mains Cottages are just off the green. The shop supplies a comprehensive range of goods.

In 1857 land was made available to the Church of England to build a school for the education of 'children of the labouring, manufacturing or other poorer classes in the said parish.' This school closed in 1964 and is used now as a village hall, offering a range of activities.

No further building has taken place and the village itself is largely unchanged. It remains a secluded, peaceful retreat in the North Tyne valley.

Slaley 🐚

Slaley, meaning 'a muddy clearing', is a parish of 7,500 acres with a central village of the same name, lying near the southern border of Northumberland. Belonging to the barony of Bolbeck in the 12th century, the southern portion was known as Bolbeck Common, being waste moorland, swampy and full of bracken. The parishioners had the use of its rough grass for grazing their own stock, the peat and brushwood they used for heating. By the 15th century the Earl of Westmorland, Sir Ralf Nevile, held the barony and he built a fortified farmhouse at Shield Hall, one wall of which is still visible today.

The parish has many signs of old disused quarries. Ladycross sandstone quarry still operates and produces excellent building and ornamental stone for the UK and the occasional export order. There are 19 burns ·running through the parish, which gave a plentiful supply of power before the introduction of steam. A water wheel drove the machinery at Dukesfield refinery and smelt mill, whilst others drove the several recorded corn mills.

Local highway names tell of bygone days. Mill Lane led to the corn, flax and fuller's mill, Coal Road to the many coal deposits used freely by inhabitants in previous centuries. Lead Road was a track used by drovers and their Galloway ponies carrying packs of lead from Dukesfield smelt mill to Gateshead, Drove Road was a track used for driven cattle between the Midlands and Scotland. Wooley Hospital Road led to the hospital built in 1916 for soldiers suffering from gas poisoning. By 1923 it was treating tuberculosis patients and by 1963 had taken on the care of the elderly, finally closing in 1980. The wards were dismantled and a private house now stands on the site.

The parish has always been primarily involved in agriculture, and many estates controlled the farmland. Today almost every farm is privately owned. The last estate in the parish, Slaley Hall estate was sold in 1985, a portion of which is now a golf course.

The church of St Mary the Virgin was rebuilt in 1832 on the site of the former 13th century Saxon church. In 1921 the lychgate was erected and the churchyard contains what is believed to be one of the oldest outside gravestones in Northumberland, dated 1635. A new Methodist chapel was built in 1900.

The village itself is a 'street', made up of buildings on both sides of the road, with a slight bend making it impossible to see from one end to the other. An old village water pump still stands in the village centre, while outlying wells and water troughs are also to be seen.

Census returns for the parish show many changes in the number of dwellings and people, the earliest in 1841 recording 45 dwellings in the village and the majority of occupations as agricultural labourers, stonemasons, thatchers, smelters and 'paupers'. The 1891 record shows 29 village dwellings and occupations of butchers, tailors, grocers, carriers, farmers, the postmaster and the headmaster. Since the Second World War there has been an increase in housing, including twelve council houses and twelve pensioners' bungalows. The present number of dwellings stands at 102, several of which are farm building conversions, and today almost everyone is employed outside the parish or in retirement. Tourism has grown over the past quarter century and the parish now boasts two caravan parks, several bed and breakfast establishments and cottages for self-catering holidays.

Sleekburn 🦡

Sleekburn began as a colliery village. The 'Old Pit' was sunk within easy reach of the river Blyth near where the Slakeburn ran into it – hence the name Slakeburn, which gradually changed to Sleekburn over the years.

Gradually streets of houses for the miners were built around the pit area. Eventually a miners' institute, a school, a Co-op, the YMCA, and in 1884 the colliery chapel, were all built, enlarging the village.

At first coals were carried on a waggon-way to Granary Point on the river Blyth, but later a railway line was laid and a station was built to carry the coals to the Tyne instead. Now Sleekburn is often referred to as Bedlington station.

As the village grew, several businesses were set up in the area such as a brickworks, a candleworks, a famous ironworks and a mineral water factory. The ironworks made railway lines for George Stephenson's *Rocket*, one of the first railway engines. Three small villages in the area became part of Sleekburn. They were East Sleekburn, Red Row and Bank Top.

The community went on thriving for many years, until the businesses began to close and eventually the 'Old Pit' was closed down in the early 1970s.

Stamfordham 🦡

The village of Stamfordham has seen many changes over the years, not the least of these being in its name. History records it in 1298 as Stanfordham, which had altered over the next 150 years to Stanwardame. From there we read of Stanerden, then Stannerton Town, finishing up 700 years later almost as it began.

This is a very attractive village, with a village green still separating the north and south sides. Stamfordham has always been an agricultural village with, until about 50 years ago, everyone living in it being involved with farming in one way or another. It has also seen its share of history. The Anglican church has looked down on many changes as major families of the district fought and feuded with each other and the Scots came on regular raids.

By 1715 the old Red Lion Inn, situated where the village store and post office now stands, had become very popular with the gentry of Northumberland, with the Earl of Derwentwater a regular visitor – this was one of the 'hot spots' in the Jacobite uprising. Twenty years on and we find the old market cross, erected by Sir John Swinburne, Bart. This was the focal point of the market where the local farmers drove their cattle and sheep to be sold before the days of cattle waggons, and for 200 years cattle could be seen on the green. Two fairs were held yearly as were the local 'hirings', one for hinds and one for unmarried servants. The board with all the details now hangs in the village hall.

The old gaol at the east end of the village was built following a meeting in The Bay Horse in 1838. The record tells us that 'Sir John Swinburne was insulted by a person. The constable was called upon, to take that person up but he had no place to put him. Sir John called the attention of the magistrates present to the necessity of a lock-up being built and offered the land and stone for the same.'

This is about the same time as we read of some of the cottages being 'let to a low class of tenant, Irish drainers, small hawkers and the like.' Houses in the village were let at between three shillings and twelve shillings a year, while the rent of two farms is given as three pounds of pepper per annum.

This is the period when the village was in its heyday as a centre of commerce, with its own brewery and seven public houses and spirit stores as well as two banks, but with the advent of motorised transport the fairs stopped and trade moved away, so that now we are left with only The Bay Horse and The Swinburne Arms while both the banks are now private houses.

The church tower dates back more than 800 years while the rest of the church was rebuilt in 1849. A son of the vicarage, Sir Arthur Bigge, later became Lord Stamfordham as a reward for his services to the king. The United Reformed church, at the east end of the village, is unusual in that it is one of the few churches without a gable end of its own as it stands in a street. Among the many ministers was the Rev William Fisken (1847–1884) who gained fame as the inventor of the steam plough as well as of a mechanical potato planter. He is buried in the churchyard.

The Roman Catholic church is situated within Cheeseburn Grange, a legacy of the persecutions, while on the south side of the village across the road from the old gaol, the Methodist church stands. This church and the URC have held joint services for more than 50 years, with the meetings alternating between the two buildings.

The original school in the village was endowed by Sir Thomas Widdrington in 1663. Education was free to the children of the poor of the village. To ensure the continuation of the trust a farm was also given. Although the original school is now a private house, the trust is still in existence. The old Catholic school at the eastern entrance to the village is now a store while over the road the old smithy is now a garage.

When the school built to replace Sir Thomas Widdrington's gift became redundant about 20 years ago it was replaced by a modern building. However, it was purchased by the people of the village and is now the heart of the community since it was converted to the village hall.

Although the village has doubled in size over the last 50 years the character of the village has remained essentially the same, in spite of the fact that agriculture is now only of minor importance. Gone are the auctioneer, the saddler and the veterinary surgeon while the slaughterhouses are closed along with the butcher's shop and the brewery. While almost all of those who have replaced them work outside the area, most take an active part in village life.

Stannington

Stannington is situated on the A1 road nine miles north of Newcastle and five miles south of Morpeth. On the west side of the village, and a landmark for miles around, is St Mary's church which was rebuilt in 1871 on the site of a Norman church dated 1190. The Ridley Arms and a large well-used village hall are both located on the east side. Other amenities include the village shop, a post office and a well attended first school. A fine monumental fountain, in Church Road, was donated by Viscount Ridley to commemorate the coronation of Edward VII in 1902.

Blagdon Hall, home of the Ridley family since 1720, lies one mile south on the river Blyth. A pleasant house, it is surrounded by parkland, woods and farmland. The present Lord Ridley is Lord Lieutenant of Northumberland.

Anyone returning to Stannington after some absence may think little has changed. They would be wrong, for village life has changed significantly. In 1945, Stannington was much the same as in 1900. A small village where everyone knew everyone else, living and working together as a whole community. Most families were involved in agriculture, many employed on the nearby Blagdon estate, or work connected within the parish. This is not so now.

Since the war, agriculture has changed dramatically – machines taking over from manpower resulting in the disappearance of the small family farm. When a farm becomes vacant the land is often added to a neighbouring farm, equipped with large machines and buildings better suited to modern farming. As a consequence of these changes, Blagdon estate is no longer the largest employer in the district. Less staff in the house, gardens, woods and especially on the farmland have meant fewer workers living in estate houses. Farm buildings unsuitable for modern farming have been converted to housing or industrial units. Nowadays, many new residents in the village have no connection with rural life and the tight-knit community spirit is missing.

However, Blagdon is still very much an integral part of the parish. The extensive grounds are used for many local activities. In the spring, the gardens are opened in aid of charity and the daffodils are a memorable sight. One large room in the hall is now a function room where charitable events are held.

Changes have been repeated all over the parish. On the western periphery stood two large hospitals. St Mary's mental hospital was opened in 1913 to care for 1,000 patients, under the administration of Gateshead Corporation. A large number of staff such as doctors, nurses, cooks and gardeners lived on the complex. Standing amid beautiful grounds with its own farm it was a self-sufficient unit, employing many local people. Sadly, it is now run under the threat of closure.

Stannington Children's Hospital was built in 1905 as a children's charity. It became a TB hospital then later reverted back to a children's establishment. This hospital also had a farm with a community in its own right. It was closed in 1985, the farm sold, the site cleared and the large sheds converted to commercial premises.

To the north east of the village just off the A1, stands Netherton Park, formerly Netherton Training School. It was built in 1857 as a reformatory for delinquent boys. The headmaster lived in a large Victorian house in the centre of the school. The staff lived in houses adjacent to the large dormitory building where the boys slept. Their communal life evolved around working on the two farms and workshops where the youngsters were taught craftsmanship. Local farmers bought their carts and gates from Netherton Training School and some employed the boys on casual farm labouring. Netherton had its own school, chapel and playing fields. It exists today as a juvenile assessment centre, with a few staff living on site. The farms have been sold to three different people and the premises converted to other uses.

Until 1945 there were only 32 houses in the village – now there are five times that number. However, the newer houses blend in with the original stone buildings and are not obtrusive. The old village school has been converted into three dwellings.

The village is fortunate to have its own vicar, who lives in a new vicarage – the old vicarage was sold in 1992. A policeman still lives in the police house but he has a much wider area to cover. Probably the most significant change is that the A1 no longer cuts the village in half. A bypass was built to the east and although it is quieter and safer to cross a village street, the new road has made access in and out of the village unsafe and been the cause of a number of accidents.

Stannington remains a very pleasant place to live with friendly and caring neighbours. The church, village shop, post office, Ridley Arms and village hall are the focal points of village life. Frequent charitable events take place and there always seems to be something of interest being arranged by a local group. Stannington has evolved well during the past 50 years and, despite great change, has retained the neatness and quietness of a Northumberland village on its way toward the 21st century.

Stobhill (Morpeth)

Morpeth is a well known ancient Market town with a long and rather turbulent history. On its fringe is Stobhill, mentioned on old maps as the Stobb Hill. In those days the area surrounding Morpeth was given over to farmland, market gardens and the common. It is hoped the latter will be preserved for posterity, but modern housing has overtaken the former agricultural land.

The Stobhill area grew from Stobhill Villas, near the mart, which was situated by the main line railway station. This has had a recent facelift revealing the original Victorian building. The mart is now an attractive housing estate, near to the cricket, hockey and tennis clubs, and Stobhillgate with its modern church of St Aidan. Several shops, schools and the British Legion club give it a village atmosphere. Stobhill

Grange, High Stobhill and Low Stobhill run into each other, making a sprawling modern village.

Until the Morpeth bypass was built, for centuries a bridge over the river Wansbeck carried all the Great North Road traffic. The present bridge, a feat of engineering by Telford, is used by a tremendous number of vehicles. Nearby is the imposing courthouse, the site of the old castle, St George's United Reformed church and the chantry chapel, which has had several uses but now, beautifully restored, houses a bagpipe museum, craft centre and information room. Annually there is the Riding of the Bounds, the New Year's Day road race to Newcastle, and a summer Fair Day when Bridge Street is closed to traffic.

The town hall, designed by Vanbrugh, houses historic treasures. The Hollin Fountain was built by public subscription in 1885 in honour of R. W. Hollin who married Mary Trotter of Morpeth. When she died after 25 years of marriage, he left money to provide a tea on 5th November for 13 goodly women and twelve men, an afternoon enjoyed to this day! Another landmark is the clock tower, near the town hall. Until recently the peal of bells rang out at 8 pm for the curfew and on a Wednesday morning for the start of the market at 10 am.

Carlisle Park, with its hilly setting and abundance of flowers, catches the eye as one enters the town from the south, passing the war memorial which on 11th November is enhanced by the autumn tints of the surrounding trees. Morpeth is a keen annual competitor in the Britain in Bloom competition and has the honour of having won this on one occasion.

The bowling greens, tennis courts, putting green, paddling pool and woods are much enjoyed in the park alongside the river, where rowing boats can be hired. The swimming pool and leisure centre in the New Market are well used for musical and dramatic evenings besides all types of sport, and there is thriving market each Wednesday.

Famous sons of Morpeth include the biologist Dr W. Turner whose *Herbal* is a prized possession, and Lord Collingwood whose house in Oldgate was a retreat for him after his famous sea battles. Thomas Burt, devout Methodist and teetotaller, who served Morpeth for 40 years as a privy councillor and rose from pitman to parliamentarian, is still remembered with affection.

King Edward VI school is well respected and the nearby psychiatric hospital of St George has done wonderful work for the mentally ill.

Stonehaugh 🦢

Stonehaugh village lies six miles west of Wark. It was built in the early 1950s to house workers for the Forestry Commission, who were helping to build up and harvest the Kielder Forest.

Originally, there should have been about 200 houses, a church, school, shop and pub, but only 35 houses were built along with a social club and village hall. One of the houses was used as a church, another for a shop/post office.

The Forestry Commission offices and workshop were on the edge of the village but were sold off when new premises were built at Bellingham. A local haulier now uses them. There are holiday chalets to the east of the village with the original Stonehaugh Shields farmhouse. Alongside this is the small camping and caravan site.

Just outside the village on the road to Wark is Crookbank Farm. Despite being only a quarter of a mile out of the village it does not have electricity from the national grid, nor do the outlying farms and houses to the west. The old school and house is a little further down the road. Before Stonehaugh was built this building was used as the meeting place for the local community. There were hunt balls, wedding receptions, monthly church services and other events held there. There is a holly or holy well sulphur spring on the outskirts of the village where the Methodist church services were held in the summer.

Even in the short history of the village there have been a lot of changes. Sadly the village hall was demolished as the foundations became unstable and the shop closed, leaving us with a part-time post office in one of the houses. The Forestry Commission has made cutbacks in recent years in their labour force so many houses were left vacant. About nine years ago these were sold to private ownership and the tenants were given the option to buy their own homes. The amenity areas in the village were passed over to the parish council to maintain.

This is a small community but we still have the social club which is open four nights a week for drinking, pool or darts and is available anytime to hold social events in. The youth club, Neighbourhood Watch and gardening club meet there regularly. The leek show is held annually with as much rivalry in the baking sections as there is in the vegetable and flower ones. The villagers also get together as the village green committee which funds the bonfire night, Easter competitions, sports day, Christmas party and annual trip. They also fund-raised for and built the new playground which replaced the old swings. Once a year in November the rural calm is broken by the revving of engines as the RAC rally comes almost to the doorstep.

Stonehaugh is within the boundaries of the National Park and the Pennine Way passes alongside the village. Naturally, as the village was built for forestry it is surrounded by the Kielder Forest, but recently a large amount of trees have been felled. A replanting programme will begin but there are more open areas planned rather than trees in every direction.

The Warksburn, an attractive tributary of the North Tyne, flows alongside the village and curves along the back where the water is deep enough to swim in on hot summer days.

There is a small waterfall which flows down to the picnic area called 'Biggyhaugh', where there are public toilets, tables and benches, with plenty of space for ball games. Here are also three carved totem poles which were originally chainsaw-carved by two local forestry workers. They were removed because they had rotted and replacement poles were again chainsaw-carved, replicas of the damaged ones, but treated wood has been used so hopefully they will last for many years. The village gained itself the nickname of 'Dodge City', thanks mainly to the totem poles, not the unruly behaviour of its residents.

There are three forest walks specially marked with coloured markers; each walk is of a different length depending on how long people wish to spend enjoying the fresh air and looking for the varied wildlife in the woods. In springtime the roads into the village are a nightmare for drivers as they seem to be alive with toads and frogs heading towards the Warksburn to breed. Walking along the riverbank you are startled by the noise these amphibians make and the water is often black with their eggs. The deer are frequent visitors into the village; dusk is a good time to see them, but in the summer they are not too popular as they eat the flowers, especially roses which they seem to favour. The most endearing wildlife are the red squirrels, which are a joy to watch.

The Forestry Commission have had hundreds of nesting boxes put into Kielder Forest to encourage the small birds to come, as the trees grown are not the type they would normally nest in.

Swarland 🦢

Although Swarland has rarely gained a mention in history books, it is nevertheless unique in two regards: its name, which means 'land heavy to plough', and its land settlement of the 1930s, which was the only such scheme in the country to be funded entirely by private monies.

Here, too, is a perfect example of the transfer of a village name to a different area when the balance of population created an increase in housing away from the original. Less than 60 years ago, the cluster of estate cottages beside the present village square was addressed as Swarland Moor, whilst the hamlet now called Low Swarland was known, as for centuries and correctly, as the village of Swarland.

There is evidence of Roman, and possibly earlier, occupation of the area in the large entrenchment near Chester Hill, but despite the lack of historical occurrences, and the consequent absence of location note on the older maps of Northumberland, Swarland has been owned throughout most of its recorded 800 years by men of repute.

Not much is written of Swarland before the 13th century, but in c1270 it became the property of Thomas de Carliolo, whose family produced many eminent citizens of Newcastle. Thomas having no sons, the husband of one of his five daughters succeeded to Swarland, and he, Peter Graper, was mayor of Newcastle six times. The estate then descended to his granddaughter, Agnes, who married John de Hesilrigge.

The Hesilrigges remained at Swarland for 300 years, and William 'The Covenanter' lies there still. Dying in 1681, he was buried in the field behind Swarland Old Hall, and his grave can be seen, surrounded by iron railings, in the exposed spot where Presbyterians held an annual service before the last war.

The estate had been forfeited because of the family's 'uncompromising attitude towards Church and Crown during the Civil War' but was restored to them in 1740 and eventually became the property of the famed Sir Arthur Hesilrigge, who conveyed Swarland to Richard Grieve of Alnwick. Richard Grieve had been awarded land on Swarland Moor, in lieu of his 'right of common of pasture' on the enclosure of Felton common in 1754, and it was here in 1765 that his son Davidson Richard Grieve built Swarland House, a beautiful mansion in the Italian style, situated about a mile from the original Swarland Hall.

In 1795, the mansion and estate were sold to Alexander Davison, personal friend and, later, prize-agent of Lord Nelson. After the battle of the Nile in 1798, Davison created a park to reflect in shape that of Aboukir Bay, and he planted it with trees and shrubs to represent the British fleet in battle order. Also, after the battle of Trafalgar he erected a dwarf obelisk beside the old A1 (then the post road). Davison died in 1829, and the estate devolved to his heir who became an absentee landlord until his death in 1873.

After this the estate was bought by Hugh Andrews (the owner of Broomhill colliery and developer of Warkworth harbour), who extended the mansion house and built the beautiful private chapel there. Around 1902, the place was again sold, this time to James E. Woods, the Newcastle banker, High Sheriff of Northumberland in 1908 and treasurer of the RVI, who was knighted in 1922, when Swarland, once more, was on the market. It was purchased by the owners of the Shilbottle, Whittle and Longframlington collieries who used the house as a miners' hostel.

By 1934, the dereliction was complete, and the central portion of the estate was bought by Clare Vyner, of Studley Royal, Ripon, for development by the Fountains Abbey Settlers' Society Limited as a land settlement for unemployed tradesmen and their families from Tyneside.

Since the end of the 19th century, land settlement had been seen as a way of providing smallholdings for men anxious to carve out for themselves a life of agriculture in the countryside, and by the mid 1930s as a partial answer to unemployment. Thus there were many land settlements throughout the country and, indeed, throughout Northumberland, but all had been provided by local authorities and by public money. Swarland was different. Funded entirely by private subscription, and designed by Miss Molly Reavell, there were 54 smallholdings built, each with an acre and a half of land. Sixteen other houses were provided, together with three shops, a magnificent sports field with tennis courts and bowling green, and a large, superbly equipped village hall.

The families who came were all tradesmen who had been out of work for some time. Work was provided for them at the Swarland brickworks at Thrunton, the Swarland sawmills and joinery at Amble and the Swarland tweed mills on the estate, where beautiful Cheviot tweeds and Harris tweed, under licence, were woven. In addition, socks, scarves and blankets were sold from the shops in the village square, at Alnwick and at Ripon, and Norman Hartnell was a contact in London.

A district nurse, too, was provided by the society, and when in 1937 a new school was opened, the settlement was approaching true village status. With the advent of war in 1939, however, all development was curtailed, and by 1945 many of the families of men whose labour had been directed back to the shipyards had returned to Tyneside. By 1947 the society had been replaced by the Fountains (Northumberland) Trust and the settlement houses were offered for sale. In that year, too, the remains of Swarland Hall were finally demolished.

In 1970, it was suggested that the paddocks attached to smallholdings be sold for building, in order to finance the construction of the 'settlement' roads, and since that time the size of the estate has doubled, with still more houses to be built. Many of the beautiful trees have been felled and the once admired spaciousness of this unusual village is disappearing fast.

It now has street lighting, a speed limit, a caravan park, and golf course with associated amenities. Swarland Old Hall still stands in its beautiful location, and six clumps of 'ship' trees can be found on the park. Settlement houses of Molly Reavell's design can be seen from the A1, but others are lost among the new buildings of recent years.

Swarland is a place where change has come, not gradually, but almost with a violence, twice within a half-century. Heavy land, indeed, but still dear to most of the people who live there.

Tarset ✤

The name Tarset is given to a village hall, a burn, a parish, a former station and the remains of a castle – but you will not find a village of that name! Tarset is a postal area comprising much of the parishes of Tarset and Greystead and encompassing the beautiful valleys of the Chirdon, Tarset and Tarret burns and part of the wider North Tyne valley. It includes the hamlets of Gatehouse, Greenhaugh, Lanehead and Greystead along with scattered farms and homesteads.

There is flat haugh land, tumbling burns edged with alder and hazel and some pretty waterfalls. Pasture and deciduous woodland on the lower slopes rise to dark green conifer forest and rough grazings of bent grass and heather. In the forest at Sidwood are remains of a Romano-British site – an enclosure with three huts inside and one outside.

The 14th century brought a turbulent period in the history of Tarset. The populace organised themselves into family groups called 'graynes' – Charltons, Robsons, Dodds and Milburns all played their part and you will still find people answering to these names today. Each man rallied to the support of his 'hedesman'. On moonlit autumn nights, the reivers set out on raids to other 'graynes', on either side of the Border, their battle cry ringing out:

'Tarset and Tarretburn,
Hard and heather-bred
Yet! Yet! Yet!'

They drove off cattle, sheep and horses, burned homes and killed the occupants. Today we'd call it robbery and murder!

The reivers built small, fortified farmhouses with stone walls five feet thick. Living quarters were on the first floor and in times of trouble animals were housed below. The remains of several of these bastles can be seen today on the Reivers Trail from Sidwood. Most need some imagination but Black Middens has been somewhat restored. Gatehouse boasts two, both late 16th century. The best preserved is to the north and privately owned but can be conveniently viewed from the highway.

Near Tarset Hall, on private land, is a grassy mound – the remains of Tarset Castle. Built around 1267 by Red Comyn, one of the great Scottish nobles, it had 'walls about four feet thick, of the finest ashlar work, and strongly cemented'. There was a turret at each corner, an outer wall and a moat. The castle commanded extensive views to south, east and west. Later it passed to the English and a garrison was stationed there to control the 'thieffs'. In 1525 the said 'theiffs' joined forces with the Scottish reivers, attacked the castle and 'brownte and killed dyvers men'. It was never rebuilt.

By the Chirdon burn stand the ruins of Dally Castle. Dating probably from 1237 and built by another Scot, David de Lindsay, it was never completed and seems to have fallen into ruin before 1542.

By 1300 the shieling system of farming was established. 'Inbye' land was cultivated and cattle and sheep driven 'outbye' to the shieling grounds in summer – hence such place-names as Shipley Shiel and Gibshiel, indicating summer grazings. After 1603 farming expanded. Long low farmhouses were built, often with a byre attached. Land was enclosed and improved by the application of lime. In the late 18th century, much of the land was ploughed, as indicated by the parallel lines of 'rigg and furrow' still visible. Today sheep and suckler herds of beef cattle are the mainstay of the farming scene.

From the late 17th century, coal was mined at High Green. Limestone was quarried and burnt in kilns at High Green and Belling Rigg near

Gatehouse. This led to a need for a more efficient transport system and by 1862 the Border Counties Railway had been laid from Hexham to Riccarton Junction. Tarset station also served as a post office. The advent of the railway must have revolutionised the lives of the inhabitants. It fell to the Beeching axe of 1956.

For centuries, large herds of cattle travelled the drove road by Slatyford and Lanehead, hence the name Drover's House, now a private home but formerly an inn and later a shop and post office. The present post office is at Greenhaugh.

In the late 19th century roads were improved and bridges built to replace fords. In 1974, iron bridges over the Tyne and Tarset were rebuilt to take construction traffic for Kielder dam.

At Greystead stands a modest, grey church with a small battlemented tower built after the breakup of the huge Simonburn parish in 1814. Over the hill at Thorneyburn stands its twin dating from 1820. Both were designed by architect H.H. Seward for the Commissioners of Greenwich Hospital. Services are still held at Thorneyburn and occasionally at Greystead. At Lanehead stands a former chapel, now a private home. Dating from 1902, it served both Methodists and Presbyterians until 1979.

In the 19th century there were dame schools at Cragend, Diamond Cottage and Gatehouse. In the early 20th century there was a council school at Emblehope. The Presbyterians built one at the Hott in 1851 and the Anglicans at Thorneyburn in 1865, both buildings now converted to private dwellings. In 1966 pupils transferred to a temporary timber-frame building at Greenhaugh. This has now been replaced by an attractive, stone-faced school on the same site catering for five to nine year old children.

Up to the 20th century, Tarset was virtually self-sufficient, having craftsmen to supply every need. Earlier uses for present buildings can be deduced from such names as Cartwright Cottage, Bought Hill Mill and Smiddy Well Rigg. These traditional craftsmen have been replaced by those more appropriate to the late 20th century – a garage mechanic, a builder, a plumber and electrician.

If you visit Tarset today, you will find exhilarating walks, beautiful scenery, a wealth of historical remains and an abundance of wildlife. You will find a variety of accommodation from self catering cottage to guest house and a warm welcome in Tarset's only pub, the Holly Bush Inn at Greenhaugh. You will find friendly folk . . . and you will find peace.

Thropton 🌿

Thropton, lying between the Coquet river and the Wreigh (or Rithe) burn, in a long valley which carries the river from the Scottish border down to the sea, was once nicknamed 'Tattie-Toon' because it was said to have been the first place in the area to grow potatoes! Farming, gardening and many other country crafts continue to be practised here; the skills of the community can be appreciated at Thropton Show each autumn, one of a number still flourishing in the valley. The show is also famous for the fell-run up Simonside, the hill which rises from the south bank of the river, a landmark for miles around, where remains may be seen of the encampments of the earliest inhabitants.

The village, now numbering about 400 souls, boasts four churches. The United Reformed, formerly Presbyterian, erected in 1863, whose unusual tower dominates the main street, lies just beyond the Roman Catholic chapel of All Saints, whose foundation dates from about 1750. On the opposite side of the main street is the meeting house of the Brethren, whose worship here goes back more than a hundred years. Along the road to Cartington, opposite the school, stands the small Anglican church of St Andrew, paid for by public subscription in 1902.

Entering Thropton from the Rothbury direction, before crossing the bridge that was built in 1810 by public subscription, you pass on the right The Cross Keys public house, and on the left, Wreighburn House. The Cross Keys, on a slight rise, overlooks the main street and the crossroads, where a right turn takes you on towards Snitter, Cartington and Netherton. Though formerly much larger, Snitter, on the hill, and Cartington, which once had a castle and parish of its own, are now small villages with few inhabitants. Wreighburn House, Thropton's 'big house', stands on the site of one of the two medieval 'hospitals', or guest houses run by monks, in the neighbourhood. The other is thought to have been on the south bank of the Coquet at Allardene, reached by an old road which formed the fourth arm of the crossroads. A lane which ascends to the moor, opposite Wreighburn House, is known as Physic Lane, possibly because the monks gathered herbs and plants there. Set into the wall of a house in the lane is a stone drinking trough with an iron cup on a chain, fed by a spring. The inscription 'Rest and Be Thankful' is engraved above it.

With the Coquet on one side and the Wreigh burn and its tributary streams on the other, it is hardly surprising that Thropton has experienced some famous floods. The most recent was in April 1991, when all the low-lying fields in the valley were under water, and the bridge impassable for a short time. The workshop of William Brown, the builder, which stands just below the bridge, was almost inundated; his family have been builders here since 1896, one of many old families still represented today. Among them are the Guthersons, the Muckles, who now occupy Wreighburn House, and the Tullys, now shopkeepers in Rothbury.

Continuing up the main street, past the churches, The Three Wheat Heads inn and the shop, opposite the garage stands the oldest building in Thropton, the pele tower, now part of a private dwelling. It was first recorded in 1415 as the property of William Grene. Another Green, who was said to have killed a priest and therefore could not be buried in hallowed ground, is commemorated by a gravestone, dated 1731, set into the front wall of a cottage. Those who live there sometimes feel that they are not alone!

Of course, Thropton has changed considerably over the years. There are still the churches and two inns, but whereas there were once several shops, including a draper's, and various tradesmen, including a blacksmith, as well as a reading room and a post office, there is now only one combined grocery and post office. The horse-drawn carts and carriages have been replaced by a bus service connecting with Alnwick and Newcastle, the 'big city'; and the village pump and horse trough have been replaced by a public telephone and conveniences! There are still several working farms in the area, although not in Thropton itself. Instead, three small developments of new homes have been built; one on land where once the horses of the Catholic clergy were stabled, appropriately called Churchfields, and another on the old Village Farm fields. This has meant that, unlike many villages which are in decline, Thropton thrives, and the community is renewed.

Tillmouth

Tillmouth is in the township of Twizell, situated four and a half miles north east of Coldstream and twelve miles from the Border town of Berwick upon Tweed. The area is 2,286 acres.

The township lies along the banks of the river Till, which is crossed by a picturesque old bridge consisting of one lofty semi-circular arch. It is said to have been erected by a lady of the Selby family, and is the same bridge over which the Earl of Surrey led an army before the battle of Flodden Field.

The manor of Twizell was held by the Bishop of Durham in the reign of Edward III, then by Sir William Riddle. From the Riddles it passed to the Heron family, and then to the Selbys and after them to the Blakes. This family claims its descent from A.P. Lake, one of the knights of King Arthur's Round Table.

On a rocky height on the banks of the Till are the ruins of Twizell Castle. It was started in 1770 by Sir Francis Blake and though untold wealth was expended in the 40 years of work it was never completed or occupied by its noble owner. The castle was denuded of nearly all its dressed stone which was used to build Tillmouth Park, a very fine house, which has now been made into a hotel.

About a mile west of Tillmouth are the traces of an ancient British encampment known as Holy Chesters.

On the angle of land where the river Till adjoins the river Tweed, stands the ruin of St Cuthbert's chapel. Legend has it that when St Cuthbert's body was being carried from its original resting place on Holy Island by the monks, it was floated down the river Tweed in a stone coffin. It came to rest at the old chapel site, and the stone coffin was left there after a chapel had been built to receive the saint. A later legend or rumour circulated that the broken stone coffin was used by a farmer for salting pork. The legend of St Cuthbert has been attributed to the Rev Lambe, vicar of Norham at one time, but it would appear to be 'a flight of fancy'. Sir Walter Scott immortalised the chapel in his literary work *Marmion*.

Tillmouth school was opened on 21st January 1878. There was a charge of twopence per child, and the attendance the first week was 25, though by February the number had increased to over 60. In 1891 Parliament provided free education by a grant in lieu of the school fees, and the children's pence were last recorded at the school on August of that year.

Excuses for pupils' absences included haymaking, lifting potatoes, killing the pig, stone collecting (a perennial occupation), plucking fowls prior to Christmas, helping mother, and very often, 'keeping the bairn'. Childhood epidemics of illness were recorded – mumps, measles, whooping cough, and also the dread report common to many schools throughout the country at this time, 'drain trouble' and the ensuing absences of children with scarlet fever.

The weather in the last two decades of the 19th century was much severer than today. There were great snowstorms in 1886, and no children present for a week. In view of the distances the children had to walk to school from outlying hamlets, this was not surprising. One child was recorded as suffering from frosted feet for several weeks. Even the school ink was frozen. Despite the bad weather and muddy state of the farm lanes the children were punished for dirty boots, the boys in particular. Often the coal stocks for the year ran out during March, and school fires were dispensed with at the end of April, even if the weather was recorded as hail and snow.

The school population fluctuated with the annual hirings of labour which took place in March, and there were changes when the farm leases expired and new farmers took over the farms. The annual summer holiday for the school was 16th August to 30th September, which enabled the children to work on the harvests of corn and potatoes. Egg rolling took place on Easter Monday.

Farm work and salmon fishing were the main forms of employment. Salmon are all caught on rod and line these days; the net and coble fishing for salmon finished in 1984 and put a lot of men out of work. Most salmon stations had been in the same families for generations.

Ulgham ৠ৾

Ulgham is a village combining old with new. The church of St John the Baptist stands at the top of a steep bank above the river Lyne. It looks old, but was rebuilt in the 1800s. However, the site is Saxon and two Norman stone windows are built into the current church walls. In the north aisle is an extraordinary stone relief of a Norman knight on horseback apparently protecting a lady from two birds shown above her shoulder. The churchyard contains tombstones from the 1600s – and one prior to the Spanish Armada!

Opposite the church is a field containing earth mounds from the original village boundary, which are unique in the country. Next to the church the farmhouse has been refurbished and the farm buildings converted into interesting homes of character, which retain the existing charm of the farm.

The old village cross still stands in the main street, although it does not have a cross arm now, in front of two very modern bungalows. This is where markets were held during the plague in Morpeth. There is a small, modern estate where the pig farm used to be, opposite the post office, which was originally a one-storey building, when Ulgham was one street and three farms.

Notorious for being 'the village with the unpronounceable name', 'Uffam' is believed to mean 'the place of owls', although there are other derivations. Sadly, the destruction of the surrounding countryside for open cast mining, and the disappearance of farm buildings and stone barns means that owls are seldom heard or seen. So the people of Ulgham have their own owls and almost every house has one. There are owls of china, glass, wood, bronze, paint and needlework, stone owls in gardens and an owl is incorporated into the sign of the village pub – The Forge.

In the middle of Park Wood, now neighboured by open cast mining, grew the Ulgham Oak, where, it is said, whisky was once distilled illicitly.

The artist Luke Clennell was born in Ulgham village in 1781. He was the son of a farmer but he went to work in his uncle's grocery shop at Morpeth and it was while he was there that his talent for drawing brought him to the notice of an influential peer who, in April 1797, had him apprenticed to Thomas Bewick at Newcastle. He became one of that great engraver's best pupils.

Clennell moved to London in 1804, having acquired much of Bewick's feeling for nature and a distinct ability for landscape and rural scenes. He went on to win awards from the Society of Arts for his wood engraving, but although his work revealed much breadth, it was uneven. Success, alas, affected his reason, and he died insane in 1840. There is a stone to his memory in St Andrew's church in Newcastle, and three of his pictures are in the Victoria and Albert Museum, South Kensington.

Ulgham has adapted well to changes in population. At one time a small farming community, it has welcomed newcomers but has managed to retain its 'small village' identity Flourishing associations include the Women's Institute, formed in 1924, and the cricket club, formed in 1977 and instrumental in the acquisition of the village playing field. The Ulgham Village Association monitors all aspects of life in Ulgham. It has published a village booklet and organises social activities from dances to footpath walking. The carpet bowls club has a large membership and provides entertainment for all, while the gardening club meets every month and arranges outings to gardens of interest throughout the county.

During the First World War the vicar of Ulgham gathered around him a few eager members of the village and they began play readings. These were held in the small village school (now converted to a residence). Much later, when the WI hut was built, the group moved to the new building and when a stage was erected short plays were produced. Eventually a county evening class for drama developed, the fees paid by members and the producer paid by the county, the members being recruited from the WI.

The class proved very popular and progressed to producing three-act plays. A play was produced each year, playing for four nights, Wednesday being exclusively for the over sixties. This was very popular and the hall was packed to capacity each night. Sadly, the evening class rates were increased and travelling expenses rose and members had reluctantly to close the Ulgham Players. The pleasure and friendly entertainment they gave over many years still lives on in the memories of the people of Ulgham and surrounding district.

Wall 🦜

Wall, with a population of around 350, lies four miles north of the abbey town of Hexham and almost *on* Hadrian's Wall.

The parish church of St Oswald in Lee is one and a half miles from the centre of Wall village and is built on the site of the battle of Heavenfield. In AD 635 King Oswald of Northumbria (later St Oswald) rallied his army to fight and scatter the troups of Cadwalla. He personally set up a Christian cross and summoned his men to pray to God for victory. Cadwalla was defeated. Thus Christianity was reintroduced to and established in the North. Bede records in *A History of the English Church and People* that monks from Hagulstad (Hexham Abbey) visited Heavenfield every year on 5th August to 'keep vigil for the benefit of Oswald's soul . . .'

The church of St George was built in the centre of Wall village in 1897 thus making it easier for villagers to attend services, most of which are now held at St George's or in the Methodist chapel which was built in 1868. In 1848 Joseph Parker (of City Temple, London) had preached on the village green, thus promoting a Christian presence which still thrives today under the guidance of Wall Christian Council.

Wall has its village green bounded on all four sides by houses and three farms. The three exits from the green could, at one time, be gated thus allowing cattle and sheep to graze on the green and the village to be defended against Border raiders. A pant, dated 1858, in the centre of

Wall village seen from Wall Fell

the green was the original water supply and is fed by a stream flowing from the fell to the east of the village. The ruin of a Bronze Age camp can be seen at the top of the fell.

Many of the houses and farms date back to the 16th and 17th centuries whilst there is also a small estate of modern houses built in 1989. Town Farm boasts a listed Dutch barn whilst there are listed houses which were once bastles. The bulk of the village is now a conservation area.

One of the most beautiful railway journeys in the country ran from Hexham to Bellingham and passed through Wall, but obviously Dr Beeching had never travelled on this line for in 1960 he had the line closed. The railway station fell into disrepair, and only recently has a new home been built on the site using a number of old railway relics. The loss of the railway was a great disadvantage as very heavy lorries now trundle through Wall carrying wood from Kielder Forest or stone from the quarry, and the local bus service is sparse.

Wall thrived at the end of the 19th and beginning of the 20th century when it boasted three shops, two hotels, two successful businesses, one of the oldest post offices in the country (opened 1844) and a flourishing school. The Hadrian Hotel, once a 17th century coaching inn, is still very popular amongst locals as well as people from many miles away.

The once overflowing village school was, against much local protest, closed in 1972. This took away an important centre of activity and community. Children now attend Humshaugh first school which is a good village school, whilst the Wall school building has been tastefully converted into a dwelling house – but the 'school atmosphere' will never return.

An active group of artists, working in the village, are involved with schools and colleges and have held several successful exhibitions.

The North Tyne Implement Works was founded in about 1800 by James Herdman and at that time employed twelve men. Now run by James's great-great-great-grandson, Ronald, it employs two men. The modern garage is run by John, the son of William Proudlock who started the business in a small corrugated iron building.

Village shops all over Britain have been deprived of business by the modern supermarkets in the local towns. Wall experienced this too, but residents do not complain because within any one week two grocery vans, a greengrocer, a butcher, a fishmonger, a library van, a chiropodist and a coal merchant visit the village. Even if one is completely housebound the basics are available.

Some of the most successful activities are held in the village hall and run on a voluntary basis. The carpet bowls club is now a village institution, together with the Lunch Club, the Women's Institute, the leek club and the ladies' choir. The recently formed Local History Society and the mother and toddler group are now well established. Many activities emanate from all these clubs and societies. Village outings, the ceilidh, Christmas parties and fairs are all part of the life of Wall whilst concerts given by the Wall ladies' choir are essential appointments for everyone.

Until recently the population tended to be elderly, but, with the influx of new and younger families, Wall can now say that it has a 'mixed age' population.

Warden 🦚

Two miles north west of Hexham, Warden lies among fields and woods in the angle formed by the confluence of the rivers North and South Tyne. It is sheltered by Warden Hill (from the Saxon 'weard dun' meaning watch hill) on which are remnants of an extensive Iron Age fort and other earthworks.

Until the last century direct access from Hexham and beyond was by fords across the two rivers. The one near waters-meet was used by workers en route to Acomb mine across the North Tyne. The ancient ferry, the West Boat, plied from the cottages on the old coach road on the Hexham side of the South Tyne across to the (still popular) Boatside Inn and cottages which mark the northern landing.

A suspension bridge, completed in 1826 (and rebuilt in 1877 after collapsing under the weight of a thresher), was finally replaced by 1903 by the present stone bridge but the old toll cottage still stands.

Trains came to Warden in 1836 with the bridging of the South Tyne to link the Newcastle and Haydon Bridge sections of the Newcastle to Carlisle line. The first bridge was a wooden structure destroyed by fired after twelve years. Then followed two successive iron bridges. For a short time before the link was complete there were stations at West Boat and at Quality Corner in Warden, where there are now four cottages.

The focal point of this scattered village is the church of St Michael and All Angels with its lychgate and lovely churchyard. Christians have worshipped here for 1,400 years; an early 7th century cross stands outside the church and in the porch are Saxon coffins and grave covers found in the churchyard. The lower part of the tower is also Saxon but the top section, probably damaged by beacons lit to warn of Border

Warden church and the river Tyne

raids, was restored when the old church was rebuilt in 1765. The first recorded vicar here was appointed in 1170.

Warden was the property of Hexham Priory from the 12th century until the Reformation when it passed to the Crown, to be sold in James I's reign to the Leadbitter and Kirsop families at Low Warden, and the Erringtons at High Warden.

Until recently Low Warden comprised the vicarage, Low Warden House, built in 1734 and home of the Leadbitter family until 1944, and three farm steadings dating from the 17th to 19th century, grouped beside the church. In the late 1950s the farms were sold, most of the land passed to the High Warden estate and almost all of the buildings have been converted sensitively for residential use.

East of Low Warden, on the banks of the North Tyne at Warden Rocks was Warden corn mill, now a private house. Above it is Netherwarden House, built in 1867 for Canon Cruddas.

North from the church, Homers' Lane follows the North Tyne valley past High Warden towards Walwick Grange and Chesters. The stump of a sanctuary cross on the roadside indicates that this was a pilgrim route. It was at a cottage on this lane that the notorious unsolved murder of Joe Hedley, a quilter, took place in 1826.

West of Low Warden and the bridge is a row of cottages at Hardhaugh, built after the opening in 1762 of Warden (now Fourstones) paper mill to house the employees. A parish school, now closed, was built here in 1829 and enlarged in 1850 when the average attendance reached 90 children. The Methodist chapel opposite was built in 1851.

Much has changed through its long history but Warden retains its quiet beauty; wildlife abounds along the river banks and in the woods. A scattered but friendly community, there are close parochial and social links with nearby Fourstones and Newbrough, including a thriving joint Village Society.

Wark on Tweed 🐟

It is hard to imagine, driving along the B6350 from Cornhill to Kelso, that the village of Wark was the site of one of the most powerful and important fortresses in England for 500 years. Today the remains of the vast curtain walls of the castle are hidden beneath the moss, scrub and trees which have been allowed to grow since the time of Elizabeth I.

As early as AD 833 there was a serious engagement between the Danes and the English on land between Wark and Carham. In 1018 a battle was fought on the flat field to the east. But the castle did not appear in records formally before 1126 when David, King of Scotland tried and failed to take it on behalf of his niece, Matilda, who was in dispute with Stephen over the succession to the crown of England.

The castle was built on a vast rocky outcrop left behind by the Ice Age. It commanded a crucial ford across the Tweed, which was large enough to take a sizeable army. There were several attempts to take it, but the defences were quite secure, and it was only taken by the Scots in 1296 when the custodian, Robert Ross, threw in his lot with the Scots after becoming enamoured of a Scottish lady, Christine Mobray. Edward I sent a force of 1,000 to arrest him. However, they camped at Pressen overnight and Robert Ross was able to surprise them and massacre the entire force.

The weekly market was established on Fridays in 1241, also an annual fair on the vigil feast and morrow of St Giles, whose church was situated west of the great tower. Most of the English monarchs of the time stayed at the castle; Edward I was there after the crowning of John Baliol at Berwick, Edward II went from it to his defeat at Bannockburn, Edward III stayed often.

Some local sources believe that the Order of the Garter was first instituted here, though that cannot be confirmed as all the records of the Garter were burned in the Middle Ages – Wark shares the distinction with Windsor and Calais though there is a strong case for Wark. Edward III was at the castle in 1333 prior to the battle of Halidon Hill. His mistress the Countess of Salisbury was also present as a member of the court. Legend has it that when the Countess lost her garter, the King picked it up. Some courtiers present giggled, knowing of the relationship. The King was said to have fixed the garter on his own leg, saying 'Honi soit qui mal y pense' (evil to him who thinks evil), and declared that the garter would become the symbol of the highest order of chivalry in the land. The King had already honoured the lady's family by confirming her brother a baron of Wark in 1331, at the rent of a single rose payable every midsummer day.

The castle changed hands some 18 times in subsequent years and was at the height of its powers in the reign of Henry VIII. After that it declined, and the remaining village never recovered. Today it is a pleasant backwater on the banks of the Tweed, giving little indication of its turbulent past.

Wark on Tyne

Wark (pronounced to rhyme with 'ark' by its inhabitants) lies on a particularly beautiful stretch of the North Tyne twelve miles north of Hexham. Apart from those who stop for a meal at the Battlesteads Hotel or a drink at The Black Bull, The Grey Bull or the sports club, it is a village that is passed through. Visitors on their way to Wark Forest, to Kielder reservoir and dam, to Bellingham and Otterburn and even to the sea by way of Rothbury and Alnwick drive through it. Large timber lorries, farm waggons, tractors, sheep and cattle and horse boxes passing through reflect the occupations of the countryside around.

In 1832 there was a population of 980, now there are about 500 on the electoral roll. Then there were 15 shops and the village was quite self-sufficient. Now there is a post office selling newspapers and sweets, general stores, a filling station with a small shop, a butcher, a hairdresser and an engineering works. A mobile library, mobile vet and a travelling shop visit, but the sawmill, bakery and grocer's shop have recently closed as well as the two banks. At one time Wark had a railway station on the line from Hexham to Scotland and buses up the valley were frequent. The railway has closed and, because of the greater use of cars, the buses are few.

About 800 years ago there was a motte and bailey castle here and Wark, as head of the lordship of Tynedale, was the chief administrative centre for a huge area bounded by Scotland, Cumberland, Hexhamshire and Redesdale. Even before these times it had a castle overlooking an important river crossing. The motte can be seen on the right, opposite the Battlesteads Hotel as you enter the village from Hexham. From 1150 to 1295 Scottish kings held court here, as Tynedale was part of Scotland. The farmhouse at the top of the mound is appropriately named Mote Hill. At the foot of the mound was the blacksmith's, his smithy being the small stone building opposite. Many a villager remembers coming to the cottage to get the accumulator for the wireless charged, for that was a job done by the blacksmith's wife.

Instead of passing through, why not halt awhile? Walk down the lane by the doctors' surgery opposite the Battlesteads Hotel. To the left is the modern school opened in 1965 which takes children up to the age of nine and in which evening classes take place and the Brownies meet. Below it can be seen the old school, rebuilt in 1805 but established in the 17th century by the will of Giles Heron, a pedlar who was a natural son of one of the Herons of Chipchase Castle. Here, when the third Duke of Northumberland bought the barony of Wark, his first court leet was held in October 1835.

Following the path, a fine iron bridge comes into view. This was built in 1878 and was a toll bridge – a penny per person and twopence for a horse and cart, though many still preferred to cross by the ford downstream. Upstream can be seen the ferryman's cottage. Before the bridge was built this was the main way to Bellingham. Wark residents are fortunate in that the landowner allows them to fish the river providing they have licences and belong to the fishing club. The ducks on the river are a delight, and the best-fed ducks around!

Just across the bridge and on the road to Barrasford is the sports club where the cricket and football teams play and where the annual terrier show takes place.

One mile outside Wark along this road stands Wark station, now a private house but once a social meeting place with The Chipchase Arms just outside it. Farmers railed their stock here as there were few cattle waggons in the old days. The track has been taken up and much of the line can be walked.

On this road too, stands Chipchase Castle, an old pele to which a Jacobean mansion was added in 1620, and Georgian alterations made in 1784. According to one source a knighted ghost, Sir Reginald Fitz-Urse, clanks around it.

In the centre of Wark itself is the village green, common land beside which travellers may rest for 24 hours but then must move on. It is dominated by a magnificent old chestnut tree planted in 1887 to celebrate Queen Victoria's Golden Jubilee. This provides beautiful flowers in spring, shade in summer and conkers for the children in autumn. Round the green are cherry trees planted to celebrate the Queen's Silver Jubilee in 1977. On Christmas Eve there is a magical atmosphere as carols are sung and a wonderful Father Christmas travelling from village to village on his equally wonderful sleigh throws out sweets for the children.

Round the green are some lovely old houses and opposite is the Mechanics' Institute which was built in 1874. This is now called Wark Town Hall and here many village activities take place – dances and discos, parties, senior citizens' dinners, concerts, Scouts, toddlers group, dog training classes and fetes.

Old Year's Night is still celebrated in the village though perhaps not as enthusiastically as in the past, when according to someone who lived four miles outside the village along a gated road, all the gates were taken off their hinges to let the New Year in. On New Year's Day the public houses remain open all day and the village hums with activity. Traditional Northumbrian music, songs, fiddlers, accordions and pipes can be heard as well as strolling guitarists, on a friendly and enjoyable day.

Abel Chapman, the famous naturalist, lived just outside Wark on what was a run-down sheep farm when he bought it in 1898. It is said that when he came to view it he saw some black objects. 'What are they?' he asked. 'Crows,' was the reply. 'No Blackcock,' said Abel and he immediately bought the property. It was he who planted the beautiful avenue of lime trees as you leave the village and head for Bellingham. He is buried in the grounds of St Michael's church which is situated just north of the village.

Warkworth 🦚

Warkworth, with the Anglo-Saxon name Werceworde, has been here for a very long time. To visit us you must leave the A1 almost midway between Newcastle upon Tyne and Berwick upon Tweed and travel eastwards towards the sea. On its way to the sea, the lovely river Coquet forms a large horseshoe bend, and therein lies Warkworth.

Along the river's wooded banks are fine old trees, and the bird-lover is in his element. Herons patiently wait for fish or, uttering their harsh squawk, flap slowly downstream. Cormorants dive; there are waterhens; swans with their cygnets, and, near the bridge, if he is lucky, the bird-watcher may catch the brilliant blue flash of a kingfisher.

The parish church, within a well tended churchyard, is dedicated to St Lawrence. It stands on the site of the early Saxon church of Ceowulf, King of Northumberland who, in AD 737, resigned his crown and joined the monks on Lindisfarne. Today, visitors come to admire the long Norman nave and the fine archway which spans the entrance to the chancel with its beautiful vaulted roof. It is said that the local miller, at the turn of the century, was approached by the churchwarden of the day and asked to contribute to a fund for the building of a new churchyard wall. Without hesitation came his reply, 'I'm saying, I'm saying, I see no need for a wall – them that's in canna come out, and them that's out doesn't want to gan in.' But the wall was built.

On leaving the church, cameras invariably come out to capture the fine view up the wide village street to the castle, built on a grassy mound which, in spring, is covered with thousands of daffodils. Over the centuries, the castle has been inextricably linked with Northumberland's great family, the Percys. Thus, Warkworth is the setting for scenes in Shakespeare's *Henry IV, Part One*. From here in 1407, Harry Hotspur bade farewell to his Lady and set out for Shrewsbury where he was mortally wounded.

One of Warkworth's rather different attractions is The Hermitage, about half a mile upstream. The popular, romantic legend tells how Bertram, a Northumbrian knight, having accidentally slain both his brother and his sweetheart, Lady Isabel Widdrington, retired from the world and, driven by remorse, spent the remainder of his life in devotion and solitude whilst he created a chapel in rock to their memory.

Strolling around the village on a summer's evening, the visitor will notice the old bridge, with two fine arches spanning the Coquet, and the 14th century gatehouse, which provided a defensive point from northern marauders for both village and castle. Bridge End House, an elegant Queen Anne residence once the home of the local squire, Thomas Clutterbuck, stands nearby.

From the market cross during the 1715 rebellion, on the morning of 7th October, James Stuart, The Pretender, was proclaimed 'king of these realms' in opposition to George I. The Earl of Derwentwater had his quarters at The Mason's Arms where, on one of the beams above the bar, we read, 'The Earl of Derwentwater and 40 of his followers dined in this house on Saturday, the 8th of October, 1715.'

Along 'the butts', by the river, archery was practised and there you will find the United Reformed church, built in 1828 by those who preferred the form of worship more akin to that of the Scottish Church. The two old schools have been converted into attractive homes so that the children now attend a school in the newer part of the village which has grown up beyond the castle.

Warkworth does much to welcome the visitors who come by coach and car during the summer. Flowers in gardens, troughs and hanging baskets bring colour to brighten the greyish stone of the old houses. There is no longer a village butcher, but there are friendly hostelries and tea shops, two art galleries and a delightful book-house, as well as two larger hotels and homely, well appointed bed and breakfast accommodation.

The visitor can hire a rowing boat on the river and there is excellent sport for the angler. By tradition, the first fish caught at the opening of the salmon fishing season on 1st February is presented to the Duke of Northumberland at Alnwick Castle. There is a nine hole golf course, overlooking sturdy farmhouses and well cultivated fields to the west, and eastwards beautiful golden sands and across to Coquet Island with its lighthouse and RSPB seabird sanctuary.

Come in August, around the 20th, and at 'The Feast' you can visit the village flower show. Since 1859, this has been a showcase for the skills of gardeners, WI cooks and craftswomen and is held in the shadow of the castle. Every weekend, there is that most English of scenes, the village cricket match.

Even in winter, with ice on the river, the bare skeletons of the trees and the black pile of the castle silhouetted against the deep apricot-coloured sky make a memorable picture as the sun sets to the west of the village.

Whalton ✤

According to the *History, Directory and Gazetteer of the Counties of Durham and Northumberland* printed in 1828, Whalton was 'one of the neatest and cleanest villages in the county'! Today, Whalton is still an exceptionally pretty village of grey stone houses lying on either side of a long, narrow village green. It is situated about six miles from the market town of Morpeth.

The village has a general store/post office and a public house, The Beresford Arms. There is a primary school, built in 1831, and a village hall, built in 1922 at a cost of £400. The area is predominantly agricultural but there are some other industries in Whalton – a blacksmith and travelling farrier, a livestock haulier and a family firm that undertakes fencing and hedging.

The church is mainly 13th century although traces of 12th century stonework can still be seen. Its most interesting architectural feature is a pier in the north chancel arcade with an unusual and elaborate dogtooth pattern on all four sides. The church contains memorials to the Ogle family who held Ogle Castle, situated about two miles to the south of Whalton, prior to the Norman Conquest and right up until 1809 when it was sold to an 'opulent' shipowner, Thomas Brown, from London.

Whalton manor house was created out of four old stone houses by Sir Edwin Lutyens in 1908–9 and the gardens were designed by Gertrude Jekyll. The old rectory is built around a fortified pele tower and the rector had his own access to the church by means of a footbridge crossing the road. The bridge was demolished in the 1940s but the steps for it can still be seen outside the churchyard.

Whalton is perhaps most famous for its Bale Fire which takes place on 4th July – Old Midsummer's Eve. It is a relic of the seasonal fires with which the ancients of many races greeted the progress of the sun throughout the year. The early Christian Church wisely chose to accept and Christianise these traditional festivals. The number of seasonal fires gradually diminished until only the midsummer festival remained. In 1825 these midsummer bonfires were still quite widespread in Northumberland but, by 1903, the Rev Walker, rector of Whalton, said he knew of no other place where the custom was still observed. That the Bale is held on Old Midsummer's Eve and not on 23rd June, the summer solstice, is a curious echo of the great nationwide argument over the correction of the calendar in 1725, when eleven days were dropped from the calendar, and 14th September followed 2nd September. The die-hards clung to their lost eleven days, and the Whalton villagers of the time kept their festival on what they argued was the correct date, though it was no longer the shortest night. In more modern times groups of morrismen have attended and entertained the bystanders. As the fire burns low, the bystanders adjourn to the village hall where a barn dance takes place to raise funds for the church.

Whitfield 🌿

Whitfield is a scatterd farming community bordering the A686 in an area of outstanding natural beauty. The road from Haydon Bridge comes to Staward station at the head of the steep descent into the Whitfield valley. The station closed many years ago but memories linger of the large parties of Tynesiders who came out into the country to picnic, also the cyclists who joined them. A memorial can be found at the foot of the steep descent from Allendale to Bearsbridge to a cyclist who was killed.

The picnickers would make their way across the fields to Gingle Pot, a small cottage that supplied hot water and refreshments. The track goes on to Staward pele, the remains of a fortress standing on a high promontory. It is reputed to be on the site of a Roman temple, certainly Roman stones can be seen in what remains of the gateway and a Roman altar with the carving of a bull's head has been found.

The road makes a steep descent down a series of hairpins; writers refer to this area as Little Switzerland. Larch and fir trees in the form of 'ER II' were planted to commemorate the Queen's coronation. At the Ninebanks end of the valley a similar planting shows 'GR VI' for her father.

The road crosses the river Allen at the narrow humpbacked Cupola Bridge, taking its name from the type of blast furnace that stood here during the lead mining era. A short distance away is the meeting of the waters where the east Allen and West Allen join. The road follows the line of the turnpike road to Alston.

The village is a small nucleus of village shop and post office, inn and the parish hall where all activities are focused, including WI meetings, indoor carpet bowls, supper dances and the annual leek show. Outdoor activities are football, quoits, the annual Country Fair and Vintage Rally.

Some way up the hill on the Haltwhistle road is the school and old church, a small gem used mainly in the summer, to economise on heating. This area was the site of the old village, sadly long vanished. In the valley is a fine Victorian church with some beautiful stained glass windows. Beyond is Whitfield Hall, set in spacious wooded grounds that are occasionally open to the public for charity funds.

Across the river are the Monk Woods of primeval oak, believed to be part of the original Caledonian Forest of natural vegetation, when Whitfield was a hunting lodge of the kings of Scotland.

Going west you climb out of the valley to the open moors towards Alston; pause at the Cumbrian border and look back to the spectacular panorama of Northumberland laid out below you.

Whittingham 🦢

Northumberland has more than its fair share of picturesque villages but even amongst these Whittingham stands out as one of its most beautiful.

Just a few houses have been added around its boundaries over the years and Whittingham has retained its picture postcard looks. Local people can remember when it was not the quiet residential village it is now, but a thriving centre for the population of the whole of Whittingham Vale. Where there is now one combined grocer's shop and post office there were seven or eight serving the needs of the local community. There was little or no need to visit Alnwick and a trip to Newcastle was almost unheard of. There was everything from a butcher and a general merchant to a blacksmith and a joiner and undertaker. Whittingham also had its own doctor and nurse and a police station with cells!

In such a strong livestock-producing area it is not surprising that there was a mart at the now closed station at the Bridge of Aln and daughters of farmers and stocksmen can remember walking the ten miles or so to Alnwick with stock to sell there.

In the more distant past, the Latter Day Fair was held on St Bartholomew's Day when livestock would be traded and merchants would arrive with all manner of things to sell. This big event also included a village feast and a variety of sideshows. This fair eventually became Whittingham Sports which attracted athletes from far and wide. A huge crowd followed a marching band from the Castle Inn to the sports field on the outskirts of the village. This event has evolved to the local show which is held every August and is still well supported by local people.

Whittingham stands on both sides of the river Aln, which at not more than a burn, gurgles and burbles its way through the abundant foliage which festoons its banks.

The village originated in Anglo-Saxon times but modern history has it as the estate village for Eslington Park. With the big house at Eslington, and Callaly Castle and Lorbottle Hall all close by, the number of domestic and estate staff in the area was huge and these people all used the services in Whittingham.

The Eslington estate was, and still is, owned by the Ravensworth family and they had a major impact on village life. They provided a library and reading room along with other services for the community and one local lady can remember as a member of the Girls Friendly Society being chauffeur-driven to Eslington Park where Lady Ravensworth's lady's maid instructed them in the skills they would need in later life.

The present day Lord and Lady Ravensworth still live in Eslington Park but the estate is greatly reduced in size. Death duties meant that a large proportion of the land was sold off in 1927 and many farms were purchased by the sitting tenants.

A feature of the village is the pant where travellers would stop to drink and to water their horses. A statue of Athole, third Earl of Ravensworth, stands watching over this central point. The Castle Inn was the posting house at which the horses were changed on the daily Edinburgh to Newcastle coaching route. It was also the scene of the estate rent day dinners which were by all accounts very social events indeed!

Another notable architectural feature is the pele tower which was erected to provide protection from the Border reivers. In 1845 it was restored to provide an almshouse for four couples who had served on the estate. They were given a pension of £10 a year and a supply of coal.

The parish church, dedicated to St Bartholomew, was founded in Anglo-Saxon times and is a major part of the village landscape and village life. The Memorial Hall was built with contributions from local people in memory of those who died in the First World War. It was, and still is to a lesser extent, a social centre for local people. Regular dances were held there with music supplied by local musicians or by bands brought in from further afield.

The site of the new school was a rifle range for the duration of both world wars and it too provided a venue for the villagers' social events.

During the Second World War the area now covered by the houses of Towerside was a prisoner of war camp. From there German and Italian prisoners were sent out to work on the farmland. For quite some time after the war the prison huts were occupied by 'displaced persons'.

With a reduced need for estate staff and with agriculture so much less labour intensive, the bustle of life in Whittingham has gone. It is now home to many retired people and those who travel daily to the towns to work, but the tranquillity this brings to the village is in keeping with the unspoilt beauty of Whittingham Vale.

Whittonstall 🐾

The origins of the village owe a great deal to the Roman occupation of Britain, as does much else in this area quite close to the wall built by the Emperor Hadrian. Whittonstall lies along the line of the Roman road (variously known as Watling or Dere Street) and was very likely the site of a military or commercial staging post.

It is a small village, as is proved by its war memorial. Normally on a village memorial you would see a list of names that even today might still bring tears to the eyes. But Whittonstall is a very small village indeed, a ribbon of houses along a 'B' road. The inhabitants were always so few that just four are recorded as having died in active service in the First World War and one in the next. Let's hope there will be no more to be recorded on any memorial.

It can be a bleak place, exposed at around 700 feet, but the views, when the air is thin, stretch southwards into County Durham and to the Cheviots in the north. All around the prospects please, however chill the day.

The name itself is a puzzle. Like much else it partly derives from the Roman occupation of Britain. An early version was Quictunestal and later there was the Saxon influence that even a thousand and more years ago produced a place named Wythonstall. The first half of the name refers to the thorn hedges which prevail and the second, 'Tonstall', to a man who long ago lived in the village and no doubt owned it.

A feature of the village is the church, which has hassocks recently embroidered by the local women in a variety of designs. Inside is a medieval tomb, perhaps 13th century, with the vestiges of a sword as the main motif – quite common at Durham Cathedral and elsewhere in the region at the time.

You would not expect Whittonstall to have played any great part in history. Yet the early owners included the Balliols, with their efforts to claim the throne of Scotland, and, much later, the Earl of Derwentwater, beheaded for his unsuccessful role in the 1715 Jacobite rebellion against the Hanoverians who still, in a sense, rule us today.

Whittonstall through the years has been connected with both lead and open cast coal mining, though fortunately there are few traces to be seen today.

Today there are hopes for the future of the Anchor Inn, closed in 1992. The village once again has a resident policeman, planning permission has been given for new houses and the 26 schoolchildren are to have a new village school.

Associated with Whittonstall, some two miles south, is Newlands, a hamlet dating from Norman times. In the 18th century there were six farms, a blacksmith's shop, and a chapel which was significant to Methodists, for the crusading John and Charles Wesley chose to preach there several times between 1740 and 1759. Today it has three farms and is the home of 16 families.

Widdrington 🌿

One of the earliest references to Widdrington concerns the castle, built in 1341 by Gerard de Widdrington (the Old English name being Woderington, meaning surrounded by woods). Next to the castle stood the 12th century Holy Trinity church, which Gerard de Widdrington extended and refurbished. The tomb where the family are buried can still be seen today, surmounted by the Widdrington coat of arms. A preceptory of Knights Templars was founded in the 14th century on part of the estates at Chibburn. The castle was pulled down in 1775 and is now marked by a low green mound, approached by a row of lime trees called the Twelve Apostles.

The village has a very historic and romantic past. In 1388 Richard Widdrington, a young squire, was immortalised in the *Ballad of Chevy Chase*:

'For Witherington my heart was woe
That ever he slain should be
For when both his legs were hewn in two
Yet he kneeled and fought on his knee.'

During the religious War of the Grand Alliance against France in 1691, the French landed on our coast, led by the privateer Jean Bart, his second in command Claude de Forbin and an English renegade named Thetford. The latter piloted the boats laden with armed men safely to the beach at Druridge. The village church and castle were plundered, an easy task as Lord Widdrington was away with his garrison fighting the Border wars. They then proceeded to the nearby preceptory, looted and set fire to it. On seeing the flames a small band of Northumbrians came prepared to fight the raiders, but were outnumbered by Bart's men firing muskets. Later it is said Forbin was shocked when he learnt he had raided the estates of a Catholic lord. The booty worth £6,000 was a rare prize for the French. To compensate for the loss, a collection was made in parish churches throughout Northumbria. In 1693 the renegade Thetford was captured, taken to Newgate prison, charged and found guilty of piloting the French raiders that ransacked Lord Widdrington's estates. He was later sent to Newcastle to be executed.

Sir Bertram, lord of Bothal Castle, loved the beautiful Isabel, daughter of the neighbouring Lord Widdrington and sought her hand in marriage. She put the constancy of Bertram to the test by sending him a splendid helmet with these words:

'Sir Knight thy lady sends thee this
And yields to be thy bride
When thou hast prov'd this maiden gift
Where sharpest blows are tried.'

Wearing the helmet, Bertram rode into battle against the Scots. When seriously wounded he was rescued by his loyal friends and taken to Wark Castle. News that her love had been wounded reached the ears of Isabel, who blamed herself for his suffering. She set forth to nurse him back to health. Travelling through the Cheviot Hills, she was captured by a Scottish chieftain, who had formerly proposed marriage to her. He carried her off to his fortress. Bertram, recovered from his wounds, set out with his brother to rescue her, one heading north and the other west. He discovered where his lady was held. Under cover of darkness he went to rescue her, only to see her descend on a ladder of ropes, assisted by a man in Highland dress. He drew his sword, shouting, 'Vile traitor! Yield that lady up.' Isabel recognising his voice cried out to him, 'It is your brother in disguise.'

Her warning came too late. She flung herself forward to avert the sword and was pierced in the breast. From her dying lips he was to hear the story of her rescue by his brother. Distraught, Bertram gave away all his wordly goods to the poor and built an oratory, hewn out of the rock on the bank of the river Coquet at Warkworth. This entrance to what is now called the Hermitage has the inscription carved above its door, 'My tears have been my meet by day and night.' Inside the oratory is an effigy of Isabel lying with her feet resting on a stone bull's head, the crest of the Widdringtons. Under an arch kneels the stone figure of Bertram, his right hand supporting his forehead, his left hand on his heart, as if in great sorrow.

The present day facilities of the village include the outstanding beauty of Druridge Bay, with its view of the Coquet Island, two wetland nature reserves, two churches, one public house and the Women's Institute hut. The WI hut was erected in 1936 then commandeered by the 86th Hertfordshire Yeomanry in 1939. Soldiers were billeted in six Nissen huts, in a field next to the church. The WI hut was used as a cook house and the regiment's cook was aptly named Sergeant Ham. On Saturday nights tables were cleared, a dance was organised, the army band played and villagers from all around danced the night away. This enlivened the dark days of war and is well remembered by locals to this day.

Wingates 🐝

Wingates is a tiny village, a hamlet really, consisting of 15 houses, a post box and a public telephone. The village stands on a hill with magnificent views of the Simonside Hills and the valleys of the rivers Coquet and Font. Towards the east can be seen part of the beautiful Northumbrian coast line.

The best known feature of bygone Wingates was the celebrated spa which was situated at Chirm Well, just outside the village. People were reputed to have come from far and near to take the beneficial waters of the spa. Unfortunately, the waters drained away from the well into the local mine workings which in their turn have been worked out.

The village was originally built for the estate workers, and it is thought it was centred around a pele house which is now a private dwelling. The buildings around this dwelling were used as the smithy, carpenter's and cobbler's which catered for the needs of the village and the local community.

Wingates has still got its old water pump, although this is no longer in working order. What is now Wingates House was once a temperance hotel and opposite this a school was built for the estate workers' children and local farming community. A small house was built alongside for the school teacher. Presumably due to the fall in population the school was closed in 1946.

A hall was built in 1915 by a Mr J. H. Straker to commemorate his daughter Edith Helen's 21st birthday and given in trust to the villagers. It is used these days mainly by the Women's Institute and in recent years a weekly bowling club has been formed which is very popular and well attended.

Wingates estate included seven farms, two of which are in the village, one at either end and these have retained most of their original buildings.

In November 1979 Mr and Mrs T. Wood had the honour of being chosen to entertain HRH the Prince of Wales and his party at South Farm, prior to his going hunting with the Morpeth Hunt, whilst he was staying in Northumberland.

On the outskirts of the village there was a thriving clay tile business and also a working sawmill which was in operation until 1990. Also outside the village is an old quarry, 'Withams Hole', so called because a certain Mr Witham, along with his horse and cart, are reputed to have completely disappeared in the bog at the bottom.

Wingate's most famous personage was a Mr Robert Morrison who was born in January 1781. Robert, who was apprenticed to his father, a last and boot maker, went on to become a keen student learning Hebrew, Latin and Greek and reading Theology. In 1813, in conjunction with William Milner, he translated the Bible into Chinese.

On 11th November 1959 the estate houses and farms were offered for sale to their respective tenants and some of the houses sold for as little as £300 each with gardens and woodland. Quite a few of the dwellings are still occupied by the families of the original tenants.

Because Wingates was built with no through road, it is a very quiet, tranquil spot, not really very much different to what it was 70 years or so ago.

Woodburn 🌿

In this beautiful part of the county, where the lovely river Rede meanders its way to join the North Tyne at Redesmouth, wildlife includes ducks, goosanders, herons and dippers. There are many lovely gardens in the parish, old and beautiful trees, and seats to take a rest and enjoy the peace and hear the call of the curlew or cock pheasant.

Woodburn is one of three villages in the parish of Corsenside, which means 'cross on the side of the hill', its oldest building being Corsenside church. Built in 1120, the church is dedicated to St Cuthbert whose body was supposed to have rested there in the 9th century, implying a much older religious building. A new church, All Saints, was built between East and West Woodburn in 1907 at a cost of £2,263 (excluding gifts of furniture) and is now the only place of worship in the village, except for the annual service at St Cuthbert's. The Methodist chapel built in 1866 and the Presbyterian church in 1894 are both closed.

Until 1830 Woodburn had been a collection of twelve thatched houses, an inn and a flour mill, but the latter went out of use in 1869 when it was sold and converted into a dwelling house. Life at this time was totally based on agriculture.

Opening up the iron ore mines at Ridsdale caused new houses to be built and Woodburn extended. The railway opened in 1865 and was responsible for much new development — the transport of iron ore was made easier, as well as the stone from newly opened quarries. The quarries were for many years the main employers of local labour. Sandstone from these quarries was used in Princes Street and government buildings in Edinburgh. Today stone still leaves the village from High Nick quarry, but the railway closed in 1966.

The mission room was built in 1842 for the use of the poor as a National school and for church services. Last to use the mission room was the Women's Institute, but because of disrepair, no water or toilet facilities, they then moved to the village hall.

The village hall is still the centre for local activities and was formally opened in 1906 with a reading room and a ladies room. No hunt balls or fancy dress dances are held now — once such memorable events, and no Saturday night hops stopping at 11.45 pm which old and young attended. Now the young have discos and there are birthday and wedding celebrations, fund-raising efforts and meetings of the WI and the parish council, the Redesdale Society, the Ladies Fellowship and a youth club.

The leek show, still a popular event, began 150 years ago and was then known as Woodburn Floral and Horticultural Society. *Gardeners Question Time* held its 891st edition at Woodburn in December 1969, a snowy night, but still a full hall.

19th century Woodburn had a boot and shoe maker, dressmaker, tailor, brick and tile manufacturers and two blacksmiths. Thirty years ago there was a post office and general store where you could buy anything from a packet of sewing needles to a pair of wellingtons. In addition there was a grocer, butcher and confectioner. The latter was known simply as 'Lizzie's', a spinster and a real local character. Her home-made ice cream was second to none. We are still lucky to have a very good general store and post office under new management.

In 1883 the school at Woodburn was enlarged at a cost of about £600 including an addition to the master's house. By 1899 about 140 children attended, including children from East Woodburn and Ridsdale. It is still used as a first school for about 25 children.

The village once had a brass band, a cricket club, football club and a tennis club. The building of 20 council houses in the early 1950s provided much needed accommodation and several new properties have been built since, but the area remains almost unspoilt. Large new developments are fiercely opposed.

Among the remaining old customs, bridal couples still have to pay a toll to have the church gates opened after the wedding ceremony and first footing is still carried out on New Year's Day.

The Roman outpost of Habitancum lies south of the village, and Robin of Risingham was once commemorated in bas relief on a large sandstone block about four foot high, but his top half was blown off by the farmer at the end of the 18th century because he objected to people visiting it! According to experts, Robin represents the Roman deity Sylvanus although local legend gives a different story. In 1983 the Redesdale Society commissioned a half-sized figure on a stone which was set up at the end of the original.

Wooler

Wooler, formerly Wulloure or Welloure, is situated above the Wooler Water and is known as the Gateway to the Cheviots. At one time it was a health resort for invalids taking a goat's whey cure.

Because of the surrounding hills and the sheep which are farmed there, it was once one of the richest townships in Northumberland and the centre of a thriving woollen industry with several mills – Carding Mill, Dye Mill, Coldgate and Earle, which existed in the 17th century.

Even earlier there stood on Tower Hill the castle of Muschamps – a barony granted by Henry I in 1107. Surrey House was so named because the Earl of Surrey was supposed to have camped there in 1513 on his way to the battle of Flodden Field.

There have been many changes and many buildings lost. Parish records of 1832 show that there were a number of schools in Wooler – a Church of England school, a Presbyterian school, a Catholic school, a grammar school, three private schools, and Wooler ragged school for pupils who could not afford to pay school fees. Nowadays there is a first school, and a middle school built on the site of a prisoner of war camp in 1954.

The Victorian social worker, Josephine Butler, is commemorated by a plaque donated by Wooler WI on the house where she died in 1906. She is buried in Kirknewton churchyard. Her grandmother must also have been a woman of vision as she was instrumental in encouraging the provision of books for the two Wooler libraries – the mechanics' reading room and the subscription library. Sir Walter Scott visited in 1791 but found the accommodation so bad in Wooler that he took excellent lodgings in a farmer's house in Langleford where he partook of the notable goat's whey.

There are a number of fire plaques on buildings around the village, such as the one at the Angel Inn provided by the Globe Insurance Company. Wooler had suffered several fires in the 19th century, largely due to the vulnerability of thatched roofs. The worst of these, in 1863, started during a gale at The Three Half Moons and, as there was no fire engine, the agent for Globe Insurance had to ride to Belford to alert the fire brigade, which took seven hours to arrive, by which time the High Street was almost demolished, though The Red Lion and Black Bull survived. In 1865 a new High Street emerged with tiled and slated roofs.

Fire, too, damaged the very early church of St Mary, probably built at the instigation of the Lindisfarne monks. In 1765 a new church was built of Doddington stone, which was enlarged in 1826 and in 1856 gained a church clock paid for by public subscription and costing £200. The manse of Cheviot Street church is now used by The Abbeyfield Trust, and West Church and Cheviot Street churches were amalgamated to form the URC and the building bought by Heart of Glendale Masonic Lodge.

Outside the village a rock known as The King's Chair overhangs the Pin Well, from where ancient kings were supposed to have directed battles. On 1st May a pagan custom was observed of dropping a crooked pin into the well while making a wish.

Kettles Camp, in the same vicinity, reveals pot-like cavities which were probably the remains of earlier dwellings. On Humbleton Hill is a 'cup and saucer camp'. This hill was the site of a battle in 1402.

The fire engine no longer takes seven hours to reach the town as there is a retained fire service as well as a police station and courtroom, although there is no resident policeman. There are many active societies in Wooler, from angling and clay pigeon shooting, to a choral society and Young Farmers Club.

Wooler Livestock Mart was established in 1887 but prior to this Glendale had relied on local fairs and markets such as the Whitsun Bank Fair, St Ninian's Fair and the High Fair. As well as these fairs were The Games – racing, wrestling, football etc. This has extended to become the popular Glendale Agricultural and Horticultural Show now held on August Bank Holiday at Haugh Head.

Wylam 🐚

The village of Wylam lies about ten miles west of Newcastle on the banks of the Tyne, just at the limit of the tidal flow.

Most of the houses in the village centre were built in the late 19th century and many are of pleasant sandstone. More modern developments have largely been tucked in behind the main street and do not spoil the rural atmosphere. Although this is a busy, thriving community, with many people commuting to Newcastle or Hexham, it is definitely a country village. There is still a working farm in the centre: three times each day traffic has to come to a halt to allow the cows to walk from the fields to the milking parlour.

The visitor to the village will find many pleasant walks, by the riverside, through woods and across farmland. There are many good picnic spots and the four pubs in the village provide bar meals. There is also a French restaurant and a delicatessen with a small café.

The village has a long history. Wylam manor house was acquired by the monks of Tynemouth in the latter years of the 11th century and the prior was lord of Wylam manor and presided over the manor court. The monks extracted coal and iron in Wylam and also used

Points Bridge at Wylam

the local timber and caught fish. During the 12th century Wylam was referred to as St Oswin's village. This was because Tynemouth priory contained the relics and shrine of St Oswin, martyr and 7th century king of Northumbria, and at that time the shrine was a popular place of pilgrimage.

No church was then built in Wylam, probably because the manor house contained a chapel, so after the Reformation the village was incorporated into the ecclesiastical parish of Ovingham. However, in 1902, a few years after the opening of a village church (built by the Hedley family as a memorial to William Hedley, one of the railway engine pioneers) Wylam became a separate parish. The church, dedicated to St Oswin, is open to visitors during the day and has some magnificent stained glass windows, including Leonard Evett's Window of Creation based on psalm 19. The church hassocks are being replaced with tapestry kneelers worked by parishioners and include many wonderful original designs by Mrs Freda Hardy. Well worth seeing, St Oswin's is one of the few churches where evensong is said every day.

It was the demand for coal during the Industrial Revolution that led to development of the village: at one time there were five coal mines, two ironworks and seven pubs. There is little sign nowadays of this part of Wylam's history; the Blackett family, who owned the mines and most of the village, put most of the spoil heaps back down the shafts at their own expense.

It was Christopher Blackett, who became squire of Wylam in 1800, who was probably responsible for so many north-eastern engineers becoming involved in the development of the steam locomotive. He ordered a locomotive to be built by John Whinfield of Pipewellgate in Gateshead from the design of Richard Trevithick's Pen-y-darran locomotive. It was completed in 1805 and ran on its own track at the Gateshead works, but was never brought to Wylam. William Hedley became viewer of Wylam colliery in 1805 and Timothy Hackworth foreman of the colliery blacksmiths in 1807. With Blackett's encouragement, they carried out experiments with locomotives on Wylam waggonway. Hedley developed many successful engines, including *Wylam Dilly* and *Puffing Billy*. Hackworth left Wylam in 1815 and later became the resident engineer and first superintendent of the first public railway, from Stockton to Darlington, which was completed in 1825, Plaques showing the sites of Hackworth's birthplace and Hedley's residence have been mounted in the village and may be seen at the eastern entrance of the playing field and on the wall of a house at the western end of Woodcroft Road.

George Stephenson is the best known of the Wylam railway engineers. A short walk from the car park (on the site of the old north station) leads to the cottage where George was born on 9th June 1781. The cottage is owned by the National Trust (for opening times, phone the tenant, Wylam 853457). Stephenson did not, of course, invent the locomotive, but he more than anyone else was instrumental in the development of public railways. His great ambition, together with that of his son, Robert (who designed the high level bridge over the Tyne at Newcastle and the Royal Border Bridge over the Tweed), was to see the north-eastern railway linking London and Edinburgh. This was completed in 1850, two years after his death.

The iron that was used in the colliery ironworks and in the ironworks of the Bell brothers established by Benjamin Thompson, was extracted from the colliery spoil heaps. Christopher Blackett also had interests in the lead mines in County Durham and created a lead shot works in Wylam by the ingenious method of adapting a disused coal shaft for dropping the lead instead of building a chimney.

There are two bridges over the Tyne at Wylam. The first was built in 1836, to make a rail link between the recently opened Newcastle to Carlisle railway on the south side of the river and the coal and ironworks north of the river. A roadway was also provided over the bridge and a toll charge was made. It was not until 100 years later, in 1936, that the bridge was acquired by the county council and freed from tolls. The toll house, now a private dwelling, still stands on the north west corner of the bridge. The other bridge – the 'points bridge' – is perhaps of greater interest. Built of wrought iron in 1876, it was the first arch-rib design bridge in the world, built to support a suspended railway track. Bridges of a similar design were later built at Newcastle upon Tyne and Sydney Harbour, Australia. The railway over the bridge is now disused but the bridge is preserved as a historic monument and the trackway is a public footpath.

There are displays illustrating the contribution of Wylam's engineers to the development of the railways, in the small museum adjacent to the car park just north of the river bridge. Booklets about Wylam are available in the post office and in the church.

Index